Mrs. Christine Garland
42 Longview Rd.
Cedar Grove, NJ 07009

G F

D1553516

Digging New Jersey's Past

Digging
New Jersey's Past

HISTORICAL ARCHAEOLOGY
IN THE GARDEN STATE

Richard Veit

Rutgers University Press

New Bunswick, New Jersey, and London

Library of Congress Cataloging-in-Publication Data

Veit, Richard Francis, 1968–
    Digging New Jersey's past : historical archaeology in the Garden State / Richard Veit.
        p. cm.
    Includes bibliographical references (p.) and index.
    ISBN 0-8135-3112-8 (cloth : alk. paper)—ISBN 0-8135-3113-6 (pbk. : alk. paper)
        1. New Jersey—Antiquities.   2. Archaeology and history—New Jersey.
    3. Excavations (Archaeology)—New Jersey.   4. New Jersey—History.
    5. Historic sites—New Jersey.   I. Title.

F136.V45 2002
974.9'01—dc21

                                                                    2001058676

British Cataloging-in-Publication information is available from the British Library.

Manufactured in the United States of America

To Terri and Douglas
for their patience and encouragement

Contents

Illustrations

Foreword

In the fall of 1936 J. C. ("Pinky") Harrington, a recent graduate student just out of the University of Chicago, was assigned by the National Park Service to take charge of the first long-term professional excavation of an important American historic site: Jamestown, Virginia (1607). From that project (1936–1941), and similar work by Harrington's colleagues during the Great Depression, the discipline of historical archaeology has spread to countless sites across the nation. Today it is the most common type of archaeology practiced in the United States and Canada.

Similar but slightly later fieldwork in Western Europe and Oceania (especially Australia) has firmly established the discipline on three continents, and professional excavations of historic sites dating after 1400 c.e. can now be found in Latin America and Africa. Work in the United States initially focused on famous and early sites: Jamestown and Williamsburg in the Chesapeake, Plymouth Plantation in New England, St. Augustine in Florida, Fort Vancouver in the Northwest, and the Spanish missions of Texas and California. Soon, however, researchers turned their attention to less traditional sites, including slave cabins, workers' housing, urban neighborhoods, and factory ruins, and they expanded their time frame to include the nineteenth century and, in the last two decades, even the twentieth century.

Today historical archaeology is well established as the archaeology of the modern world (1400 c.e. to the present) and has a growing visibility. Nevertheless, this new type of research has a mixed record of success. On two levels it stands out, while on a third it has fallen far short of its own goals. Thousands of sites have been excavated and well reported in technical site reports, which are the basis of any descriptive science. At the other end of production, historical archaeology is impressive as a theoretical field. Work by historical archaeologists like the late James Deetz has greatly influenced the nature of interpretation and theoretical debate within general archaeology.

Yet as dynamic as the field is in describing its own data and talking to itself, it is noticeably less successful in the middle ground of synthesis. Except for a few popular books by Deetz and Ivor Noël Hume, historical archaeology has not summarized its findings in a way that would interest other scholars and the public. Few books tell us what archaeology has to say about historic regions, individual states, or major American cities. Only one state, Texas, has such a volume and only two cities, Philadelphia and New York, have such a summation. A volume on Denver is forthcoming. The public is more familiar with historical archaeology through museum exhibits, restored historic sites such as Williamsburg, and documentary films on public television.

Richard Veit has undertaken to resolve this problem for New Jersey. He has not produced an encyclopedic listing of every project and site excavated in the Garden State, though such a handbook might have pleased his professional colleagues. Rather, Veit takes a selective approach and weaves together the excitement of archaeological discovery with the stories these discoveries can tell us about key events and major topics in successive periods of the state's history.

New Jersey is indeed rich in its archaeological heritage. On a worldwide level, historical archaeology has been developing around several basic themes: the radical changes in Old World cultures (especially Western Europe) after 1400 C.E., the overseas colonies of these cultures, their interactions with native peoples around the globe, and the transformation of this complex system during the industrialization of the nineteenth and twentieth centuries. Archaeological remains of all these basic building blocks of the modern world are found in New Jersey, and the state was more than once a primary center for such developments. Europeans arriving in the seventeenth century confronted the area's native peoples, the Delaware. Well established by the eighteenth century, the colony witnessed many battles, military and political, during the birth of the new republic. The state served a central role as well in another revolution, the American Industrial Revolution, which has enduring consequences for our own time and culture.

Veit guides the reader on a well-organized tour through these four hundred years of New Jersey's development as seen though archaeology. Contact sites on the Delaware River, colonial Quaker settlements in the south and Dutch sites in the north, famous Revolutionary War battlefields and camps, industrial remains of canals, railroads, and lighthouses, along with historic cemeteries and African American communities, are just some of the stories he explores.

Digging New Jersey's Past reflects the state of archaeological research in the region. Some topics have been well explored and reported, while others have yet to be approached by excavators. In providing this first synthesis, Veit both highlights the unfolding story and contribution of archaeology to New Jersey history and clearly shows that the mystery and excitement of discovery await us all.

Robert L. Schuyler
University of Pennsylvania Museum of Archaeology and Anthropology
Philadelphia

Acknowledgments

Although there is only one author listed on the cover of this book, archaeology is not a solitary profession. No one can dig a site alone; the challenges—physical, intellectual, and financial—are too great. I deeply appreciate of the assistance of numerous colleagues and friends.

My colleagues in the Department of History and Anthropology at Monmouth University, particularly my department chair, Brian Greenberg, and fellow anthropologists Bill Mitchell and Glenn King, have been a constant source of encouragement. The university also provided me with a generous Creativity Grant, which helped defray the cost of reproducing graphics and carrying out some of the research.

My colleagues in the archaeological community were incredibly helpful and stood up well to my seemingly endless questions and requests for information. I especially want to thank those individuals who read and commented on sections of the text, including Marshall Becker, Charles Bello, Deborah Fimbel, Robin French, Michael Gall, Joan Geismar, Michael Gregg, Gregory Lattanzi, R. Alan Mounier, Edward Rutsch, Gerard Scharfenberger, Paul Schopp, Dan Sivilich, Megan Springate, and Matthew Tomaso. This work is much stronger thanks to their help.

The gathering of appropriate illustrations was made considerably easier by the assistance of Charles Bello of the Archaeological Society of New Jersey; Ian Burrough and Richard Hunter of Hunter Research, Inc.; Edward Lenik of Sheffield Archaeological Consultants; Patt Martinelli from Historic Batsto Village; Peter Primavera of the Cultural Resource Consulting Group; Gerard Scharfenberger of Louis Berger and Associates; Daniel Sivilich of BRAVO; Megan Springate and Bernadette Rogoff from the Monmouth County Historical Association; Ronald Thomas from Middle Atlantic Archaeological Research; Matthew Tomaso from Montclair State University; David Vecchioli and Joni Rowe from Morristown National Historical Park; and Gordon Watts and Aaron Ziemann of the Trailside Museums. A special thanks to Gerard Scharfenberger for allowing me to reproduce Rob Tucher's fine photograph of the Luyster colander on the cover of this book. Timothy McConville was also a great help in securing reproducible digital photographs. John Martin of Gannett Fleming provided valuable encouragement. The New Jersey Department of Transportation, working in conjunction with the Federal Highway Administration, has been responsible for a considerable amount of archaeological research in the state. Lauralee Rappleye Marsett was a tremendous help in procuring photographs of some of the department's projects. John McCarthy also shared his work on the Burlington Friends Meetinghouse. The Archaeological Society of New Jersey, Council for Northeast Historical Archaeology, Princeton University Library, the Society for Industrial Archaeology, and the Saint Louis Museum of Art all allowed me to reproduce materials from their collections and publications.

I also wish to thank my editors at Rutgers University Press, Helen Hsu and Marlie Wasserman, as well as Jill Stuart for their assistance, guidance, and encouragement. Gretchen Oberfranc's comments and edits helped clarify innumerable points in the text and produced a much more readable manuscript. A great debt is owed to the many students who have participated in Monmouth University's annual summer field schools in archaeology over the past five years. Without their hard work, sweat, and dedication, many of the sites discussed here would never have come to light.

My wife, Terri, and son Douglas, as well as my mother and brother, allowed me to indulge my interests in New Jersey's past and historical archaeology. Thanks to everyone for helping me bring this book to fruition.

In closing, let me quote from William Camden, author of *Brittania* (1637) and one of the first scholars to describe British archaeological remains: "To accomplish this worke the whole main of my Industrie hath been implied. . . . I right willingly acknowledge that I may erre much. Who shooting all day long doth always hit the mark? . . . Others may be more skillful and more exactly observe the particularities of the places where they are conversant; if they, or any other, whosoever will advertise mee wherein I am mistaken, I will amend it with manifold thanks . . . if it proceed from good meaning, and not from a spirit of contradiction and quarrelling, which does not befit such as are well bred, and affect the truth."

Digging New Jersey's Past

CHAPTER ONE

History Underfoot

A Short Introduction to Historical Archaeology

Archaeology: the word brings to mind thoughts of adventures in exotic lands, fraught with danger. Thanks in part to Indiana Jones, star of several Steven Spielberg epics, archaeologists are often perceived as dashing characters wearing fedoras or pith helmets and armed with whips. Personally, I have never had the opportunity to use a whip in a professional capacity.

Adventure and intrigue are only the tip of the archaeological iceberg. Archaeology is the systematic scientific study of past cultures and societies. Most archaeologists trained in America are anthropologists with an interest in past peoples and their societies; others, particularly those educated in Europe, may be trained as historians or solely as archaeologists. Although some archaeologists study the impressive ancient civilizations of Greece, Rome, Egypt, Central and South America, others focus on locations closer to home and cultures far less exotic. *Digging New Jersey's Past* is about that latter group of archaeologists, and particularly about historical archaeology in New Jersey. Historical archaeology focuses on the modern world, a period rather broadly defined as beginning with the arrival of the first Europeans in the New World roughly five hundred years ago and continuing into our modern era. (For definitions of historical archaeology, see Schuyler 1999; Leone and Potter 1994; Beaudry 1996.)

Some people might question the usefulness of archaeology as a tool for understanding the modern world. Why on earth would an archaeologist want to study an eighteenth-century house, or a Revolutionary War fortification, or, even less appealing, a nineteenth-century privy? The answer is quite simple: these archaeological features and the artifacts associated with them have the potential to provide insights into the past that are available nowhere else. Artifacts and archaeological features offer unique, tangible sources of information that can complement written documents and oral histories. Taken together, these objects contribute to a much more robust interpretation of history than could be constructed from any one source alone.

In New Jersey the historic or modern period began in the early seventeenth century with the arrival of the first Dutch and Swedish settlers. Although New Jersey has a rich heritage of prehistoric Native American archaeological sites that predate the colonists, those sites are not discussed here. (Readers interested in New Jersey prehistory should consult the publications of the late Herbert C. Kraft [1986]; the annual *Bulletin of the Archaeological Society of New Jersey*; and Mounier, *Looking Beneath the Surface* [forthcoming].) The sites that are discussed in this book, ranging from a Dutch trading post to a lost nineteenth-century lighthouse, are just the tip of the archaeological iceberg. My goal in writing *Digging New Jersey's Past* is not to provide an encyclopedia of all the sites that historical archaeologists have probed in the state, but rather to introduce a selection of the more interesting ones and discuss what we have learned or are learning from them. Some of these sites— Monmouth Battlefield, Twin Lights, and Jockey Hollow, for example—are well known from history books, and the archaeological excavations at them have received considerable attention. Other sites, though no less important, have enjoyed only a brief moment of fame in a scholarly journal, an academic dissertation, or a hard-to-find report prepared by a professional archaeologist for a readership smaller than the average baseball team. Here we revisit a sample of famous and less famous sites, all of which highlight important facets of New Jersey's history.

Despite more than a century of research, many time periods, topics, and regions of the state have been the subject of little archaeological study. The opportunity to help fill in these voids is not limited to the professional archaeologist. Many local colleges and universities, including Monmouth University, Montclair State University, Rutgers University, and Drew University, offer summer field programs in archaeology. Membership in the Archaeological Society of New Jersey is another way to participate in local historical archaeology (http://www.asnj.org). The society holds regular meetings where archaeologists talk about their research, and it publishes an annual bulletin that highlights the latest archaeological finds. The New Jersey State Museum maintains an active registry of archaeological sites in the state, and amateur archaeologists are encouraged to identify and register sites in their neighborhoods.

Sites versus Sights

Before going any further we should get a bit of vocabulary out of the way. Archaeologists dig *sites*. These are locations that contain the remains of past human activities. The diverse archaeological sites we shall visit in this book range from massive ironworks to the sooty remains of ephemeral charcoal kilns. At the most basic level, we can divide sites into several general categories: domestic, military, industrial, and religious (Noël Hume 1976). Domestic sites are houses or other places where people once lived. Monmouth Battlefield, discussed in Chapter 4, is a military site, as is an army's encampment. Industrial sites include mills, iron-works, glassworks, and often transportation-related sites like canals, railroads, and turnpikes. We shall look at transportation and manufacturing sites separately in Chapters 6 and 7. Religious sites include churches, synagogues, cemeteries, shrines, and other holy places. Chapter 5 is devoted to cemeteries.

Sites often contain *artifacts*, which are things made, used, or modified by humans. In 1922 archaeologist Howard Carter made the find of a lifetime. When he first cracked through the sealed door to the tomb of the Egyptian pharaoh Tutankhamen and peered inside, his sponsor, Lord Carnarvon, asked if he saw anything. Carter replied, "Yes, wonderful things."

The artifacts found by historical archaeologists are generally less than wonderful: bits of broken crockery, shards of nineteenth-century glass, tobacco pipe stems (the cigarette butts of early America), clam and oyster shells and animal bones—the remains of meals long forgotten—and, of course, the occasional coin. Though unimpressive in themselves, these artifacts, when taken together, can provide a wealth of information about the food people ate, the beverages they consumed, the medicines they took, the clothes they wore, the tools they used, and the buildings they lived and worked in.

Often archaeologists will divide the artifacts they find into several broad categories for ease of analysis and comparison with other sites. These categories generally include ceramics, glass, and small finds—a catchall category containing everything from dominoes to zippers. Other categories include plant or *floral remains*, and the bones of animals, called *faunal remains*. Artifacts are the building blocks of archaeological interpretations and it takes considerable expertise to identify them correctly.

Artifacts are portable. Other, nonportable forms of evidence for human activities may also be uncovered on a site, including: wells; the remains of outhouses; root cellars; middens (scatters of trash); cisterns for water storage; foundations; the stains left by wooden posts in the ground; and much more. Archaeologists call these clusters of archaeological evidence *features*.

Historical Archaeology: What Is It Good For?

Historical archaeologist Kathleen Deagan, one of archaeology's leading scholars and the discoverer of Christopher Columbus's lost settlement of La Navidad on the island of Hispaniola, notes that historical archaeology can contribute to our understanding of the past on several different levels. It can be a rich source of information about the initial colonization of the New World, provide us with new data about how the landscape was transformed over the past five hundred years, and offer glimpses into the lives of individuals who slipped between the pages of history. Historical archaeology may also reveal evidence of individuals who purposefully hid or failed to document certain activities, and it can tell us about the health and hygiene of our forebears (Deagan 1991). In this book we shall look at sites that fall into all these categories and more.

In Chapter 2, for instance, we survey some sites associated with New Jersey's first European settlers, including a seventeenth-century Dutch settlement on Burlington Island and the house of John Reading, a prominent colonial official in Gloucester City. Although the Dutch on the Delaware and even John Reading himself appear in standard histories of the state, the artifacts recovered from these sites allow archaeologists to develop interpretations that go beyond the limited printed sources that survive from New Jersey's formative period.

We shall also look at sites that provide us with information about the physical world of the past. What did the Pinelands look like in 1850? In Chapter 7 we examine some charcoal-making sites in the Pinelands (Mounier 1997). Sites like these highlight the fact that, historically, the Pinelands area was not a pristine wilderness but rather one of the leading iron- and glass-producing regions in the Northeast. Smoke billowed from furnaces smelting iron, and the din of trip hammers rang through the forest. Large swaths of timber were clear-cut to feed the ironworks' voracious appetite for charcoal fuel. Archaeology can give us a glimpse of that forgotten world.

Historical archaeology can also tell us about health and nutrition in the past. Before the days of bureaucratic health management organizations, the day-to-day realities of health, sickness, and death were considerably less well documented than they are today. Archaeologists can tell us about the health of our early American ancestors from analysis of their bones, which often bear evidence of malnutrition, injuries, and other physical insults suffered over a person's lifetime. Similarly, analysis of the night soil left behind in privies—or outhouses, as they are more commonly known—may reveal traces of the parasites that plagued our ancestors or tell us about the food they ate and the health care they received or, more often, failed to receive. In Chapter 8 we shall discuss one unusual archaeological assemblage that contained a physician's toolkit from the late nineteenth century.

Although it may be easy for a person to lie on a questionnaire or hide the evidence of misdeeds, trash never lies. When archaeologist William Rathje examined modern trash from locations around Tucson, Arizona, and compared what people had discarded with what they claimed on questionnaires to have thrown away, the results were strikingly dissimilar (Rathje 1975). For instance, no one admitted to drinking to excess, yet numerous households discarded large quantities of empty beer bottles and cans. Why the disparity? Perhaps the respondents tried to give Rathje the answers they assumed he wanted. Or maybe they lied. It is also possible that they thought the whole idea of someone investigating their trash was absurd. As you will see, the artifacts tell the rest of the story.

Historical archaeology can reveal all sorts of secrets that people once tried to keep hidden. In Chapter 6 we shall examine an unusual collection of artifacts found tucked away in a railroad roundhouse. Although railroad managers worked hard to eliminate drinking among their employees, the workers at the Central Railroad of New Jersey's Lakehurst Shops appear to have ignored the temperance message and imbibed while on the job. Apparently their behavior went unnoticed until, years later, an archaeological excavation revealed the bottles.

This sort of surprising discovery is more the norm than the exception. In a similar case, archaeologist Charles Bello found dozens of patent medicine bottles squirreled away in a blocked-up fireplace at Shippen Manor, a historic house in Warren County (Bello 1997, pers. comm.). A nineteenth-century resident was apparently treating a malady, either real or imagined, with a potent patent medicine and discarding the empty bottles where it seemed likely that they never would be found. The result for Bello and his colleagues was an archaeological jackpot.

Historical archaeology can also tell us about the disenfranchised members of our society, the individuals we might accurately call America's hidden majority. They include all of the people whose lives are not well represented in traditional histories: workers, slaves, farmers, women, and new immigrants. We shall examine the colonial farmstead of the Luyster family in Middletown and the lives of anonymous factory workers in Feltville. Although neither site is widely known, both have the potential to inform us about the transformation of American life during the nineteenth century. Another important site is Skunk Hollow, an early-nineteenth-century community of free African Americans located along the Palisades of northern New Jersey (see Chapter 8). It provides a rare glimpse of the lives of African Americans in the years before the Civil War.

Why Dig Historic Sites?

Historic sites in New Jersey have been the subjects of study for more than a hundred years. The first people to look at them were typically interested in the lives of New Jersey's Native American inhabitants and had come to historical archaeology in a roundabout way. In the 1890s, for example, Charles Conrad Abbott, a naturalist, archaeologist, and expert on Native Americans, carried out one of the first excavations on a colonial site in the state. During the early 1900s, Max Schrabisch, a German émigré, dug at a Revolutionary War site, General Henry Knox's Park of Artillery at Pluckemin (Lenik 1998:70). Schrabisch, better known for his work on Native American sites, dug at the behest of a wealthy, history-minded landowner. More recently, and with much more informative results, archaeologist John Seidel revisited the same site. The resulting collection of artifacts and information is probably the most complete from a Revolutionary War site in New Jersey.

Later still, during the Great Depression, the National Park Service joined with the Civilian Conservation Corps (CCC) to employ hundreds of out-of-work men as archaeologists in and around Morristown National Historic Park. They relocated sites associated with the American Army's encampments during the winters of 1777–1778 and 1779–1780. Little did these men know that they were working at one of the first large-scale excavations of a historic site. These early forays into historical archaeology by Abbott, Schrabisch, and the CCC were exceptional; most archaeologists at the time were focused on the state's prehistoric past.

That focus began to change with the passage in 1966 of the National Historic Preservation Act (NHPA). This legislation built upon the Antiquities Act of 1906, which preserved archaeological sites on federally owned lands, and the Historic Sites and Buildings Act of 1935. The latter directed the secretary of the interior to secure data, make surveys, acquire properties, and restore and mark historic buildings and sites (Murtagh 1997:209). The NHPA created the National Register of Historic Places, a list of significant properties fitting one or more of the following four criteria: an association with important events in American history; a connection to the lives of significant individuals in our past; the embodiment of distinctive characteristics of a type, period, or method of construction; or the likelihood to yield information important in prehistory or history (Murtagh 1997:183). The NHPA also created an Advisory Council on Historic Preservation and, most important, was responsible for having archaeological surveys carried out on thousands of sites in New Jersey and throughout the United States. The act states that federal agencies that issue licenses, permits, or funding for construction-related projects must take into account "the effect of the undertaking on any district, site, building, structure, or object that is included in the National Register" (Murtagh 1997:178).

Although the NHPA did not, and does not, stop development, it provided a way of documenting those pieces of our past that were about to be lost. It also led to the development of a unique business known as cultural resource management, or CRM. Instead of hiring thousands of government archaeologists, historians, and architectural historians to identify and assess the importance of various historic and archaeological resources, state historic preservation offices were established to administer these surveys, most of which, at least in New Jersey, are performed by private firms. Archaeology, once primarily an avocation of the wealthy, was transformed into a viable, if highly competitive and not particularly well paid, career. Today a variety of firms, ranging from small mom-and-pop operations to university-sponsored research centers and international engineering companies, are actively carrying out archaeological research in New Jersey and throughout the United States.

The nature of contract archaeology has turned many archaeologists into nomads, working at one site in June and another in October. They may see a dozen or more projects over the course of a year. Although this sort of approach is necessary for a company to remain profitable, it can mean that an archaeologist will never have more than a superficial feel for the history and prehistory of a particular area. Often, the best archaeologist for a cultural resources management job is one who has a track record of working in a region.

Although some of the more spectacular projects generate considerable public interest and result in tours and glossy publications designed to share the results with local citizens, the reality is that most CRM work goes unnoticed. Surveys are carried out, excavations performed, and reports written and filed with the appropriate agencies. The recovered artifacts, in the best-case scenario, end up at a museum or historical society where they are cared for and preserved for future researchers. All too often, however, the artifacts languish in warehouses and labs, all but forgotten. The project reports—called "gray literature" by archaeologists, as though the print were fading and scarcely visible— represent an incredible source of information about New Jersey's past. But they too are often filed into oblivion. One of my goals in writing this book is to put the gray literature under the spotlight so that it, its authors, and their contributions are not forgotten.

The legal basis for archaeology in New Jersey is evolving. Federal, state, and local ordinances may all contain relevant provisions. During the 1980s and 1990s a considerable amount of archaeology was performed as a result of CAFRA legislation (Coastal Areas Facilities Review Act). The Waterfront Development Act, Freshwater Wetlands Act, and New Jersey Register of Historic Places Act all contain provisions pertaining to archaeology. In recent years the state has seen several excellent large-scale archaeological studies funded by the

Federal Highway Administration, New Jersey Division Office, under contract to the New Jersey Department of Transportation, with oversight from archaeologists of the Bureau of Environmental Analysis. These projects included several massive studies: the Route 29 "Tunnel Project" in Trenton, performed by archaeologists from two firms (Hunter Research, Inc., and Gannett Fleming); and Raritan Landing in Piscataway, carried out by four archaeology companies (Gannett Fleming, URS Corporation, John Milner and Associates, and Karen Hartgen Associates).

More recent federal laws, such as the Native American Graves Protection and Repatriation Act (NAGPRA), enacted in 1990, are also affecting the ways in which archaeologists carry out their research. Undoubtedly, the legal landscape of a hundred years from now will be different still. With luck, archaeological sites will continue to be protected.

Of course, not all archaeological studies are directly mandated by state or federal legislation. Some archaeological excavations discussed here are aptly termed pure research projects. Archaeologist Joan Geismar's study of Skunk Hollow was done to complete the degree requirements for a doctorate in anthropology at Columbia University (Geismar 1982). Gerard Scharfenberger's study of the Luyster House, an eighteenth- and nineteenth-century Dutch farm in Middletown, was a salvage project performed without any funding, simply because Scharfenberger wanted to record an important site before it was lost to development (Scharfenberger and Veit 1999).

Most summers see groups of young people heading for the field at various sites in New Jersey, eager to learn the craft of archaeology. Although some field schools are tied to cultural resource management projects, others are motivated simply by a professor's research interest in a particular site, era, or topic. All of these excavations—academic, salvage, and professional—can and do provide new information about the past. Here we shall draw upon examples from all three fields.

Dig We Must!

All archaeologists—whether uncovering Mayan temples in the steaming jungles of Belize, tracing Mesopotamian irrigation networks in dusty Iraq, or surveying Dutch farmhouses in verdant central New Jersey—share certain techniques in common. What follows is a brief introduction to those techniques (for more information, see the many detailed treatises on how to excavate an archaeological site).

The first step in excavating a historic site should never be digging—at least in the ground. Rather, one must delve into the wealth of documents at a library, archive, or other repository. Excavation is hard and sometimes tedious work. It is made easier and considerably more effective by good historical research. Before excavating, the archaeologist or a historian should gather as much information as possible about the site under investigation. If it is a farm, there may be property deeds, census and tax records, and household inventories (documents compiled when a homeowner died, listing all possessions, which can provide clues as to how rooms were arranged and furnished). Maps and old photographs show the locations and details of buildings that no longer survive. County histories and atlases, published during the late nineteenth and early twentieth centuries, often contain accounts of a region's first settlers and prominent local landowners. Interviews with knowledgeable local individuals may yield information that is simply unavailable anywhere else.

Parts of New Jersey have been fairly well mapped since the American Revolution. Detailed insurance records from the nineteenth century, particularly Sanborn fire insurance maps, document the evolution of the state's cities. Aerial photographs from the early twentieth century offer vivid evidence of the gradual urbanization of the landscape. Decades of archaeological research have resulted in a massive collection of cultural resource studies housed at the State Historic Preservation Office in Trenton. A few days of concerted research can result in a much more effective effort in the field. After the bulk of the research is done, fieldwork begins. I say the bulk of the research because new questions or lines of investigation tend to emerge as a project develops.

One other step often precedes actual excavation: remote sensing. *Remote sensing* is a term used by archaeologist to refer to a battery of techniques designed to help determine the presence, location, and extent of archaeological sites without actual excavation. Some of these procedures are simple and inexpensive; others are complicated and costly. None is foolproof. One simple technique is the use of a probing rod—a pointed metal rod with a cross-bar handle—which is used to locate buried foundations, particularly in rock-free soils. Metal detectors can also be used effectively to locate archaeological sites, particularly military ones, such as battlefields, where ephemeral material traces are likely. Ground-penetrating radar and soil resistivity may be employed, although these techniques must be followed up by excavation. Otherwise, a twentieth-century utility pipe may be mistaken for a feature of much greater age and importance. Nonetheless, whenever possible, it is wise to employ remote-sensing techniques prior to excavation.

Sometimes a surface, or pedestrian, survey is conducted before excavation. The suspected site is systematically walked, and surface features and artifact scatters are recorded. The presence of artifacts and the remnants of gnarled old fruit trees or rose bushes or other ornamental plantings may show where people once lived, even though buildings no longer survive. Dry patches in the grass might indicate buried foundations near the surface. The more looking an archaeologist does before starting to dig, the more effective the digging is likely to be.

Furthermore, archaeology is not the random retrieval of objects from the soil. The critical difference is context. *Context* means identifying an object in terms of the location where it was found, including depth, the time period in which it was used, and what it was used for. Before breaking ground, an archaeologist will typically establish a grid across the site. The grid, which may be marked out with string on the ground or simply inferred between marked points, enables the archaeologist to keep track of where artifacts are found. In the case of particularly complicated sites, where the archaeologist wants to extract as much information as possible, he or she may record the exact location of every single artifact using surveyor's tools like a transit, total station, or even global positioning systems (GPS). Whether the methods are simple or complex, the goal is the same: to record precisely where the site and its components, particularly artifacts, are located.

Excavations are typically one of two types: probing or clearing. *Probing excavations*, as the name implies, extend deep into the soil in an attempt to determine the presence, nature, and depth of the cultural deposits. Typical forms of probing excavations in New Jersey include *shovel tests*—typically round holes, eighteen inches in diameter, excavated with a spade well into the subsoil on a regular interval grid, such as a fifty-foot-grid. *Excavation units*, measuring a meter square or, alternatively, three or five feet square, can also be used to investigate archaeological deposits.

Probing excavations are excellent for getting a glimpse of what lies below, but they make it hard to interpret the overall configuration of archaeological features. *Clearing excavations*, which reveal large areas of a site at once, are much better for seeing the extent of archaeological features such as houses, privies, and middens. They take more time to complete, however, and can be more costly.

Regardless of the excavation method used, archaeologists rarely excavate an entire site. The preference is to excavate a representative sample. Of course, given that we cannot see what is underground, *representative sample* is somewhat ambiguous term. An archaeologist might miss the most informative deposits at a site or stumble upon a rich feature that is in no way representative of the site as a whole. Yet sampling is a must—for several reasons. First, excavating a site is like reading a book, taking notes, and then burning the original. The notes are all that survive. With today's improved techniques, we can extract much more information from a site than even our most talented predecessors could; presumably future archaeologists will be able to employ even better methods, techniques, and theories. By excavating only a sample of the site, we leave the rest of a finite resource for future archaeologists.

Another pragmatic reason for digging only selected areas of a site is that excavation is the fun part. Almost everyone likes to find artifacts. Only a dedicated few have the commitment to wash, label, and catalog them, and to write a report summarizing the work. Although ratios vary, in general it seems that every day in the field results in two or three days in the lab and an equal amount of time writing. A particularly interesting and productive site can potentially yield information for years' worth of analysis and writing.

The rare exception to the sampling rule occurs when a site of preeminent importance will be totally lost. With careful planning, however, it is often possible to find a middle ground. For instance, archaeologists from a private firm, the Cultural Resource Consulting Group, found very rich mid-eighteenth-century deposits all around the General John Frelinghuysen House in Raritan Borough, Somerset County (figure 1.1). Typically, the findings would be cause for celebration. Here, though, the dignified old house serves as the borough's library, and at the time it desperately needed an addition. Excavating all of the deposits would have been prohibitively expensive. As a solution, the archaeologists and architects developed a plan to excavate a sample of the eighteenth-century deposit and then to fill the excavation units (holes) with piers to support the library addition. The result is an addition that literally floats over the archaeological remains (figure 1.2). Sampling and thoughtful planning paid off: the library was able to expand, and the archaeological deposits were preserved (Cultural Resource Consulting Group 1994).

The tools archaeologists employ to excavate vary from site to site and range from dental picks to backhoes. The former are used to dissect the most complicated deposits, while backhoes may be required in urban locations that have been paved over and repeatedly built upon. Mason's trowels, particularly those made by the Marshalltown Company of Marshalltown, Iowa, are inarguably the archaeologist's tool of choice. Often their edges are honed to a razor edge—creating something of a hazard for individuals who carry them in their back pockets. These handy tools are used to peel away layers of soil, carefully revealing artifacts where they lie.

Most of the excavated soil from sites is sifted through a wire mesh (figure 1.3). Although their designs vary, from the old reliable wooden screen that

Figure 1.1. The General John Frelinghuysen House in Raritan Borough, Somerset County. The house, which dates from the mid-eighteenth century, serves as the borough's public library. Excavations to the rear of the structure revealed extensive archaeological deposits from the 1760s. Photograph by the author.

stands on two legs to massive screens powered by chugging gas engines, all screens serve the same function: to ensure that even the smallest artifacts are recovered. Again, context is everything. The importance of knowing where an artifact was found and being able to ascertain its function cannot be overestimated. Typically, artifacts are bagged in the field, often with a tag identifying where they came from and what they are. This labeling allows researchers in the laboratory to piece the finds back together and understand their relationship to one another. Extensive notes and photographs documenting the course of excavation are also critical. A collection without this accompanying information is almost impossible to interpret.

Archaeologists and Dating

Archaeologists are known for their ability to date artifacts. A misidentified or erroneously dated artifact can skew the date for an entire site. The techniques used to determine the ages of archaeological finds fall into two basic categories:

relative and absolute dating. The term *relative dating* might conjure up a variety of comical images. For archaeologists, however, it has nothing to do with cousins, but rather means the placement of artifacts and archaeological deposits in relation to one another. Simply put, artifacts found together tend to have been deposited at the same time. Archaeologists call this concept the Law of Association. Many archaeological sites are stratified, with different layers of soil laid down at different times. In general, artifacts found in deeper layers were deposited earlier than those in higher layers (figure 1.4). The first American archaeologist to note this fact was Thomas Jefferson, who is generally regarded as the father of American archaeology (Bahn 1996:79).

When excavating, the archaeologist attempts to unearth the deposits in reverse chronological order starting with the most recent and working down toward the oldest. In cases where the natural stratigraphy is invisible or indecipherable, levels of an arbitrary depth may be used. Even so, deeper layers tend to be older than ones closer to the surface. The Harris Matrix is one system of visually recording and tracking the relationship of one layer to another (Harris 1989). Although the Harris Matrix will not reveal the exact age of a level or of the artifacts in it, the system allows archaeologists to see which levels and artifacts are earlier or later than others.

Another form of relative dating is *seriation*. Seriation involves arranging artifacts in order by either time or popularity, and it is based on the fact that artifact styles and forms have changed or evolved through time. These changes often seem gradual, if not exactly predictable. For example, tobacco pipes in the early seventeenth century had tiny bowls, short stems, and wide bore diameters. Over the course of the eighteenth century their stems became longer, the bowls larger, and the bore diameters more narrow (figure 1.5). Archaeologist J. C. "Pinky" Harrington, who is widely regarded as one of historical archaeology's founders, discovered that the holes or bores through tobacco pipe stems— ubiquitous artifacts on historic sites—gradually and predictably evolved from very large to very small between 1620 and 1800 (Harrington 1954). Lewis Binford, working with Harrington's seriation scheme, was able to derive a mathematical formula for calculating the approximate age of a group of tobacco pipes (Binford 1962). Archaeologists James Deetz and Edwin Dethlefsen later seriated—arranged in order—the colonial gravestones in New England. The same methods are applied to some of New Jersey's early gravemarkers in Chapter 5.

Absolute dates, in distinction from relative dates, give the date, or at least a range of years, during which an artifact was either made or used. For example, a New Jersey copper one-cent piece excavated from the foundation trench of a house indicates that the trench must have been dug in 1786 or later, because

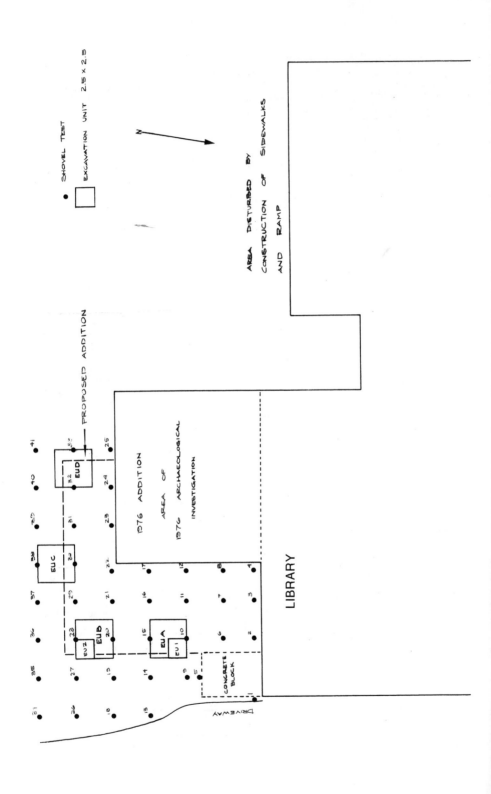

SHOVEL TEST

EXCAVATION UNIT 2.5 × 2.5

N

AREA DISTURBED BY
CONSTRUCTION OF SIDEWALKS
AND RAMP

PROPOSED ADDITION

41

32

26

EUD

40

32

24

39

31

25

EUC

29

23

1976 ADDITION

AREA OF

1976 ARCHAEOLOGICAL

INVESTIGATION

38

30

22

17

12

8

4

37

29

21

16

11

7

3

36

28

20

35

27

15

10

EU3

EUB

EUA

34

18

14

9

6

2

EU2

13

EU1

5

1

33

CONCRETE
BLOCK

LIBRARY

DRIVEWAY

Figure 1.3. A group of Monmouth University students and volunteers excavating at the Parker Farm, an eighteenth-century farmstead in Little Silver, Monmouth County. Note that only one student is actually digging. The others are screening for artifacts, taking notes, and assisting the excavator. Digging, though critical, is only a part of what archaeologists do. Photograph by the author.

New Jersey coppers were minted only from 1786 to 1788. This evidence provides what archaeologists call a *terminus post quem*, or "date after which," for the deposit.

Similarly, the techniques employed in the manufacture of various items allow them to be dated accurately. Machines that could cut nails out of bar iron were not in common use until about 1820, so a machine-cut nail recovered archaeologically should postdate 1820.

Although some scientific dating techniques such as radiocarbon dating, thermoluminescence dating, and potassium-argon dating are valuable primarily for

Figure 1.2. (opposite) This map shows the location of shovel tests and excavation units dug at the Frelinghuysen House prior to construction of the library's addition. By setting the new section on piers instead of a full foundation, it was possible to preserve most of the archaeological deposits in place. Courtesy of the Cultural Resource Consulting Group.

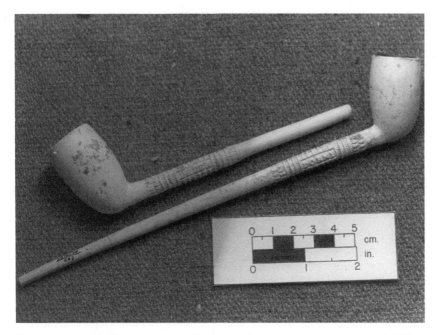

Figure 1.5. A pair of reconstructed mid-nineteenth-century tobacco pipes, marked Peter Dorni. They were recovered during an archaeological excavation in New Brunswick. Courtesy of the Cultural Resource Consulting Group.

prehistoric sites, another absolute dating technique employed by historical archaeologists is *dendrochronology*, or tree-ring dating. This technique allows the archaeologist to date a piece of timber from the frame of a house, for example, to the year in which the tree was cut down. As every schoolchild knows, trees produce annual growth rings, and some trees that are more susceptible to environmental fluctuations produce rings of varying width depending upon the amount of precipitation and other factors over the course of the growth cycle. In the early twentieth century, A. E. Douglass, an astronomer studying climate change, began collecting tree-ring data in the American Southwest. Using data from living trees, he was able to make calculations going back only about five hundred years. Interested in extending the sequence, Douglass began working with archaeologists and was eventually able to put together a series of tree rings

Figure 1.4. (opposite) Stratigraphy, as seen in the excavation of a Native American burial mound on the plantation of William Feriday, Concordia Parish, Louisiana, ca. 1850. This painting by John Egan clearly depicts the different layers of soil in the mound and is one of the earliest renderings of an archaeological excavation in North America. Reproduced by permission of the Saint Louis Art Museum.

dating back more than a thousand years. When segments of ring patterns from timbers of unknown dates are matched to the reference sequence, a date for the unknown sample is revealed.

On the East Coast, the best-developed tree-ring chronology is for oaks. Although archaeologists do not often recover timbers from their sites, they can use this technique to date standing buildings. For instance, the Rahway Historical Society, which operates the Merchants and Drovers Tavern Museum, had long debated the exact age of the tavern, an imposing three-story frame building that towers over the intersection of Westfield Avenue and St. Georges Avenue in Rahway (figure 1.6). Some experts argued for an early-eighteenth-century date; others concluded, based on architectural style, that a date closer to 1800 was more likely for the oldest part of the building. In the spring of 1999 wood samples were taken from thirteen locations within the structure (Veit 1999). The samples, removed with a hollow-pointed drill, measure roughly the length of a pencil (figure 1.7). Scientists associated with Columbia University's Lamont Dougherty Earth Sciences Observatory examined the samples and compared them with regional tree-ring chronologies. The results indicate two construction episodes, one in 1795–1796, followed by another in 1818–1819. Although it is

NORTHEAST ELEVATION

Figure 1.6. Merchants and Drovers Tavern, Rahway. Dendrochronology, also known as tree-ring dating, helped determine that the earliest section of the tavern was constructed in 1795–1796. Library of Congress, Prints and Photographs Division (HABS, NJ,20-RAH,16-36).

Figure 1.7. Scott Wieczorek taking a wood sample from a historic building for tree-ring dating. The drill removes a core that is roughly the size of a pencil. Photograph by the author.

possible that an earlier tavern stood on this well-traveled corner, it is unlikely that the current building existed before 1795. Probably not coincidentally, this date corresponds closely with the date of the first tavern license issued to innkeeper John Anderson in 1798 (Bertland 1998:11).

Back to the Lab

After the fieldwork is done, artifacts are taken back to the laboratory and cleaned according to their material and condition. They are generally labeled and painted with small numbers to identify their *provenience*, that is, their exact location on the site. Although ceramics and glass can endure years of burial with minimal decay, artifacts of wood, plaster, bone, and metal may require immediate conservation attention to ensure that they survive the transition from burial underground to storage in museum boxes. Objects of iron and other ferrous metals, if left untreated, have a tendency to fragment away so that within a short time they become unrecognizable. Conservation is a complex, acquired skill that draws on knowledge of chemistry and physics and often involves the use of volatile chemicals. Conservation is critical to ensuring the survival of archaeological collections into the future.

Unfortunately, the result of some excavations is a collection of artifacts tucked away in a dusty corner of a museum or historic society. If, as I have argued, artifacts are documents that provide direct information about the past, a collection that is inaccessible or forgotten is of little use to anyone. Displaying artifacts, creating finding aids to collections, publishing excavation reports, and ensuring access to them by interested and knowledgeable individuals is paramount.

In the following chapters we shall look at sites associated with New Jersey's seventeenth-century colonists, eighteenth-century elites, Revolutionary War record, historic graveyards and cemeteries, early transportation networks, industrial revolution, and nineteenth-century growth. Although these diverse sites do not necessarily reflect all facets of the state's history, they do provide windows into the past. As more archaeologists turn their attention and trowels to the Garden State's fertile soils, it seems likely that these windows will become larger and clearer.

 # "A Good Land to Behold"
In Search of New Jersey's
First Settlers

Many archaeologists are afflicted with a strange malady: the desire to find the oldest or first archaeological site of a particular kind. For historical archaeologists working in New Jersey, these "oldest" sites date to the seventeenth century, the period of initial interaction between European colonists and Native Americans. Sites from this period are extremely rare, in part because New Jersey was sparsely populated in the seventeenth century, having fewer than twenty thousand settlers by 1700 (Wacker 1975:132). Making matters even worse for archaeologists, many of the first colonial settlements were situated in choice locations and grew into such major cities as Newark, Elizabeth, Perth Amboy, and Burlington. Continuous development over more than three hundred years has erased or deeply buried the archaeological remnants of these earliest communities.

Nonetheless, archaeologists have discovered a few of these early sites. The ones examined here illustrate what might be called the "frontier period" of New Jersey's history. They include the house of a wealthy Dutch official on Burlington Island, a Quaker meetinghouse, and the home of John Reading, a West Jersey proprietor (figure 2.1). (Some additional early sites are explored in Chapter 3, which focuses on eighteenth-century life.)

New Jersey's written history began in 1524 when Giovanni da Verrazano, an Italian mariner in the employ of the French king, sailed along the coast of what is today known as the Jersey Shore. Nearly one hundred years later, in 1609, Captain Henry Hudson, an Englishman exploring for the Dutch, sailed north along the same coast. He is believed to have sighted the high hills of the Navesink on September 2, 1609 (Smith 1963:6). Robert Juet, his first mate, described the Highlands as "Very pleasant and high and bold" (Juet in Wacker 1975:19). Although Hudson and his crew were clearly impressed with what they

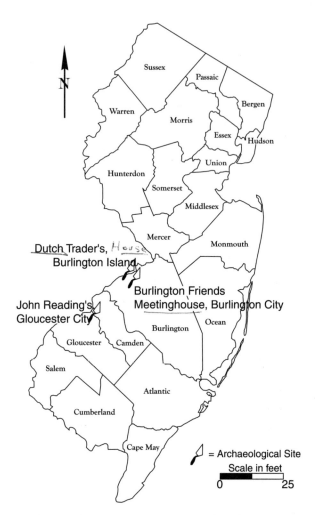

Figure 2.1. Map showing the approximate locations of Burlington Island, site of the Dutch Trader's House; Burlington City, home to the Burlington Friends Meetinghouse; and Gloucester City, site of the John Reading House. These three sites represent the earliest phase of colonial life in New Jersey.

saw, it was not until the 1620s that the Dutch began to establish small trading posts along the North (Hudson) and South (Delaware) Rivers.

The land that Hudson and his predecessors had "discovered" was far from uninhabited. New Jersey and adjacent sections of what today are the states of New York, Delaware, and Pennsylvania were home to diverse groups of Native Americans. Today these groups are often lumped together under the term *Lenape*, which in their dialects of a language known as Eastern Algonkian means "ordinary" or "common people." (See Kraft 1986, Grumet 1995, and Becker 1983, 1986, for detailed analyses of the various groups that historically lived in New Jersey.) They called themselves by various names depending upon where they lived: Raritans, Navasinks, Aquackanoncks, Esopus Minisinks, among others (Goddard 1978:213). Their ancestors had lived in New Jersey for more than ten thousand years. During this period their lifestyle had evolved from a mobile hunting and gathering pattern to a somewhat more settled existence that included foraging for food and, in the northwestern corner of the state, some horticulture.

In the years immediately preceding contact with European settlers, some of New Jersey's Native Americans lived in small communities of bark-covered lodges. In the northwestern portion of the state archaeologist Herbert Kraft found the remains of longhouses like those constructed by the Iroquois and other Native Americans in New York State (Kraft 1986:124; 1975:73–86). The archaeological traces of less formal dwellings, such as wigwams, have been found at sites in the Delaware Valley (Becker 1993). The Native Americans were fine craftsmen who worked with cloth, wood, quills, shell, pottery, and stone. Unfortunately, much of what they produced was perishable and rarely found by archaeologists.

Although an extended discussion of the prehistoric lives of New Jersey's Native Americans is beyond the scope of this book, over one hundred years of archaeological research, much carried out by talented amateurs, has revealed a wealth of information about this state's first inhabitants. (For more on this topic, the interested reader should see Kraft 1986, Grumet 1995, and Mounier [forthcoming].) At most, a thousand Native Americans may have lived in New Jersey in 1600 c.e. In the following 150 years, they would lose much of their land to European colonists. Disease and warfare, exacerbated by social breakdown, further reduced their population, and by the 1750s they had become a persecuted minority in their own homeland.

Based on Hudson's explorations of 1609, the Dutch claimed an area called New Netherland that stretched from Maine south to Delaware Bay, and they established many trading stations. This was the golden age of Dutch commercial power (Huey 1991:25). In 1614 the Dutch New Netherland Company established a small trading post on Castle Island, near today's Albany, New York. The Dutch West India Company took over the monopoly on New World trade in 1621 (Huey 1991:29).

Both the English and the Dutch scrambled to lay claim to the Delaware River. In 1610 the English navigator Samuel Argall sailed into Delaware Bay, claimed it for Great Britain, and named it after the English governor of Virginia, Lord de la Ware. Six years later, probably unaware of Argall's voyage, the Dutch sea captain Cornelis Hendricksen explored the Delaware River and reported his discoveries in the Netherlands. Cornelis Jacobsen Mey, for whom Cape May is named, also visited the Delaware River in 1616 and again in 1620 (Weslager 1961:45). Despite these visits, the Dutch did not establish a settlement on the Delaware until 1624. That settlement, though it proved short-lived, was located on Burlington Island.

Charles Conrad Abbott and the Dutch Trader's House on Burlington Island

In the 1890s, while walking the shores of Burlington Island looking for Native American artifacts, Charles Conrad Abbott happened upon the remains of a seventeenth-century site associated with the Dutch settlement of the island. This chance discovery and Abbott's subsequent actions made him the state's first historical archaeologist (figure 2.2). He amassed a noteworthy collection of colonial Dutch artifacts that languished unrecognized and forgotten for nearly one hundred years in the storerooms of the University of Pennsylvania Museum and the Peabody Museum of Archaeology and Ethnology at Harvard University. The story of Abbott's initial discovery, and of the rediscovery and reanalysis of the collection by myself and Charles Bello (1999), provides an opportunity to examine how archaeological practices have matured over the past century. At the same time Abbott's story highlights how luck and being in the right place at the right time have characterized so many great archaeological finds.

The story of Burlington Island's settlement has been recounted by Adrian Leiby (1964:6):

> In March, 1624, the [Dutch West India Company] sent out Captain Cornelis Jacobsen Mey . . . in the *Nieu Netherland*, a vessel of 260 tons, with about thirty families aboard, the first Dutch settlers of America. All of them were Walloons, religious refugees who had come to Holland from the French-speaking provinces of the Spanish Netherlands. In the late summer of 1624, Mey settled eighteen of his passengers at Fort Orange (Albany), two families and six single men at the Fresh [Connecticut] River and two families and eight single men, the first settlers of New Jersey, on an island in the Delaware River which is now called Burlington Island, a good distance inland from the sea.

Unfortunately, very little is known about these pioneering settlers. According to historian Henry Bisbee (1972:11), "a palisaded fort was built on the down river end of the island."

Figure 2.2. Charles Conrad Abbott strolling in Trenton about the·time of his Burlington Island excavations. Abbott was the first archaeologist to dig a historic site in New Jersey. Courtesy of the Manuscripts Division, Rare Books and Special Collections, Princeton University Library.

During the mid-seventeenth century both the Dutch and the Swedes, who had established a small, poorly supported colony in the Delaware Valley in the 1630s, used the Burlington Island settlement as a trading post (Nelson 1886:214), but friction over trade led to conflict between the groups. In 1655 Peter Stuyvesant, the famous Dutch governor of New Netherland, dispatched an expedition to the Delaware Valley to remove the Swedish threat to Dutch trade on the river. Shortly thereafter, Alexander d'Hinoyossia, vice director of New Netherland, moved his family to Burlington Island and "made it a pleasure ground or garden, built good houses upon it, and sowed and planted it" (James and Jameson 1959:98).

The Delaware Valley, and in fact all of the East Coast of today's United States, was contested ground in the seventeenth century, claimed by the English, Dutch, and Swedes. In this turbulent state of affairs, D'Hinoyossia's tenure proved short. When the English conquered New Netherland in 1664, one of the plums picked by Sir Robert Carr, the duke of York's representative on the scene, was Burlington Island. After a series of land transfers, Robert Stacey, a prominent Quaker, obtained a seven-year lease to Burlington Island from the governor in New York.

Questions soon arose regarding the validity of Stacey's title. In 1682 the West Jersey Assembly passed an act setting aside "all rents, issues, and profits" from the island "for the maintaining of a school for the education of the youth within the said town, and in the First and Second Tenths" (Leaming and Spicer 1758:455). Through most of the eighteenth and nineteenth centuries the island was farmed and the proceeds used to support various educational endeavors in the town. While the city of Burlington flourished, the island remained largely undeveloped. During the early twentieth century, it was a popular family resort with extensive picnic grounds.

The largely undisturbed landscape of Burlington Island was radically altered in 1955 when the Warner Company began mining gravel from the southern end. The work created a large, unsightly basin and likely removed most, if not all, of the remaining archaeological deposits. Even so, Charles Conrad Abbott's publications, and the artifacts he recovered from the island, provide a tantalizing glimpse of life on the colonial frontier in seventeenth-century New Jersey.

Charles Conrad Abbott was born in Trenton on June 4, 1843. Although trained as a physician, Abbott is best known today for his writings on natural history and archaeology. He and his wife, Julia Boggs Olden, lived on a farm just south of Trenton, which they called "Three Beeches" (Kraft 1993; Aiello 1967). Like many other members of the rural gentry, Abbott collected artifacts as a pastime. He read widely and was aware that archaeologists in Europe had demonstrated the coexistence of man with various species of ancient and extinct animals. Digging on his farm, Abbott found crude stone tools, which he called paleoliths—literally, old stones. He believed that these ancient-looking artifacts dated to glacial times, some twelve thousand years ago or more.

Frederick Ward Putnam, the distinguished curator of the Peabody Museum at Harvard University, was impressed with Abbott's work and became his mentor and patron. Pleased by the attention, Abbott sent more than twenty-five thousand artifacts to Cambridge (Kraft 1993:3), where they still compose a major portion of the Peabody Museum's little-studied New Jersey collection. In 1889 Abbott was appointed as the first curator of archaeology at the University of Pennsylvania Museum in Philadelphia, then known as the Free Museum of Art and Science. Unfortunately, the irascible and opinionated Abbott alienated the other anthropologists in Philadelphia, and in October 1892 he was fired (Hinsley 1985:66).

Abbott's misfortune has proved a boon to present-day archaeologists. After losing his position at the museum, he spent several years digging on Burlington Island. In his book *Recent Rambles* (1899:314), Abbott tells how he found the site:

> During a recent ramble I found a yellow brick upon the sand; and looking far-ther, another, and curious old red bricks and bits of roofing tiles, and pipe-stems; scattered everywhere odds and ends that could only have come from some old house near by. But where? It needed but to ask the question to change from aimless rambler to explorer, and then my troubles began. It was not enough to search for the spot whereon had stood the house, for this was soon found; but who lived here; when did he build; when and why did he leave? A hundred questions plagued me at once and I took refuge in the book-stack.

Abbott's reading apparently led him to conclude that the site was either a Dutch trading post or a tavern built by Peter Jegou (Veit and Bello 1999:100).

We know little of Abbott's excavation methods. In fact, the only description of his fieldwork is encapsulated within his discussion of the site (1899:316–19):

> I would that some one had written a learned essay on the art of digging. It is something more than mere shoveling of dirt, pitching aside with a spade sand, gravel, and clay. It may mean important discovery at any moment and the bringing again to light of day of long-buried treasure. . . . Sitting upon the damp sand, dotted with bits of the old house and pipe-stems, I burrowed into the low bank with a garden-trowel, making little horizontal holes that would have pleased the swallows, saving them half the labor of nest-building. But at last the steel struck a resisting object that was not a stone, but a curious, long, thin brick. This was the outlier of the treasure beyond, and the digging henceforth was a pleasure notwithstanding the many tree roots that had en-viously wrapped about the one-time belongings of the defunct Dutchman. A part of the wall was finally exposed, and many small, pale-yellow bricks. The larger red ones were generally perfect, but every yellow one was broken. Next came a part of the roof, still intact, three large curved tiles, and beneath them

portions of what I took to be a charred beam. Hand-wrought iron spikes were found, all twisted out of shape, the effect of heating when the house was burned.

Apparently the site was quite productive. As Abbott later wrote, "there were beer mugs, and schnapps bottles and wineglasses . . . and then the pipes and pipe stems! I have a pile of over five hundred" (1899:321). In 1894 he sent much of the collection to the Peabody Museum. One curved red clay roof tile remained at the University of Pennsylvania Museum. It was that artifact which led to the rediscovery of the collection by myself and Charles Bello.

Today 194 artifacts survive from the "Dutch Trader's House" on Burlington Island. They include fragments of black (actually very dark green) glass bottles, more than fifty glass trade beads, sixty-one stem and bowl fragments from tobacco pipes, as well as hand-wrought iron nails, fragments of window glass, roof tiles, and a variety of Native American items. Although it is not possible to describe all of these artifacts in detail here, some merit further discussion.

Among the most interesting are fragments from four pottery roof tiles. Brick red in color, the tiles strongly resemble ones recovered from seventeenth-century deposits at Fort Orange in Albany, New York, and from Manhattan (figure 2.3). Clay tiles were commonly used for roofs in urban areas of the Netherlands be-

Figure 2.3. A Dutch pan or roof tile recovered by Abbott during his Burlington Island excavations (object no. 9186). Courtesy of the University of Pennsylvania Museum, Philadelphia.

cause they provided considerable fire protection. The presence of such roof tiles at this site hints at Dutch occupancy.

The fragmentary tobacco pipe stems recovered at the site provide one of the best tools for dating its occupation. Although Abbott claimed to have recovered five hundred, today only sixty-one are present in the collection. Fifty-six of these were manufactured from white ball clay, sometimes incorrectly called kaolin. The remaining five were made from reddish brown clay that probably originated locally. The white clay fragments include both bowls and stems, and several are stamped with maker's marks: fifteen have heels embossed with the letters "EB," and one is marked "IS." The "EB" pipes were most likely produced by Edward Bird, an English-born pipe maker based in the Netherlands; the pipe marked "IS" may be the work of John Sinderling, who was active in Bristol, England, between 1668 and 1699 (Hurry and Keeler 1991:68–69).

As noted in Chapter 1, archaeologists J. C. Harrington and Lewis Binford developed techniques for dating collections of pipe stems that rely upon the changing diameter of the bore, or hole, through the center of the stem. The bore diameters of English pipes, for example, became gradually smaller during the seventeenth and eighteenth centuries. When applied to Abbott's Burlington Island collection, these techniques yield a mean date of 1660, which corresponds fairly well with the historical record, despite the rather small sample size.

The five red clay pipe stems are even more interesting (figure 2.4). In terms of form and finish, they are identical to the white clay pipes, but they appear to have been made from local clays. None is marked. A note in Abbott's handwriting found with one of the pipes reads, "This is a pipe made in New Jersey about 1700, and probably first pipes [sic] for smoking tobacco made in this country." Abbott's interpretation is supported by a promotional pamphlet published in 1685 by Thomas Budd, a former inhabitant of Burlington, who asserted that "[t]here are several sorts of good clay, of which bricks, earthen-ware, and tobacco pipes are made" (Budd 1685:8).

Similar pipes, often designated terra-cotta pipes, have been recovered from seventeenth-century sites in Virginia and Maryland and have led to considerable discussion among archaeologists. They may have been manufactured by Native Americans, African Americans, European colonists, or all three (Mouer 1993). Such pipes are often elaborately decorated and were most commonly made between 1660 and 1720 (Henry 1979:35).

Based on Veit and Bello's reanalysis of the collection, it appears that Abbott was correct in assigning the site a date in the 1660s. Although it is not the site of the first settlement on Burlington Island, the Dutch Trader's House is one of

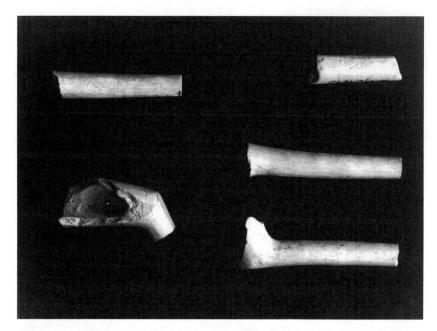

Figure 2.4. A selection of red clay tobacco pipes found by Charles Conrad Abbott at the site he called the Dutch Trader's House on Burlington Island (catalog no. 10/43026). Courtesy of the Peabody Museum, Harvard University, Cambridge.

the oldest historical archaeological sites in the state. Most likely it was one of the houses built by Governor d'Hinoyossia.

When he described the site in 1898, Abbott wrote, "How completely history and pre-history here overlapped! We know pretty much everything about Dutchmen, but how much do we really know of the Native Americans?" (1898:171). The sentiment is ironic to us today, for it is clear just how much more there is to learn about the Dutch, as well as the English and the Swedes, who met Native Americans and each other in the Delaware Valley in the seventeenth century. Thanks to Charles Conrad Abbott, we have a bit more information to help unravel these mysteries.

Quaker Zion on the Delaware: The Burlington Meetinghouse

To understand how Burlington City was founded, it is necessary to know something about how New Jersey was settled. The desire for religious freedom motivated Puritans to emigrate to New England, and the cash crops of tobacco, cotton, rice, and indigo made English settlement of Virginia and the Carolinas profitable. New Jersey's settlers, on the other hand, were drawn by the opportunity to acquire land cheaply. Many also hoped to benefit from the subsequent resale of their lands for substantial profit.

In 1664 James, duke of York, dispatched Colonel Richard Nicolls and an expeditionary force of 450 soldiers to stake England's claim to the Middle Atlantic. Nicolls convinced the burghers of New Amsterdam to surrender without firing a shot. As resourceful as he was energetic, Nicolls then set about enticing settlers to the colony by distributing land patents. Events in England, however, were moving faster than even he could have predicted. Unbeknownst to Nicolls, the duke of York had already granted to his powerful allies Sir George Carteret and John, Lord Berkeley, all the territory between the Hudson and Delaware Rivers. The duke, who mistakenly believed the province was an island, renamed the territory New Caesarea, or New Jersey, in honor of Carteret's defense of Royalists on the Isle of Jersey during the English Civil War.

Carteret and Berkeley dispatched Philip Carteret, a cousin of Sir George, to govern their new colony and collect quitrents. The colonists refused to pay, claiming that Carteret lacked the authority to collect them. To make a long and convoluted story short, Lord Berkeley, in an attempt to make some money from a colony he cared little about, sold his half of New Jersey to Quaker Edward Byllynge in 1674 for £1,000. Byllynge, however, was bankrupt and beholden for the money to another Quaker, John Fenwick (Pomfret 1964:21). Soon Fenwick and Byllynge had a falling out. Three members of the London Friends, including William Penn, agreed to serve as trustees for the purchase. The eventual result was that West Jersey, Berkeley's former half of the colony, was divided into one hundred proprietary shares (Wacker 1975:275). Although more legal maneuvering followed, the Byllynge/Fenwick purchase opened West Jersey to settlement by Quakers seeking refuge from persecution in England (Pomfret 1964:66–69). Other settlers, probably from New England, had arrived earlier in the century.

In 1677 a group of 230 English Quakers disembarked at the site of today's Burlington City, beginning nearly a century of strong influence on the developing politics and culture of the Delaware Valley. Roughly half of these settlers hailed from Yorkshire, Derbyshire, and Nottinghamshire; the others came from London and Middlesex (see Fischer 1989:441; Wacker 1975:288). When they laid out their settlement at Burlington, they built on two sides of a stream. Not surprisingly, the bridges that spanned it were called London Bridge and York Bridge (Fischer 1989:441). The ten Yorkshire proprietors built on the north side of Market Street, while the London proprietors constructed their houses on the south side (Wacker 1975:289).

The Quakers' success in the New World was owing in large part to the strong institutional organization that they developed. According to David Hackett Fischer, "The Society of Friends was organized as a complex structure of meetings—men's meetings and women's meetings, meetings for worship and meetings for business, monthly meetings, quarterly meetings and yearly meetings. They recognized a need for leadership by elders and overseers, whose task was to teach, counsel and support" (1989:428). Although Burlington would be quickly superseded by Philadelphia, the city was the early center of Quaker religious life in the New World; the first yearly meeting of Friends in North America occurred there in 1681 (Grummere 1884:17–18).

Initially, the Friends worshiped in private homes, but by 1682 the membership had outgrown these informal quarters. The meeting thus "ordered that a new meetinghouse be built." Francis Collins, a carpenter and member of the meeting, undertook the work, which was finally completed five years later, in 1687 (McCarthy and Ward 1999:3; Ward and O'Reilly 2000:3). Friends from throughout the region came to the Burlington Meetinghouse for weekly worship, as well as for quarterly and yearly meetings, which could last, respectively, for a full day to several days. In addition to the opportunity to discuss broader issues of religious policy and doctrine, the meetings also provided an obvious opportunity for socializing (McCarthy and Ward 1999:2).

The description from the meeting's minutes, as well as some historic sketches, indicate that the meetinghouse was likely hexagonal in form, with steeply sloping roof planes that met under a central cupola (figure 2.5). By 1783 the meeting had outgrown this home as well, and a substantial rectangular brick building (still standing) was constructed to replace it (Grummere 1884:68). Its predecessor was dismantled in the 1790s, and at least some of the materials were reused in other buildings.

In the spring of 1994, when a conference center was scheduled to be built on what was reputed to be the site of the original Burlington Meetinghouse, historical archaeologists Jeanne A. Ward and John P. McCarthy volunteered their services in an effort to determine whether any remains of the unusual building could be found and to salvage any archaeological data that might otherwise be lost. (The following discussion is based primarily upon McCarthy and Ward 1999; O'Reilly et al. 1999; and Ward and O'Reilly 2000). The excavations took place in two stages. During the first phase of work, archaeologists laid out and excavated twenty-two shovel tests on a ten-foot grid in the area likely to contain evidence (Ward and O'Reilly 2000:4). In three of these tests they encountered a deposit of

Figure 2.5. The hexagonal Burlington Meetinghouse (1687–1783) as depicted in a nineteenth-century woodcut.

yellowish brown sandy soil that contained seventeenth- and eighteenth-century artifacts. They surmised that this archaeological feature might be the remains of the original meetinghouse.

Further excavations, carried out with the assistance of interested Friends and local students, included digging several larger excavation units within a five-foot grid. These excavations revealed both a hexagonal pit, measuring 48 feet across and between 23 and 25 feet on a side, as well as stone footings probably associated with an addition to the structure built in the 1720s (McCarthy and Ward 1999:5). Apparently, after the original structure served out its useful life, the frugal Quakers salvaged the bricks and stones. Interestingly, one of the fragmentary bricks recovered from within the former cellar hole was a molded brick, which would have formed one corner of the building. Also found were nearly three thousand artifacts. Most were architectural items, though artifacts related to cooking and eating were also recovered. They were deposited in the hole left by the removal of the structure and appear to have been tossed in when the building was demolished.

The artifacts include window glass, rosehead and T-head nails (commonly used during the eighteenth century), brick rubble, mortar, and fragments of roofing slate (Ward and O'Reilly 2000:5). Ceramics such as Chinese export porcelain, British brown stoneware, domestic gray stoneware, Buckley coarse earthenware, redware, and tin-glazed earthenware were all recovered from the cellar hole. Two coins, a George II farthing produced between 1730 and 1739 and a George I Irish halfpenny with a date of 1723, were also recovered, corroborating the eighteenth-century date of the assemblage. An average date of 1784 was calculated for the ceramic fragments present (Ward and O'Reilly 2000:6), which conforms with the hypothesis that the deposit dates to the late eighteenth century and is related to the original meetinghouse. The ceramics found at the site, along with a small quantity of food remains, animal bones, and shells, probably indicate that the Friends ate meals at their meetings, a practice that continues among modern Friends (O'Reilly et al. 1999:11). The generally undecorated ceramics also reflect the conservative tastes of the Quakers, who were known for their "plainness" (Ward and O'Reilly 2000:9).

One of the puzzles that McCarthy and Ward had to address was the hexagonal design. In their research they found no seventeenth-century British antecedents for a hexagonal Friends meetinghouse; most were rectangular and plain in style. Friends in northeastern New Jersey and New York did build the occasional octagonal meetinghouse, which may have inspired the Burlington Friends. Moreover, the unusual design highlights the fact that "the late seventeenth century was a time of experimentation in meetinghouse form" (O'Reilly et al. 1999:10).

Thanks to the volunteer excavations of John McCarthy and Jeanne Ward, and the subsequent artifact analysis by Ward and Carey O'Reilly, we have an archaeological glimpse of a significant and unusual colonial structure and the activities that occurred around and in it.

The House of John Reading, a West Jersey Proprietor

In many of New Jersey's older towns there still stand houses believed to date to the first decades of the state's settlement. Marked with bronze plaques proclaiming their venerable origins, they remind us of the families and individuals who carved the first communities out of the wilderness. Many of these houses, however, are not quite as old as they purport to be. In fact, very few structures built before 1725 have been confidently dated in this state. Furthermore, despite years of archaeological research, only a handful of seventeenth-century houses has been found by archaeologists. (See Epperson 1992 and Louis Berger and Associates 1998:27–100, 167–203, for exceptions.) One of the most interesting of these was excavated in Gloucester City, Camden County, by archaeologist Ronald Thomas of Middle Atlantic Archaeological Research (MAAR) and a team of skilled professionals and volunteers. Although this site (designated

28Ca50) was first occupied approximately eight thousand years ago by Native Americans, the deposits that will interest us here date from the mid and late 1600s.

Andrew Stanzeski, a local resident who also happens to be an archaeologist, discovered the site on the weekend of April 9–10, 1983 (MAAR 1985:I-1). He noticed that a construction project on the property had uncovered a variety of prehistoric and early colonial artifacts. Aware of their importance, he brought these finds to the attention of the Archaeological Society of New Jersey. Working together, volunteers from the society and professional archaeologists attempted to "rescue from destruction important archaeological information that . . . would otherwise be lost" (MAAR 1985:I-1). Despite their efforts, it appeared that the site was too large to be effectively salvaged by volunteers. Timely intervention by the New Jersey State Museum and the National Park Service resulted in a professional archaeological excavation of the site by MAAR.

Thomas and his staff researched the site's history while excavations were underway so that they would be able to link the archaeological remains with the people who left them. Doing research on early colonial Camden County is challenging, however, because many important documents are missing or hard to find. Immediately relevant to this study, a fire early in eighteenth century at the house of John Reading, the first county clerk, is known to have destroyed very early land records (MAAR 1985:I-25).

Gloucester Town was one of the first planned communities in West Jersey. (Other early settlements were Salem and Burlington.) It was located near the site of Fort Nassau, one of the earliest European settlements on the Delaware. Established by the Dutch, this fortified fur-trading post was occupied intermittently between 1626 and 1651 and has been the subject of unsuccessful searches since the mid-1800s. One of the most intensive searches, carried out by a committee of the New Jersey Historical Society in the 1850s (Mulford 1853), combined map research, interviews with elderly local residents, and an inspection of likely locations. In fact, they did everything but dig. Fort Nassau, if its remains still survive, has yet to be excavated.

Thomas Sharp laid out the town, now city, of Gloucester in 1687. As planned, it consisted of "three areas: the Town, the Suburbs and the Town Bounds or Liberties" (MAAR 1985:I-29). The town itself contained eighty-eight lots, six of which were investigated by Ronald Thomas and his team. John Reading, a West Jersey proprietor and "Clerk of the Court at Gloucester from 1688 to 1702" had a dwelling somewhere within the study area (MAAR 1985:I-25).

Excavations on the property, which had already been disturbed by construction activities, revealed the partial brick foundations of a house and an interesting assortment of artifacts dating to the period between 1670 and 1710 (Thomas and Schiek 1988:3). The parts of the foundation that survived allowed the archaeologists to infer what the structure looked like. The foundation was one-and-one-half bricks thick and probably supported a timber-framed super-structure (figure 2.6; Thomas and Schiek 1988:4). The house itself was quite small, measuring only 26 feet by 12 feet, and was probably constructed on a two-room hall and parlor plan, with the hall serving a variety of public func-tions and the parlor providing a more private space.

Unlike many settlers' houses, this one had lead casement windows—a rare and costly touch on the frontier. Thomas and his team found 124 pieces of lead that once held the glass panes in place (Thomas and Schiek 1988:6). Sixty-nine of these "window leads," or *kames*, were imprinted with the manufacturer's name and the year. Most of these bear the stamp EW WILLIAM PVRVOVR: 1678 (MAAR 1985:IV-8–IV-9).

Figure 2.6. An artist's interpretation of the seventeenth-century house discovered on John Reading's property in Gloucester City. The sketch is based on archaeological evidence from MAAR's excavations. Drawn by Rich Green; reproduced courtesy of Middle Atlantic Archaeological Research and the Archaeological Society of New Jersey.

The numerous tobacco pipe stem fragments recovered—890 in all—also suggest a late-seventeenth-century occupation of this house. The ceramics from the site include lead-glazed red earthenware, likely produced in the Delaware Valley, as well as buff-colored earthenware made in England and Westerwald salt-glazed stoneware mugs made in Germany (Thomas and Schiek 1988:407). Some tin-glazed earthenwares, probably made in the Netherlands or England, were also recovered.

Also found were several pieces of fragmentary glass stemware, probably dating to the seventeenth century (MAAR 1985:IV-6). If seventeenth-century sites are rare to begin with, those containing stemware are rarer still. These glass fragments may indicate that someone of particularly high status lived at the site—probably John Reading.

Other items in the large collection include two British trade tokens dating to the 1660s (Thomas and Schiek 1988:9; Thomas 1994:111). Tokens, roughly the equivalent of today's store coupons, served in place of small change in the poorly supplied colonies. Also found were two coins, one of which was minted, probably in the 1680s, in either Lima, Peru, or Potosi, Bolivia.

What all these artifacts reveal—ceramics, glass, coins, and window leads—is the participation of the house's inhabitants in the growing global economic system. Far from being self-sufficient frontiersmen, crafting all that they needed from the forests and fields around them, John Reading and his successors purchased and brought most of their material possessions from Europe.

Excavating at the Gloucester City site, probably the home of the West Jersey proprietor John Reading, Ronald Thomas and his fellow archaeologists salvaged a rich assemblage of seventeenth-century artifacts that enables us to better understand life in the colonial Delaware Valley, particularly among the highest levels of society. Moreover, in this present age of economic and cultural globalization, their findings highlight the beginnings of our capitalist world system and its local manifestations.

In 1677 John Crips, a resident of Burlington, wrote to his friend Henry Stacy in England. Crips was more than pleased with his new home: "For the Country, in short, I like it very well: And I do believe that this River of Delaware, is as good a River as most is in the World; it exceeds the River of Thames by Many Degrees." He was so smug in his approval of the region that he said of prospective settlers, "if they cannot Live Here, they can hardly live in any Place in the World" (Crips, quoted in Weiss and Weiss 1964:39). John Crips's glowing appraisal of New Jersey was shared by many of his contemporaries in the seventeenth century.

Although Dutch, Swedish, and English explorers all claimed parts of present-day New Jersey as their own, it was not until the English conquest of New Netherland in 1664 that colonists began to settle the area in earnest. In this chapter, we have examined three early colonial sites, each of which highlights a different aspect of colonial culture in the Delaware Valley. The Dutch Trader's House found by pioneer archaeologist Charles Conrad Abbott may not have been a trading post at all but rather a house associated with a prominent Dutch settler. Although the location of the house Abbott excavated has again been lost to time, the artifacts he recovered and his writings give us a glimpse of how historical archaeology developed in the state. McCarthy and Ward's excavations at the Burlington Friends' hexagonal meetinghouse remind us of the religious practices of the Quakers, who were so influential in the settlement of New Jersey. The artifacts from the seventeenth-century house associated with John Reading, a prominent official in Gloucester Town, provide a glimpse of life in the upper echelons of colonial society. Whoever owned the home had ready access to fine imported ceramics and glassware.

Archaeologists have much to offer when it comes to understanding the earliest years of settlement and colonization in New Jersey. They can provide physical evidence that corroborates or refutes written histories. Perhaps, in the years to come, more informative sites from this period will be excavated, giving us a better understanding of colonial settlement in northern and eastern New Jersey as well as in the Delaware Valley.

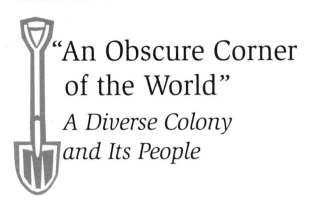

CHAPTER THREE

"An Obscure Corner of the World"
A Diverse Colony and Its People

Writing in 1747, the newly appointed royal governor of New Jersey, Jonathan Belcher, lamented his assignment, describing the colony as the "Wilderness of Nova Caesarea" and an "obscure corner of the world" (Batinski 1982:63). Belcher, who had previously served the English crown as governor of Massachusetts and New Hampshire, arrived to find a colony wracked by land riots and home to a diverse and independent-minded population. This chapter examines life in colonial New Jersey, focusing on the various ethnic groups that then inhabited the state. Five eighteenth-century sites, each representative of a particular aspect of life in the colony, will illustrate the cultural and economic diversity: Raritan Landing, a port town on the Raritan River; the Allen House, a rural tavern in Shrewsbury; the Luyster House, a Dutch-American farmstead in Middletown; Morven, the palatial home of the Stockton family in Princeton; and the Burr-Haines site, an unusual Native American dwelling in the Pinelands (figure 3.1).

It must be emphasized that these are only a few of the dozens of noteworthy eighteenth-century sites excavated in New Jersey over the past thirty years. Large-scale excavations have been carried out at the home of Revolutionary War General William Alexander, Lord Stirling, in the Somerset Hills, and other important sites have been studied in and around Trenton and at Beverwyck in Parsippany–Troy Hills. Because fieldwork at these sites has only recently been completed and reports have not yet been produced, it would be premature to discuss them in any great detail. We can also look forward to reading about the research along the Route 29 Trenton corridor by two firms, Hunter Research, Inc., and Gannett Fleming, Inc., which uncovered a variety of eighteenth-century structures, including warehouses, bake ovens, and even the kiln of a colonial potter.

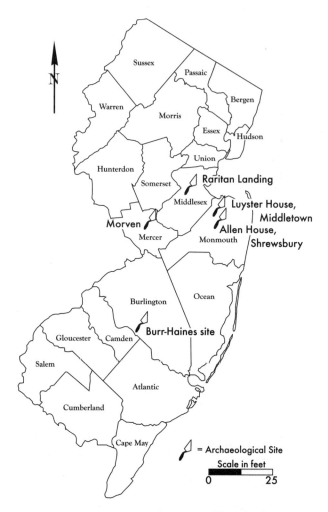

Figure 3.1. *Map showing the locations of Raritan Landing, the Allen House, the Luyster House, Morven, and the Burr-Haines site. Map by Dawn Turner.*

Archaeologists working at Beverwyck found substantial remains associated with the plantation of Dutch merchant Lucas von Beverhoudt (Silber and Catts 2001). Among the hundreds of artifacts recovered, perhaps the most intriguing find was a pair of rusted but still recognizable manacles or handcuffs. Although local histories note that both Beverhoudt and the previous owner of the property, William Kelly, were slaveowners, archaeological evidence for the brutal treatment of slaves was unexpected. This property, which had been slated for development as a commuter parking lot, is now being preserved for continued archaeological study. One can only guess what other secrets it will reveal to the probing trowels of archaeologists.

Raritan Landing and the Development of a Regional Culture

New Jersey is often ridiculed as a state without an identity, the butt of jokes inspired by the often unappealing views from the Turnpike between Philadelphia and New York. In fact, archaeological excavations at Raritan Landing, a colonial port on the Raritan River, show that New Jersey had developed its own distinct culture as early as the mid-eighteenth century.

Raritan Landing, located near New Brunswick at the high point of navigation on the Raritan River, once served as an important port for the farmers and merchants of central New Jersey. Since the 1970s, numerous professional archaeological firms have worked at the site, making it the most intensively studied colonial community in the state (Grossman and Porter 1979; Springsted et al. 1980; Grossman 1982; Mudge and Zmoda 1982; Zmoda 1985; Yamin 1988; Howson et al. 1995; Porter et al. 1995; Hartwick and Cavallo 1997). Recently, Terry Klein and Rebecca Yamin directed a team of four archaeology firms, Gannett Fleming, URS Corporation, John Milner and Associates, and Karen Hartgen Associates, in an extensive examination of a portion of the community that will be lost when Route 18 is extended from New Brunswick into Piscataway. As the results of that study become available, they will undoubtedly refine our understanding of eighteenth-century life in the Raritan Valley.

Established at the end of the seventeenth century, Raritan Landing flourished, despite its rural setting, owing to its convenient location. At its height in the mid-eighteenth century, the community counted about one hundred households (Yamin 1989a:50). Warehouses and craftsmen's shops lined its roads (figure 3.2). Although this area of Middlesex County was settled primarily by Baptists emigrating southward from New England and Scottish settlers hoping to establish a major city in Perth Amboy (Landsman 1985), Raritan Landing was more diverse. Many of the residents were of Dutch descent and had close family ties to New York (Vermeule 1936).

Only two houses contemporary with the original community remain today. The Cornelius Low House is an impressive stone mansion built in the fashionable Georgian style on a bluff overlooking the town. Low, a wealthy New York City merchant, moved to the Landing in 1738 (figure 3.3; Bailey 1968:390–91). Also surviving is the Metlar Bodine House, a small frame structure—today much enlarged—built by Peter Bodine, one of the town's founders.

During the American Revolution, British soldiers and their Hessian auxiliaries

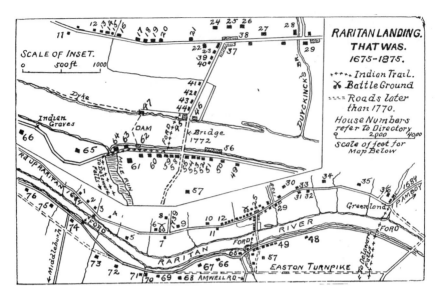

Figure 3.2. "Raritan Landing That Was, 1675–1875." This map shows Raritan Landing as it may have looked at its height. Note the houses, stores, and warehouses along River Road and Metlars Lane. Today much of the site lies under the grassy fields of Johnson Park. Courtesy of The New Jersey Historical Society.

occupied the town from December 1776 until June 1777 (Baurmeister 1973:87; Ewald 1979:51). Although the community recovered from the devastation of the war, the growth of New Brunswick in the early nineteenth century far out-stripped that of Raritan Landing. The Delaware and Raritan Canal, completed in 1834, had its eastern terminus at New Brunswick, and the Camden and Amboy Railroad laid track through town in 1836. Cut off from developing transportation routes, the Landing's fate was sealed. By the mid-nineteenth century the once-bustling community had largely disappeared.

Recent excavations at the site, funded by the New Jersey Department of Transportation and the Federal Highway Administration, addressed a variety of topics, including the community's layout, the ethnicity of its settlers, and its Revolutionary War experience. This work is likely to revolutionize our under-standing of life in the colonial Raritan Valley.

Earlier excavations at Raritan Landing by Rebecca Yamin presented a tan-talizing glimpse of life in the riverside community (Yamin 1988, 1989a, 1992–1993). Yamin's research examined the changing relationship between the Landing's inhabitants and those of nearby New York City. She discovered strong evidence that Raritan Landing traders had developed their own distinctive regional culture by the late eighteenth century. This finding refutes the commonly held assumption that New Jersey was "an amorphous land caught between New York and Philadelphia with no clear identity of its own and certainly no commerce free of its neighbors" (Yamin 1989a:49).

Yamin's conclusions were based upon archaeological evidence, particularly colonial ceramics, uncovered during 1979 excavations at the site by the Rutgers University Archaeological Survey Office. She also conducted extensive research into the historic documents that survive from the community. Yamin found that the inhabitants of Raritan Landing, a town whose fortunes were closely tied to trade, did not acquire the fashionable new ceramics, such as white salt-glazed stoneware and creamware, that were gracing New York City's tables in the 1760s and 1770s. Instead, they chose more colorful but less fashionable slip-decorated buff earthenware (Yamin 1989a:51). Why this difference? After careful research, Yamin concluded that Raritan Landing's residents, despite ready access to the

Figure 3.3. The Cornelius Low House (ca. 1738), one of two remaining structures from the height of Raritan Landing's prosperity in the mid-eighteenth century. Today the restored house is a museum run by the Middlesex County Cultural and Heritage Commission. Photograph by the author.

latest merchandise, simply had tastes distinct from those of their cousins in New York. Their actions left behind archaeological deposits reflective of their local culture. Although some economic historians would have us believe that eastern New Jersey was an economic suburb of New York during the eighteenth century, Rebecca Yamin has shown that it was not.

An Early New Jersey Rest Stop: The Blue Ball Tavern

In the eighteenth century, as today, New Jersey was an important transportation nexus. Nowadays, rest areas, service stations, fast-food restaurants, and neon-lit motels cater to hungry and weary travelers crossing the Garden State. In the eighteenth century, taverns served all of these functions and more.

In addition to satisfying thirst and hunger, taverns were important centers for entertainment and community gatherings, and they often served as informal courthouses and military recruiting stations. Inventories and travelers' descriptions indicate that several colonial New Jersey taverns even had small libraries for their patrons' edification (Bertland 1998:33). It is also worth noting that, for local residents, the travelers who passed through were a welcome source of entertainment and news about the outside world.

Archaeologists have studied several of New Jersey's historic taverns, including: the Blue Ball Tavern (now known as the Allen House) in Shrewsbury, Monmouth County; the Merchants and Drovers Tavern in Rahway (Bertland 1998); the Village Inn in Englishtown, Monmouth County; Widow Wood's Tavern in Franklin Township, Somerset County; and the Cherry Valley Tavern in Hanover Township, Burlington County. The Blue Ball Tavern, our subject here, is one of several historic structures owned by the Monmouth County Historical Association (MCHA). Excavations there have been conducted as an educational summer camp for youths ages twelve to fifteen, supervised by Project Archaeologist Megan Springate (figure 3.4).

The property where the Allen House now stands, located at the busy intersection of Sycamore Avenue and Route 35 in Shrewsbury, was first purchased by a Quaker named Judah Allen around 1680 (Springate 2000:3). He probably did not build the structure that today occupies site, but may have lived elsewhere on his extensive holding. A later owner, Richard Stillwell, built part of the current structure around 1740. He sold the tract in 1754 to Josiah and Zilpha Halstead, who turned the structure, presumably a dwelling house, into a tavern (Springate 2000:3). It is likely that a blue ball or globe decorated the tavern's sign and gave the place its name. Located at what was even then a busy intersection, the Blue Ball was almost immediately successful. Halstead expanded

Figure 3.4. The Allen House, formerly the Blue Ball Tavern, in Shrewsbury, Monmouth County. Owned and operated by the Monmouth County Historical Association, the Allen House is the site of an annual archaeological summer camp. Photograph by Megan Springate; reproduced courtesy of the Monmouth County Historical Association.

the structure, adding an attached kitchen with a large brick fireplace and two beehive ovens (Springate and Rogoff 1999:3). Sadly, shortly after this expansion, Zilpha Halstead, only thirty years old, died. She was buried across the street in Christ Church Cemetery.

Josiah Halstead, now a single parent caring for six children and running a busy tavern, did not remain a bachelor long. Within a year he married Anna Throckmorton. Although, as Springate and Rogoff point out, "his haste to re-marry may seem callous, the need for a wife to assist in the operation of a large tavern was paramount" (Springate and Rogoff 1999:3). Wives were vital part-ners for tavern keepers. They prepared meals, tended bar, aided travelers, and did everything else necessary to run the establishment. In fact, tavern keeping was one of the few occupations seen as appropriate work for either a man or a woman. Anna Halstead died in 1760, and six years later Josiah again remarried, this time to Lydia Worthley (Springate and Rogoff 1999:4).

During the 1760s, the Monmouth County Circuit Court met at Halstead's tav-ern, as did the Christ Church Vestry and the Shrewsbury Library Company. De-spite the Blue Ball's apparent popularity, Halstead suffered significant financial reversals, owing in part to a deepening recession in the colony. In 1765 he advertised the tavern for sale in the *Pennsylvania Gazette*, describing it as:

> A Compleat small Farm, lying the Center of the Town of Shrewsbury, New-Jersey, containing 56 Acres of very good Land and Meadow with a good Dwelling House, Garden, and Orchards of excellent Fruit, Stables, and other Out-houses, all in good Repair, and in compleat order for a Tavern, it being the Place where the most noted one in Shrewsbury, hath been kept for many Years, and is a proper place for a Store, Tradesman, or any other public Business. (Quoted in Nelson 1917:484–85)

The unfortunate Halstead was not able to find a buyer and again offered the tavern for sale in March 1768, without success (Springate and Rogoff 1999:5). In 1772 Halstead was committed to debtor's prison for failure to pay his excise taxes.

Stephen Tallman Jr., a prominent local landowner, acquired the property and rented the tavern to a series of tenant innkeepers. This pattern was not uncommon in early America. Although towns desperately needed taverns—indeed, since 1688, each town was legally required to have a tavern—the business required considerable capital and entailed substantial financial risks. A rapid turnover of tenants was common (Springate and Rogoff 1999:6), and a long line of innkeepers circulated through the Blue Ball until 1814, when Dr. Edmund Allen purchased the property (Springate and Rogoff 1999:8). His descendants retained ownership of the structure until 1927. After a few subsequent transfers, the Monmouth County Historical Association acquired it in 1968.

The earliest excavations at the Allen House occurred in the early 1970s, when the MCHA staff and trustees dug in and around the building during its restoration. Although a fascinating collection of eighteenth- and nineteenth-century artifacts was recovered, documentation of the excavations was limited, constraining the usefulness of the collection (Springate and Sinclair-Smith 2000:14). The most recent excavations, begun in 1998, have two main goals: to document the archaeological potential of one of Monmouth County's best-known historic sites; and to expose youths to the archaeological process in a carefully controlled, professionally supervised setting. On both levels, the MCHA Allen House Archaeology Camp has been an unequivocal success.

During the initial season of work, a large colonial garbage deposit, or midden, was excavated directly outside the tavern's back door. Middens are common features at historic sites. Archaeologist Stanley South, working at the ruins of Brunswick Town in North Carolina between 1958 and 1968, discovered that residents simply discarded their refuse out the front and, more commonly, the back doors of their houses. He named the resulting pattern of trash disposal the Brunswick Pattern (South 1977:47). This pattern is not by any means unique to North Carolina and has been documented at British-American sites up and down the eastern seaboard.

The midden at the Allen House is a similar sort of deposit, dating from 1780 to about 1814. It probably represents the kitchen refuse discarded by one of the many tenant tavern keepers at the Blue Ball. Two five-foot-square units were excavated in the midden, and more than 8,500 artifacts were recovered (Springate and Sinclair-Smith 2000:10). Most relate to the preparation and serving of food. Almost 40 percent of the artifacts found can be lumped into a category archaeologists call faunal material, consisting of animal bones and shells. It is no surprise, given the site's proximity to the tidal Shrewsbury River, that shells from clams and oysters composed 82 percent of the faunal material.

The broken ceramics in the midden include locally produced redwares, such as milk pans and serving plates. Fancier dishes, such as blue- and green-edged pearlware plates, which would have graced the Blue Ball's tables, are also present, along with pieces of bottle glass and cutlery (Springate and Rogoff 1999:8). The ceramics, while colorful, would have been quite inexpensive, and nowhere near the quality of transfer print or Chinese export porcelain. Despite their shaky finances, it appears that the tenant tavern keepers tried to set an attractive table (Springate and Rogoff 1999:11).

The large quantity of ceramics and faunal material in the midden, and the relative paucity of tobacco pipes, supports a hypothesis first presented by archaeologists Diana Rockman and Nan Rothschild (1984). They argued that urban taverns served primarily as places for meeting and socializing, which is why their archaeological remains tend to have a high proportion of tobacco pipes and beverage bottles. Rural taverns, on the other hand, were places where food was of central importance, and thus will yield a higher proportion of ceramic containers. This appears to have been the case at the Blue Ball.

The Allen House excavations are slowly but surely uncovering the history of this important historic site and, at the same time, training a new generation of student archaeologists (Springate and Sinclair-Smith 2000). It is a model for how excavations supervised by qualified archaeologists can be used to teach students about both archaeology and their own local history.

Salvage Archaeology at the Luyster House

Eighteenth-century travelers heading north out of Shrewsbury next came to one of New Jersey's first settlements, Middletown, home to the Johannes Luyster

House (figure 3.5). This rare surviving example of an early-eighteenth-century Dutch house was the site of a massive all-volunteer salvage archaeological excavation in the 1990s, making it the most thoroughly excavated eighteenth-century Dutch farmstead in the state.

The Luyster House was to be moved as part of the expansion of the AT&T (now Lucent) facilities in Middletown and preserved at a new location about one-quarter mile east of its original site on Red Hill Road. There it would be offered for sale to the general public. Until Gerard Scharfenberger of the Middletown Landmarks Commission became involved, no steps had been taken to deal with the extensive archaeological deposits likely to exist on the property. In fact, because the site was situated on private property, and the construction and expansion of the AT&T complex was being undertaken with private funds, no archaeological surveys were required. Nevertheless, with the support of the landmarks commission, permission was secured to conduct the excavation (Scharfenberger and Veit 1999).

The study, directed by Scharfenberger and assisted by me, several of my students from Monmouth University, and a cadre of skilled volunteers, began in September 1997. Originally, the time frame for completing the archaeological survey was approximately three months, with the understanding that excavations could continue after the structure was moved. Once structural repairs began on the house, the digging beneath the floorboards unearthed a large number of artifacts, many of which were complete or nearly complete. Protected by the house, they were found in an excellent state of preservation. The "three-month window" thus evolved into fifteen months of weekend excavations. The additional time enabled the archaeologists to expand their level of study considerably.

Scharfenberger and I developed a research design that focused on two questions: When was the house constructed, and would the archaeological deposits reflect Luyster's Dutch heritage? Dating the house at first seemed a straightforward matter. When the excavations began, the building's façade displayed a plaque assigning it a date of 1680. Yet extensive historical research by Joseph W. Hammond determined that Johannes Luyster and his brother-in-law Jan Brower did not acquire the original 149 acres until January 1, 1717 (Hammond 1998). Luyster and Brower, who were originally from Long Island, farmed the land together for some eighteen years before subdividing the property.

A survey drawn in 1730 shows a one-and-one-half-story Dutch colonial or Anglo-Dutch farmhouse already on the property (Hammond 1998). Originally, the house was rectangular in plan. Later, two wings were added to its rear: one dates from the 1850s, the other from the twentieth century. The colonial

Figure 3.5. *The modern and original appearance of the Luyster House, an eighteenth-century Dutch house in Middletown. Library of Congress, Prints and Photographs Division (HABS, NJ,13-HOL,2).*

building stood on a very shallow unmortared fieldstone foundation, only one to two courses deep. The house had shingled sides, a steeply pitched gable roof with flared eaves, and two interior end chimneys on the main block. Notably, the pitch of the front of the gable roof differs from that of the rear—a feature found on Dutch houses on Long Island but uncommon among those of northern New Jersey. Although the building currently has a single central doorway, with paired windows on either side, it originally had two divided doors. The interior of the oldest section of the house displays Dutch-style H-bent framing and once had a jambless (unenclosed) fireplace. Architecturally, it was the quintessential Anglo-Dutch house.

The descendants of Johannes Luyster retained ownership of the property until the 1940s. Even though it has since passed through a number of owners, a substantial collection of original furnishings survives. These include an eighteenth-century painting by Daniel Hendrickson depicting Peter Luyster, one of the house's owners, with a basket of eggs (figure 3.6). (Paintings that showed prominent landowners with the sources of their wealth were common at the end of the eighteenth century; see St. George 1998:353.) Apparently, Luyster and some of his northern Monmouth county neighbors specialized in supplying eggs to the New York City market (Wacker and Clemens 1995:206–7). A spectacularly painted Dutch *kas* (cabinet) from about 1720 (figure 3.7) and a charming hanging cabinet dated 1722, as well as a variety of family documents, also survive in the MCHA collections. Taken together, the written sources, the furnishings from the house, and the estimated twenty thousand artifacts found in and around it present a robust body of evidence from which archaeologists can interpret this family's life.

Excavations at the house revealed approximately twenty archaeological features, including post molds, buried walkways, wells, fence posts, stone foundations, and a trash pit. Although it is impossible to discuss all of them here, several deserve special note. The first feature discovered by the archaeologists was a series of post molds—stains left by wooden posts that have rotted away—located immediately east of the front doorstep and adjacent to the building's foundation. Based on their location, the archaeologists surmised that these post molds were part of an earlier support system for the house, or possibly the remnants of a "pioneer" house erected before the permanent structure (Scharfenberger and Veit 1999:5).

As noted, the archaeologists were able to excavate within the crawl space under the floor of the Luyster House before it was moved. Preservation within the house was exceptional, and wooden items rarely found on archaeological sites in the eastern United States were recovered intact. These included several

Figure 3.6. Peter Luyster owned the Luyster House from 1719 to 1810. This painting by his neighbor Daniel Hendrickson shows him with one of the sources of his wealth. Courtesy of the Monmouth County Historical Association.

wooden spatulas discarded beneath the floorboards of what was the original room of the house, a child's toy sailboat whittled from a wooden block, as well as several well-preserved two-tined bone-handled forks.

Trench 1, located just east of the house, yielded the greatest number of artifacts. It is probably the in-filled foundation of an outkitchen. While digging shovel tests to the east of the house, volunteers unearthed an extremely dense deposit of historic ceramics and animal bones—presumably the remains of many meals consumed by the Luysters. The collection includes bowls, plates, teacups, and porringers that appear to have been deposited whole, with breakage occurring through dumping and pressure from overlying deposits and surface activity. Moreover, pieces from several sets of early-nineteenth-century ceramics were present. Why the Luysters divested themselves of a large number

Figure 3.7. A painted kas (cabinet) associated with the Luyster family of Middletown (ca. 1720–1722). Courtesy of the Monmouth County Historical Association.

of matching and apparently functional ceramics is not known. One explanation could be a mass purging of all possibly contaminated items during a time of severe epidemic (Scharfenberger and Veit 1999).

The age of the deposit is still unclear. The deepest and earliest levels contain late-eighteenth-century materials, while the upper levels contain a disproportionate amount of pearlware, a type of ceramic popular between 1775 and 1820. It seems likely that the cellar hole was filled in during the 1830s.

A Dutch-style colander used to clean shellfish, found in Trench 1, is one of the only artifacts that clearly reflects the known ethnicity of the homeowners (figure 3.8). The example from the Luyster House was made from redware and is nearly complete. While its form is quintessentially Dutch, its rather crude appearance may indicate local manufacture. The vessel seems strangely out of place among the fine imported English ceramics that make up most of the deposit.

Clay pipe fragments are ubiquitous at most historic sites, and Scharfenberger and his team recovered several hundred from the Luyster House. Numerous whole and fragmented pipe bowls were found, including examples bearing the initials RT, the mark of one of three Bristol pipe makers named Robert Tippet, who were active from 1660 to 1720, and LE, Llewelyn Evans (ca 1661–1688), also of Bristol. The presence of very early pipes may indicate that the site was occupied in the late seventeenth or very early eighteenth century and that an earlier structure stood there.

Fifteen months of archaeological excavations at the Luyster House generated an impressive collection of eighteenth- and nineteenth-century artifacts. Interestingly, with the exception of the colander, the assemblage is not significantly different from that found at contemporary English sites in Monmouth County. Although the Luysters lived in a Dutch-framed house and kept their family records in Dutch into the nineteenth century, they set their table with the finest ceramics from Staffordshire, smoked tobacco pipes from Bristol, and, judging by the fragments of several teapots, enjoyed drinking tea just like their

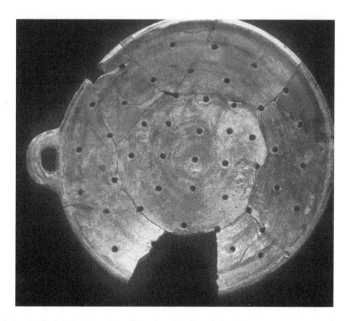

Figure 3.8. A distinctive Dutch-style colander found in Feature 10, next to the Luyster House. This is one of the few Dutch artifacts found at the site. It was reconstructed from eighteen sherds. Photograph by Rob Tucher; reproduced courtesy of Gerard Scharfenberger.

English neighbors. One wonders whether their choices reflect the English domination of the market for refined goods or the changing culture of the Luysters themselves. Although we can only speculate while analysis of the collection continues, it appears that the process of acculturation in colonial Monmouth County was uneven, with some aspects of culture, such as ceramics, changing much more quickly than others, such as architecture and perhaps language.

Even with the substantial collection of artifacts, the assignment of a date to the construction of the Luyster House remains a challenge. The artifacts indicate a long-term occupation beginning in the early eighteenth century, if not before. They do not provide a clear date for the initial settlement of the site. In an effort to confirm when the house was constructed, dendrochronology (tree-ring dating) was performed on several timbers removed from the house during its restoration. These samples all dated to 1724. Therefore, at least some of the timbers used when the house was built were cut in that year.

All in all, the Luyster House excavation was a success. The volunteers, supervised by Scharfenberger and myself, succeeded in recovering thousands of artifacts that would have otherwise been lost when the house was moved. Their finds provide a glimpse of Dutch life in colonial New Jersey. At the same time, the house survived being lifted from its original foundation and transported down the road to a new site. With luck, the Luyster House will last another three centuries or more in its new location, a vivid reminder in shingle and frame of Monmouth County's early Dutch settlers.

The Power Gardens of Morven

If the Luysters represent a successful rural farming family of the eighteenth century, their wealth pales in comparison with that of the Stocktons of Princeton. Nor does the distinctive vernacular Luyster House resemble Morven, the home of Richard and Annis Stockton, constructed in the 1760s. That house began its life as a fashionable brick Georgian mansion with flanking dependencies (figure 3.9). The style was popular for much of the eighteenth century, during the reigns of Kings George I, II, and III. Symmetrical and well balanced, it represented a clear break with the postmedieval architecture previously popular in the colonies. Wealthy merchants and planters displayed their taste and social status by constructing houses inspired by the work of architects Andrea Palladio and Inigo Jones.

Morven's first owner, Richard Stockton, was one of New Jersey's signers of the Declaration of Independence. Later the house was home to Commodore Robert Field Stockton, commander of the Pacific Squadron during the Mexican

Figure 3.9. Morven, the home of Robert and Annis Stockton, as it appears today. Photograph by the author.

War. From 1944 until 1981, the house served as the governor's mansion (Bill et al. 1978). Today, Drumthwacket, another noteworthy Princeton house, holds that honor, while Morven is open to the public as a historic house administered by the New Jersey State Museum.

In the late 1980s a team of archaeologists directed by Anne Yentsch of Historic Annapolis, Inc., studied the grounds around Morven as part of a larger effort to preserve and restore the property (Goodwin et al. 1995:35; Yamin 1989). The team included historical archaeologists, ethnobotanists (specialists who study plant remains), and a phytolitharian (a scientist knowledgeable in the rather arcane field of minute plant stones, microscopic mineral bodies formed during the growth of certain types of plants). The goal of their study was to determine whether enough of the Stocktons' original two gardens survived to warrant their restoration.

The gardens at Morven, like those at other palatial eighteenth-century homes in both Europe and North America, did not just provide produce for the table but were intended to complement the house. They served as important and highly visible status symbols. Laid out on a geometric plan, with manicured lawns and carefully selected plantings, these gardens presented a "vision of nature that was productive, harmonious, and controlled" (Kryder-Reid 1995:104). They were physical manifestations of their owners' knowledge, power, and control. Historical archaeologist Mark Leone notes:

Gardens in England, from the early Georgian times on, were to be built according to the skillful use of the rules of perspective; in England, they frequently carried a particular message, such as individual liberty, through their iconography and were to so engage a visitor's emotional reaction by entertaining the eye through the illusions and allusions in them, that the message appeared to have a more real existence by being copied in nature. (1988:252)

Some of Leone's excavations at the William Paca mansion in Annapolis, Maryland, have focused on that property's magnificent garden, which stretched out from the house, gradually descending through four terraces (Leone 1996:379). The first three terraces were laid out geometrically, with neatly arranged plantings and manicured lawns. In contrast, the last terrace, at the rear of the property, was a veritable wilderness. Though not unplanned, it appeared unkempt and natural to viewers. The terraces, falls, and optical illusions were intended to be "public experiments . . . attempts to show that their builders understood the natural, and thus the social order" (Leone 1988:252). We should not be surprised that individuals like William Paca and Richard Stockton, who were crafting a new social and political order, were also constructing elaborate and well-ordered gardens, which highlighted their understanding of and ability to control the forces of nature and man.

Gardens are considerably more complicated to excavate than other more substantial features. The very processes of maintaining a garden tend to erode the deposits found there. Moreover, the subtle signatures of past plantings can be quite elusive. They may be buried under feet of fill or obscured by more recent plantings.

At Morven, archaeologists employed an array of techniques, ranging from the simple to the complex, in their efforts to reconstruct the historic landscape. They began with ground-penetrating radar. When a radar antenna is pulled across the ground, the time it takes the electromagnetic pulses sent into the ground to be reflected back to the receiver depends on what is encountered and how deeply it is buried. The results can be used to determine where buried structures and other cultural or natural features are located. Although ground-penetrating radar has proved useful at other sites, the results at Morven were disappointing. Modern features, such as buried pipes, were found, but not the expected historic deposits (Goodwin et al. 1995:39).

Excavation proved more revealing. The techniques varied from simple probing with a hollow-pointed or split spoon auger to inspect soil conditions and stratigraphy, to using a steel T-probe to find buried walkways and foundations

(Goodwin et al. 1995:40). A post-hole digger was used to test deep fill in some locations, and five-foot-square excavation units were also dug to provide clear stratigraphic profiles. Arguably, the most successful technique employed at Morven was the excavation of several five-foot-wide trenches, which provided the large-scale data needed to understand the features present underground. Artifacts recovered in the garden deposits allowed the archaeologists to infer the ages of the deposits.

Other research focused on garden plants, particularly trees, as clues to changes in the Morven garden. In 1987 Naomi Miller carried out a survey aimed at locating trees on the property that might have been alive in the nineteenth century. Obviously, the most accurate way to determine a tree's age is to cut it down and count the rings. Such a destructive measure was not acceptable at Morven, of course; instead, Lawrence Lockwood of Lockwood Associates drilled cores from twenty-five of the largest trees on the property (Yentsch et al. 1987:17). The results were surprising. For instance, a grove of towering Norway spruces, assumed to be of venerable age, proved to date only to the early twentieth century. A large and imposing tulip tree, long believed to be "one of two that Richard Stockton and his wife Annis planted" (Bill et al. 1978:21), was shown to have been planted in the mid-nineteenth century. The horse chestnuts that line the lane leading to the house were reputedly planted with seeds brought by Samuel and Lewis Pintard, French Huguenot émigrés who married into the Stockton family in the 1770s (Yentsch et al. 1987:19). These young-looking horse chestnuts proved to be roughly two hundred years old, a bit later than the Pintards, but older than expected. Clearly, looks and oral history can be deceiving.

The attention to detail in the excavations at Morven is noteworthy. Soil samples were taken from excavations, as well as from excavated planting holes and garden beds in the hope of recovering silica bodies known as phytoliths, which occur in plant tissues (Yentsch et al. 1987:22). Many families of plants produce distinct phytoliths, making it possible to identify the types of plantings once present. Moreover, because they are quite literally "plant stones," phytoliths can survive for long periods of time buried underground. Analysis of soil samples from the site revealed an abundance of phytoliths from trees, grasses, weeds, and vegetables, information that might be used to reconstruct the historic plantings at Morven.

Most important, the archaeologists were able to define the plan of the Stocktons' garden. Like its cousin in Maryland, it was terraced and laid out on geometric principles. All measurements were made in perches, an archaic unit that equals 16.5 feet, or one rod.

The interdisciplinary study of the Morven gardens brought together historical archaeologists, architectural historians, historians of eighteenth-century life,
and specialists in a variety of fields. Although the Stocktons' gardens have not
yet been restored, the careful work of this team has given us a much better understanding of New Jersey's historic landscape. At the same time, their findings
provide a glimpse of how eighteenth-century elites used carefully designed
gardens filled with exotic plants to show their mastery over nature, to impress
their neighbors, and to establish their own place in the social hierarchy of the
time.

The Burr-Haines Site

The lives of the relatively few Native Americans still residing in New Jersey during the eighteenth century present a striking contrast to the lives of the Stocktons in Princeton. Since the early seventeenth century, disease and conflict had
reduced their numbers, and as the small colonial settlements along the coast
and major waterways of New Jersey grew, some Native Americans left the state
and moved west to Pennsylvania and Ohio. Very few Native American sites survive from this period of rapid change in colonial New Jersey (but see Kraft 1986;
Lenik 1989; Pietak 1999; Santone 1998, 1999). Although eighteenth-century Native American cemeteries have been the subject of archaeological analysis (Volk
1911; Heye and Pepper 1915; Cross 1941), it is clear that the grave goods found
with the burials are not representative of day-to-day activities (Pietak 1995).
One important site with the potential to reveal this kind of information is the
Burr-Haines site in rural Burlington County. Here archaeologists found the remains of a briefly occupied residence dating to the period 1745–1765 (Cosans-
Zebooker and Thomas 1993:13). Their serendipitous find provides us with a
tantalizing glimpse of Native American life in colonial New Jersey. (The site is
named for the historic owners of the property. The names of the Native Americans who lived there remain unknown.)

By 1750, New Jersey's Native Americans had been dispossessed from much
of their land (see Kraft 1986:229). Many felt defrauded by the infamous walking purchase of 1737, whereby they lost twelve hundred square miles of territory in eastern Pennsylvania to John and Thomas Penn and James Logan
(Grumet 1995:239). By the time of the French and Indian War (1754–1763), the
number of recorded Native Americans living in New Jersey had fallen to about
one thousand; at the same time, the white population was growing rapidly
(Kraft 1986:229). During the war some Munsee sided with the French and attempted to exact revenge upon the English settlers of the region. Others, often

peaceful Christian converts, found themselves ready targets for the misguided vigilante justice of their neighbors.

In 1758 a pair of treaties irrevocably changed the situation of New Jersey's remaining Native Americans. The first was signed at Crosswicks in February, when representatives of the Delaware and from the colonial legislature met to resolve conflicting land claims (Kraft 1986:230). As a result, the legislature approved the purchase of outstanding native land claims and acquired a tract of 3,044 acres at Edgepillock, in Burlington County, to serve as a reservation for Native Americans living south of the Raritan River (Grumet 1995:240). At the second conference, held at Easton, Pennsylvania, the remaining native-owned lands in northern New Jersey were sold to the colony in return for one thousand Spanish silver dollars, wampum belts, and a variety of other goods (Kraft 1986:230).

Governor Francis Bernard named the Edgepillock tract Brotherton. By 1761, Brotherton's population numbered roughly one hundred Native Americans, and homes, a sawmill, a school, and a church had been constructed. Despite these early indications of success, the community began to falter: the mill was destroyed by fire, and over time the population was demoralized (Kraft 1986:232). As conditions continued to deteriorate, local Quakers began supplying food and clothing to the Native Americans. A German scientist, J.F.H. Autenreith, who visited the community in 1795, described a dejected population of roughly nine families, who had lost most of their traditional beliefs and were struggling to survive (Kammler 1996).

Although no substantial excavations have taken place at Brotherton, the nearby Burr-Haines site provides a glimpse of Native American life during this period. The site was discovered by R. Alan Mounier during a roadside archaeological survey in the Pinelands. Often, surveys like this—a series of regularly spaced shovel tests dug to determine whether archaeological materials are present before roadwork begins—are mind-numbingly unproductive. Archaeologists may dig dozens or even hundreds of shovel tests and be rewarded only with the detritus of modern American car culture—beer cans, cigarette butts, and plastic bags. But this particular survey was different. Mounier found an unusual collection of colonial artifacts. A second study, and later a full-scale archaeological data recovery performed by archaeologists from Middle Atlantic Archaeological Research (MAAR), revealed a trash-filled feature measuring about eleven feet across.

The excavations concentrated on the area that would be disturbed by improvements to the road. From a trench 25 feet long and 3 feet wide (Cosans-Zebooker and Thomas 1993:14), some 1,313 artifacts were recovered, all dating to the mid-eighteenth century. They came from a trash-filled pit, designated Feature

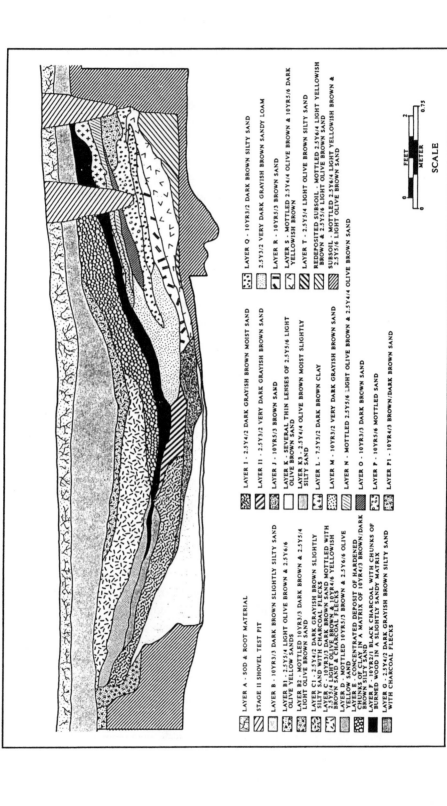

LAYER A - SOD & ROOT MATERIAL

STAGE II SHOVEL TEST PIT

LAYER B - 10YR3/3 DARK BROWN SLIGHTLY SILTY SAND

LAYER B1 - 2.5Y5/4 LIGHT OLIVE BROWN & 2.5Y6/6 OLIVE YELLOW SANDS

LAYER B2 - MOTTLED 10YR3/3 DARK BROWN & 2.5Y5/4 LIGHT OLIVE BROWN SAND

LAYER C1 - 2.5Y4/2 DARK GRAYISH BROWN SLIGHTLY SILTY SAND WITH CHARCOAL FLECKS

LAYER C - 10YR3/3 DARK BROWN SAND MOTTLED WITH 2.5Y5/4 LIGHT OLIVE BROWN & 10YR4/6 YELLOWISH BROWN SAND & CHARCOAL FLECKS

LAYER D - MOTTLED 10YR5/3 BROWN & 2.5Y6/6 OLIVE YELLOW SAND

LAYER E - CONCENTRATED DEPOSIT OF HARDENED CHUNKS OF CLAY IN A MATRIX OF 10YR4/3 BROWN/DARK BROWN SILTY SAND

LAYER F - 10YR2/1 BLACK CHARCOAL WITH CHUNKS OF BURNED WOOD IN A SLIGHTLY SANDY MATRIX

LAYER G - 2.5Y4/2 DARK GRAYISH BROWN SILTY SAND WITH CHARCOAL FLECKS

LAYER I - 2.5Y4/2 DARK GRAYISH BROWN MOIST SAND

LAYER II - 2.5Y3/2 VERY DARK GRAYISH BROWN SAND

LAYER J - 10YR3/3 BROWN SAND

LAYER K - SEVERAL THIN LENSES OF 2.5Y5/6 LIGHT OLIVE BROWN SAND

LAYER K3 - 2.5Y4/4 OLIVE BROWN MOIST SLIGHTLY SILTY SAND

LAYER L - 7.5Y3/2 DARK BROWN CLAY

LAYER M - 10YR3/2 VERY DARK GRAYISH BROWN SAND

LAYER N - MOTTLED 2.5Y5/6 LIGHT OLIVE BROWN & 2.5Y4/4 OLIVE BROWN SAND

LAYER O - 10YR3/3 DARK BROWN SAND

LAYER P - 10YR5/6 MOTTLED SAND

LAYER P1 - 10YR4/3 BROWN/DARK BROWN SAND

LAYER Q - 10YR3/2 DARK BROWN SILTY SAND

2.5Y3/2 VERY DARK GRAYISH BROWN SANDY LOAM

LAYER R - 10YR5/3 BROWN SAND

LAYER S - MOTTLED 2.5Y4/4 OLIVE BROWN & 10YR5/6 DARK YELLOWISH BROWN

LAYER T - 2.5Y5/4 LIGHT OLIVE BROWN SILTY SAND

REDEPOSITED SUBSOIL - MOTTLED 2.5Y6/4 LIGHT YELLOWISH BROWN & 2.5Y5/6 LIGHT OLIVE BROWN SAND

SUBSOIL - MOTTLED 2.5Y6/4 LIGHT YELLOWISH BROWN & 2.5Y5/6 LIGHT OLIVE BROWN SAND

SCALE

1, no deeper than 3.6 feet and measuring 10.35 feet wide in the excavation (Cosans-Zebooker and Thomas 1993:15). The full width of the pit is unknown because it extended beyond the study area and under the road (figure 3.10). It may be the filled-in cellar from a house (Cosans-Zebooker and Thomas 1993:15).

The artifacts include white clay tobacco pipes and typical eighteenth-century ceramics, such as white salt-glazed stoneware, scratch blue stoneware, and locally produced redwares. Among the clothing-related artifacts are brass straight pins, buttons, buckles, and at least two sets of cuff links. The pins were likely associated with women's clothing or possibly sewing; the cuff links would have been worn with better-quality men's shirts. Hand-wrought nails, fragments of several spoons, a hasp knife, several glass trade beads, and lead shot were also recovered. Other interesting artifacts include antler tools, probably used in the manufacture of stone projectile points, several flakes of stone, and at least two projectile points. Nearly a third of the artifacts are faunal remains. They include bones from white-tailed deer, elk, bear, squirrels, rabbit, fish, shellfish, and turtles (Cosans-Zebooker 1992:61). Conspicuously absent are the remains of sheep, cattle, and chickens, which are typically found on colonial farmsteads. The only remains of domestic animals were from pigs.

The artifact assemblage suggests a Native American occupation. The site is roughly contemporaneous with Brotherton, includes both European and Native American artifacts, and suggests a diet primarily of wild game. The buttons, cuff links, and pins indicate that both sexes were present at the site. Although the archaeologists' excavations were limited by the physical constraints of the study area, their findings offer a glimpse of what was probably a Native American family's dwelling in the mid-eighteenth century. They had adapted many of the trappings of their European neighbors but still manufactured and used some stone tools and consumed a diet not significantly different from that of their prehistoric ancestors.

The eighteenth century was a time of great change in New Jersey and throughout England's New World colonies. At the beginning of the century, much of New Jersey was an untamed wilderness. Small settlements had been established by the Dutch, Swedes, English, and Scots in areas with ready access to major waterways. The populations of Native Americans and settlers

Figure 3.10. (opposite) A profile showing Feature 1 at the Burr-Haines site. The feature is apparently what remains of a partially underground Native American house. Drawn by Rich Green; reproduced courtesy of Middle Atlantic Archaeological Research and the Archaeological Society of New Jersey.

were small. Government was controlled by an elite group of wealthy landholders. By the century's end, New Jersey had witnessed a staggering increase in population, and the frontier had moved west toward the Alleghenies.

During this time, New Jerseyans fought in the French and Indian War (1754–1763) and the American Revolution (1775–1783). Although the colony and then state remained primarily agrarian and rural, major towns were developing at Newark, Elizabeth, Perth Amboy, Trenton, and Burlington. Entrepreneurs established mills, potteries, ironworks, and glassworks. Several regional cultures developed as well: a strong German influence in northwestern New Jersey; important Dutch settlements in northeastern New Jersey and in Somerset and Monmouth Counties; Quaker settlements in the south; and a reservation for Native Americans in the Pinelands.

The five archaeological sites examined here provide insights into the life of colonial New Jersey. At Raritan Landing, historical archaeologist Rebecca Yamin has teased out the first glimmerings of a distinct, regional New Jersey culture. At the Allen House in Shrewsbury, once the Blue Ball Tavern, ongoing excavations are reconstructing the story of tenant tavern keepers and offering young people an opportunity literally and figuratively to get their hands on the past. Further north in Monmouth County, the Luyster House is a good example of salvage archaeology. The work by Gerard Scharfenberger and his team has shown that the Dutch settlers of the area set their tables with the same ceramics and smoked the same pipes as their English neighbors, even as they continued to speak Dutch and live in a house of distinctly Dutch design. In Princeton, at the Stocktons' family home, archaeologists have found evidence for what might be termed a power garden. More than just a testimony to the Stocktons' good taste, it served as a visual reminder and a physical symbol of their mastery over nature and scientific knowledge. While the Stocktons lived the life of country gentry, the Native American inhabitants of the Burr-Haines site deep in the Pinelands were struggling to survive as their traditional way of life was quickly eroding.

Each of these sites represents a different aspect of life in colonial New Jersey—from diverse ethnic groups re-creating and slowly changing their traditional lifestyles to the powerful elite changing nature to reflect their social position. The excavation of more eighteenth-century sites can only enhance our understanding of this critical period.

CHAPTER FOUR

"Cockpit of the Revolution"
Unearthing the War
of Independence

Writing in 1940, historian Leonard Lundin characterized New Jersey as the "Cockpit of the Revolution." Indeed, although one of the smallest of Great Britain's seaboard colonies, New Jersey was the scene of several significant battles, including those at Trenton, Princeton, Red Bank, Monmouth, and Springfield (figure 4.1). In addition to these major encounters between the regular armies, numerous skirmishes occurred throughout the war as troops foraged and moved from one theater of battle to the next. During the winters of 1777–1778 and 1779–1780, Morristown housed the winter cantonments of the Continental Army. Though less well known, Middlebrook, near present-day Bound Brook, served as the main army's cantonment during the winter of 1778–1779, and nearby Pluckemin was the site of the Continental School of Artillery, a predecessor of West Point.

Situated between New York City (held by the British from September 1776 until November 1783) and Philadelphia (capital of the thirteen colonies), New Jersey was also a state whose citizens were truly divided in their loyalties. While the Presbyterian ministers of Essex and Morris Counties preached revolution, Loyalists were a strong presence in Monmouth County and, with British support, held Sandy Hook for the duration of the war.

When the war ended, much of the state was left in desolation and ruin. A survey by the state legislature in 1782 enumerated more than two thousand British and Hessian depredations, with nearly a third in Middlesex County (Cunningham 1966:115). Nor were American troops blameless; they too had plundered the homes of Loyalists and suspected Loyalists. At war's end, many citizens still loyal to the crown left to begin new lives in Canada or, if their finances permitted it, Great Britain.

Few topics have received as much scholarly attention as the American Revolution, and its local effects continue to engage researchers. Historians have

Figure 4.1. Map showing the locations of Pluckemin, Morristown National Historical Park, the Old Barracks, Monmouth Battlefield, and the Baylor Massacre site. Map by Dawn Turner.

studied military operations in New Jersey, the politics of the war, the role of Loyalists, and the lives of numerous participants (see particularly Bill 1964; Fleming 1973; Leiby 1962; Lundin 1940).

Max Schrabisch Finds General Henry Knox's Artillery Park

Not until the early twentieth century did anyone undertake a true archaeological investigation at a Revolutionary War site in New Jersey. In 1916 and 1917

Max Schrabisch, a German émigré, carried out excavations at the site of General Henry Knox's artillery park, or cantonment, in Pluckemin, Somerset County. A cantonment is "a group of buildings constructed primarily for the purpose of housing troops"; the terms "camp" and "encampment," on the other hand, refer to troops quartered in their regimental or brigade lines (Seidel 1987:152). Knox established this cantonment for the Continental artillery in the winter of 1778. The previous year, most of the Continental Army had gone into winter quarters at Valley Forge, Pennsylvania, some eighteen miles northwest of Philadelphia. Political infighting in Congress and a breakdown in the supply chain caused terrible hardships for the troops quartered there (see Parrington et al. 1984).

In comparison with the trying times at Valley Forge, conditions the following winter in Somerset County, New Jersey, were vastly improved. Washington divided his army into four groups, not counting Pluckemin. While they remained close enough to support each other in the unlikely event of an attack, they were dispersed to pose less of a burden on local civilian populations. The main body of troops was quartered at the Middlebrook Encampment near present-day Bound Brook and Somerville. Washington took the newly built home of a wealthy Philadelphia merchant, John Wallace, as his headquarters. Baron Friedrich von Steuben stayed at the home of Abraham Staats in South Bound Brook, General Nathanael Greene moved into the home of Derrick Van Veghten, and Knox occupied the home of Jacobus Vanderveer near Pluckemin (Prince 1958:16–17). In addition to the troops at Middlebrook, smaller contingents of the Continental Army were stationed at Fort Arnold—present-day West Point, New York—and at Redding near Danbury, Connecticut. The New Jersey Brigade under General William Maxwell was encamped in Elizabethtown, much closer to British-held New York. There they provided a first line of defense for the rest of the army.

Washington had selected an excellent location for an encampment. Strategically located at the southern end of the Watchung Mountains, Middlebrook offered his troops ready access to food supplies from the farms of central New Jersey, and their presence provided some measure of protection for the ironworks of northern New Jersey. The troops stationed at Middlebrook included divisions from Virginia, Maryland, and Pennsylvania, and a regiment from Delaware. Hospitals were established in New Brunswick and Millstone; the quartermaster's stores were situated in Bound Brook; and the artillery, under Knox, was moved some seven miles north of Bound Brook to a spot just southwest of Pluckemin, a strong and easily defensible position (Seidel 1987:142–45).

Upon their arrival at Pluckemin on December 7, the artillerymen began building barracks. Even with a double ration of rum, the work went slowly in the cold weather (Prince 1958:59). It was not until January 10, 1779, that General Knox was able to report that his "poor rebels in mourning" had "got into their barracks which are comfortable and on an elegant plan" (quoted in Prince 1958:59). Despite the superiority of the barracks, problems remained. Food and clothing, particularly shoes, were in short supply, and even ammunition was scarce. Morale, not surprisingly, was also poor. Part of the problem was apparently the quartering of some officers in nearby private houses. Unlike Washington, according to historian Carl Prince, "Knox was not at all insistent that the officers rejoin their men. . . . Field officers were altogether exempted from residence as no barracks were constructed for them" (Prince 1958:60).

The most imposing structure at the camp was the academy (figure 4.2), which may have been constructed before the encampment began. It served as a lecture hall for the soldiers and as a gathering place for religious services. According to a contemporary description:

> [It] was raised several feet above the other buildings, and capped with a smart cupola, which had a very good effect. The great room was fifty feet by thirty, arched in an agreeable manner, and neatly plastered within. At the lower end of the room was a small enclosure elevated above the company, where the preceptor of the Park gave his military lessons. (Quoted in Prince 1958:62)

The Irish-born preceptor, Christopher Colles, who became a noted mapmaker after the war, lectured on mathematics and ballistics (Sekel 1972:74). The academy can be considered the army's first school of artillery and engineering, a function now served by the United States Military Academy at West Point (Seidel 1987, 1995).

Life for the troops in camp was strictly regimented according to the manual, or "Blue Book," imposed by Baron von Steuben the previous winter at Valley Forge (Seidel 1990:189). Daily activities included drilling and guard duty—both in camp and at St. Paul's Church in Pluckemin Village, which was used as an ammunition depot. Men might also be assigned to specific tasks, such as constructing and maintaining buildings, digging latrines, and transporting supplies. Armorers repaired hundreds of broken muskets and bayonets, and skilled soldiers filled 156,036 musket cartridges and made numerous cartridges for the artillery (Seidel 1987:238; Sekel 1972:app. H). Officers were relieved of the more onerous and physically taxing camp duties. They would have been busy supervising construction projects, attending to their men, and presumably studying in the academy. Despite Knox's best efforts, poor discipline plagued the camp.

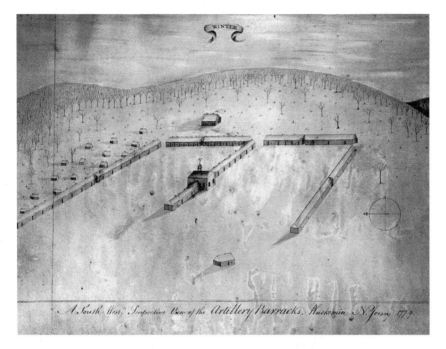

Figure 4.2. Contemporary perspective drawing by Captain John Lillie showing the barracks and academy at Pluckemin, 1779. Courtesy of Morristown National Historical Park.

Apparently, some of the barracks at the camp's rear served as unofficial taverns, and gambling was widespread.

As the spring of 1779 wore on, the troops at Middlebrook prepared for the summer campaign, and the artillery units were dispersed to other parts of the army. General Knox and his staff left on June 3. Even after his departure, Pluckemin was not entirely abandoned by the Continental Army. Artificers continued to repair wagons, and armorers labored over broken muskets (Seidel 1987:241). The site also served as a depot for munitions and supplies. After the troops deployed from Pluckemin, the sick and wounded from Middlebrook moved into the newly vacant quarters, which then took on a second career as one of the three general hospitals in New Jersey. Nearly one hundred sick and wounded men remained quartered at Pluckemin until 1780, when the site was probably abandoned.

After the war, Pluckemin reverted to its former existence as a sleepy rural town, and the original owners reclaimed their land. The barracks, once full of troops learning the technical skills needed by eighteenth-century officers, stood vacant (Sekel 1972:86). It seems likely that the buildings were scavenged for their wood and hardware. By the mid-nineteenth century little physical evidence remained to indicate the vital part the artillery park at Pluckemin had played in the Revolutionary War.

The exact location of the cantonment remained forgotten until the arrival of Max Schrabisch, one of New Jersey's first archaeologists (figure 4.3). Born in Stettin, Germany, on March 1, 1869, Schrabisch attended the Royal Real Gymnasium in Berlin, the University of Berlin, and the University of Munich (Lenik 1998:5). Between 1900 and 1940, following his arrival in America, Schrabisch located and documented hundreds of prehistoric sites in northern New Jersey and adjacent areas of Pennsylvania and New York. Although we do not know

Figure 4.3. Max Schrabisch, the pioneering archaeologist who carried out the first documented excavation of a Revolutionary War site in New Jersey, at Pluckemin. Courtesy of the Trailside Museums, Bear Mountain, N.Y.

what sparked his interest in archaeology, his particular fascination with cave sites and rock shelters is not surprising. During the 1860s and 1870s, archaeologists working in France and Germany found the remains of Neanderthals (*Homo sapiens neanderthalensis*) and stone tools tens of thousands of years old (Daniel 1967:56). Schrabisch may have hoped for similar finds in the caves and rock shelters of the Northeast.

By today's standards, Schrabisch's excavation techniques were primitive, limiting the amount of information that could be gleaned from a site. But this limitation did not prevent him from publishing prolifically. By his death in 1949 he had some 150 professional books and popular newspaper and journal articles to his credit, including five books written for general audiences. Even today, archaeologists working in the Garden State regard his Indian Site Survey volumes, published by the New Jersey Geological Survey, as basic reference tools (Schrabisch 1915; Skinner and Schrabisch 1913).

Schrabisch rarely dug on sites from the historic period, but in 1916 and again in 1917 he was retained by Grant Schley, a wealthy landowner from Pluckemin, to search for the remains of General Knox's artillery park. The site was by then quite overgrown. Schrabisch spent eleven weeks in 1916 exploring the area and "undertook to make a thorough study of this old landmark, the purpose being to restore it as far as possible and also to secure the remains left behind" (Schrabisch 1917:162).

Schrabisch went to work excavating twenty small mounds present on the site. As he dug, it became clear that they were what remained of the soldiers' huts. Of the twelve he excavated, almost all contained central fireplaces, clearly demarcated by ashes, charcoal, and fire-stained rocks. Small quantities of artifacts, particularly fragments of animal bones, nails, and pottery, were found within and around the structures (Schrabisch 1917:163). The huts fell into two groups: small ones measuring eight by seven feet; and larger ones, about fifteen feet square (Schrabisch 1917:163). Schrabisch believed that the larger huts housed groups of soldiers, while the smaller ones housed individuals.

In addition to the soldiers' huts, Schrabisch also located what he believed was a large blacksmith shop. There, large quantities of "ox and horse shoes were dug up, along with hundreds of nails, hooks, iron rods, sheet iron, and many curiously shaped pieces of iron" (Schrabisch 1917:164). His interpretation may be correct. We know that among the troops at Pluckemin were skilled craftsmen who repaired thousands of wagons. An alternative explanation is that Schrabisch had stumbled upon the remains of the workshop where armorers repaired guns and prepared munitions.

Further testing uncovered several trash heaps full of oyster shells, bottle glass, bones, scraps of iron, and pottery fragments (Schrabisch 1917:164). The pits appear to have been carefully located and sealed over with stones. Several small ovens were also found. All told, Schrabisch excavated twelve mounds, four refuse pits, ten small fireplaces, and "restored" twenty-one small hut sites. Unfortunately, in the intervening years the collection of artifacts he recovered was lost.

Most of Schrabisch's finds related to the daily life of the soldiers. For instance, food remains, ranging from mundane oyster shells to turkey and bear bones, were found—evidence that the soldiers were able to supplement their rations. Military artifacts were also common, including lead shot and numerous buttons marked with regimental numbers and the initials "U.S.A." Schrabisch also found many Continental artillery buttons showing a cannon and a flagstaff.

There is no indication that Schrabisch kept detailed field notes describing what he found and where; nor did he map the locations he excavated. Some of his excavation techniques, particularly rebuilding hearths and foundations, have caused problems for later archaeologists, who are hard pressed to differentiate his crude reconstructions from the actual handiwork of the Continental artillerists. Schrabisch published several articles on his excavation; however, they were almost all short pieces in local newspapers and failed to make a lasting impression on the scholarly community.

Pluckemin Redux

In 1917, following the death of Grant Schley, Max Schrabisch left Pluckemin and returned to his first love, the archaeological study of Native American rock shelters and campsites. The Pluckemin cantonment again slipped into obscurity, until the early 1960s, when historian Clifford Sekel began studying Knox's artillery park (Sekel 1972). It took considerable legwork to relocate the camp. Once he had found it, Sekel tried to interest archaeologists in the site. In the late 1970s, archaeologist John Seidel joined forces with Sekel. Seidel's meticulous fieldwork provides the basis for much of the following discussion (Seidel 1987).

Fieldwork at Pluckemin began in 1979 and continued through 1986. Financial support came from the not-for-profit Pluckemin Archaeological Project and from the Hills Development Corporation, which owned the site. In a unique cooperative effort, the archaeologists worked with the community and the developer to investigate and preserve the core of the site, while facilitating construction on other portions of the property. At different times, students from Drew University, Somerset County College, and Rutgers University all worked at the site (Seidel 1987:iv).

The first step was to clear the brush and establish a series of grid points across the property. Mapping the site and recording the locations of artifact scatters and landscape features followed. The surface collection of artifacts revealed that the southeast portion of the site was the likely location of the forge operations and possibly a tinsmith's shop (Seidel 1987:366). The northern area contained considerably more artifacts associated with the tasks of cooking and preparing food, and was probably the location of a line of barracks.

Seidel employed a wide range of technologies to document the site thoroughly. These included low-level aerial photography using a camera suspended between two tripods. This system allowed the project photographers to record complicated patterns of artifacts rapidly. Seidel and his team also employed two of the most common and effective remote-sensing techniques: ground-penetrating radar (GPR) and magnetometry. In contrast to GPR, which detects buried archaeological deposits by sending radar pulses directly into the ground, magnetometry employs an instrument that is able to discern minor variations in soil magnetism. The magnetometer takes readings at regular intervals across a site, which are then converted into a sort of contour map that shows areas of high and low magnetism. Transitions in magnetic intensity may indicate archaeological features. With magnetometry, GPR, and other forms of remote sensing, it is generally necessary to do some excavating in order to "ground truth" the results.

The goal of the magnetometer survey at Pluckemin was to identify the remains of a line of barracks shown on a 1779 drawing (see figure 4.2). This line would have paralleled the one identified during the surface collection. The magnetometer survey identified several underground areas where the natural soils seemed to have been disturbed. The same area was then tested using GPR (Seidel 1987:479). Subsequent excavations showed that the anomalies noted by the remote-sensing techniques were either natural features or more recent disturbances.

Seidel and his team nevertheless went on to determine the probable location of the academy and identified some trash deposits likely associated with officers quartered at the camp. As might be expected, these show a much higher concentration of expensive porcelain and fine imported English teawares than in the deposits associated with the troops. As Seidel points out, this evidence highlights the social gulf between the officers and enlisted men, who seem to have maintained their differences despite the common cause that engaged them (1987:527; see also Seidel 1995).

The ceramics recovered at Pluckemin also provide another interesting insight into life during the Revolution. Seidel's team recovered 101 fragments of a ceramic called china glaze or pearlware (1987:680). Pearlware is a refined, thin-bodied earthenware developed in the 1770s by English potter and entrepreneur Josiah Wedgewood. Small amounts of cobalt were added to the glaze, imparting a pale blue tint, particularly in crevices. Although pearlware is common at late-eighteenth- and early-nineteenth-century sites, most scholars believed that it was first imported to the United States after the Revolution. The presence of what was one of the newest and most fashionable ceramics on the English market at a Continental Army artillery cantonment in rural New Jersey was surprising, particularly because legal trade with Great Britain was impossible. Obviously, trade, even if surreptitious, continued during the war. The ceramics also show that fashion-conscious American soldiers, probably officers, were aware of the latest trends in London tableware (Seidel 1990:82–95).

Among the most interesting discoveries was what remained of an armorer's shop. Although the outline of the building was hard to trace, the team found glass from windows (necessary to light the workplace) and a large quantity of artifacts lost or discarded by the gunsmiths (Seidel 1987:635). The gun parts recovered indicate that as late as 1778, the Continental troops employed a wide variety of armaments. British and German gun parts were present; but, not surprisingly, given Benjamin Franklin's purchase of a large quantity of French muskets in 1777, French parts were most common. More were purchased at other times, and some arrived with the French troops who served during the war. The lack of standardization challenged the gunsmiths' ingenuity. One problem appears to have been fitting British bayonets onto French Charleville muskets. The solution devised by the resourceful gunsmiths was to cut off the base of the British bayonets so that they could fit over the muzzles of the French guns. Several cut-off bases of British bayonets were recovered near the armorer's shop (Seidel 1987:654).

General Knox's artillery cantonment at Pluckemin has yielded more information than many other Revolutionary War sites. John Seidel's painstaking excavations recovered a variety of artifacts and features that highlight the experience of General Knox's artillerists. Moreover, Seidel's work demonstrates the advances in archaeological techniques and theories since Max Schrabisch's time and points out the value of carefully controlled excavations.

Morristown and Jockey Hollow

Some of Washington's troops returned to New Jersey for a third winter in 1779–1780. In 1777, following the victories at Trenton and Princeton, Washington had moved some of his troops north to Morristown, which at the time was a village of roughly 250 people, many of whom had roots in New England and were very patriotic.

The Continental Army's first encampment at Morristown has been the subject of little archaeological attention, in part, perhaps, because the main body of the army spent that difficult winter quartered at Valley Forge (Parrington et al. 1984). During the first winter in Morristown, Washington chose the Arnold Tavern as his headquarters and domicile (Weig and Craig 1955:5). Many of his men were billeted with local families in town and in the nearby communities of Madison and Chatham. An encampment of log huts is reputed to have existed on the farms of John Easton and Isaac Pierson in the Loantaka Brook Valley. It has yet to see archaeological investigation.

Conditions during the winter of 1777 were appalling. Enlistments were about to expire, and many of the soldiers were homesick. As the winter wore on, more and more went home. Washington wrote, "The fluctuating state of any Army, composed Chiefly of Militia, bids fair to reduce us to the Situation in which we were some little time ago, that is, of scarce having any Army at all, except (if) Reinforcements speedily arrive" (quoted in Weig and Craig 1955:7). Food and clothing were also in short supply. Washington spoke of troops "[m]arching over Frost and Snow, many without a Shoe, Stocking or Blanket" (quoted in Weig and Craig 1955:7). On February 22, 1777, General William Maxwell reported to Washington that his men were starving. Smallpox also struck the troops. Washington responded by ordering a massive inoculation program. Although the project was generally successful, a fair number of the patients did not survive, and many who did live bore the scars of their ordeal on their faces for the rest of their lives.

Despite these misfortunes, Washington and his troops returned to Morristown in the winter of 1779–1780. Although the Continental Army had seen some successes in the intervening two and a half years, including victories at Monmouth Courthouse and Saratoga, the overall situation was still grim. The finances of the young United States were in disarray (Weig and Craig 1955:11), many soldiers were nearing the end of their enlistments, and supplies were scarce. While Washington stayed in Morristown, most of the troops were quartered about three miles to the southwest in Jockey Hollow. Explaining his selection of the site to the Continental Congress, Washington noted that Morristown was the closest place available "compatible with our security which could also supply water and wood for covering and fuel" (quoted in Weig and Craig 1955:12).

The troops began to arrive in Morristown during the first week of December. All told, between 10,000 and 12,000 men occupied Jockey Hollow during the winter (Weig and Craig 1955:12). Other infantry brigades made encampments on Mount Kemble and near Mendham. The commander in chief and his personal bodyguard occupied the Ford Mansion, the large Georgian home of the widow Theodosia Ford.

The men arrived to find the ground frozen and snow-covered. Dr. James Thatcher would later state, "notwithstanding large fires, we can scarcely keep from freezing" (cited in Weig and Craig 1955:14). Nonetheless, the soldiers set about constructing huts on the hillsides. These rather primitive log cabins with board and shingle roofs were arranged in rows of eight and designed to house twelve men. Officers had larger huts and were allowed more creativity in their design.

The winter was widely regarded as the coldest in memory, and some twenty-eight snowfalls were recorded. The Delaware and Hudson Rivers froze solid, and the supply chain quickly broke down. Washington wrote that the men went "Five or Six days together without bread. At other times as many days without meat, and once or twice two or three days without either" (quoted in Weig and Craig 1955:18). Not surprisingly, the number of desertions climbed.

One bright spot in this otherwise gloomy scene occurred on May 10, 1780, when the Marquis de Lafayette arrived in Morristown and informed Washington that Louis XVI of France was sending more troops and a fleet to aid the America cause. That spring, the troops from the Morristown encampment began to disperse: the Maryland brigades went south, and the New York brigade was sent north to the Hudson Highlands. Some six brigades of men remained at Jockey Hollow until June 25, 1780.

The following winter, 1780–1781, a small number of troops, primarily the Pennsylvania Line, consisting of ten infantry regiments and one artillery regiment, returned to Jockey Hollow. Once again, conditions were poor. Many of the troops had not been paid in over a year, and they were also short on clothes and equipment. Despite repeated requests by their commander, Major General Anthony Wayne, no steps were taken to redress the situation. On New Year's Day 1781, the troops mutinied. One captain was killed and two other officers were wounded before the troops marched off in an attempt to deliver their grievances to Congress. In Princeton, representatives of Congress and the state of Pennsylvania met with the mutineers and agreed to secure the requested clothing and back pay. Men who had served their three-year enlistments were discharged.

The last encampment at Morristown occurred during the winter of 1781–1782, when the New Jersey Brigade was quartered a short distance south of the Wick House in Jockey Hollow (Weig and Craig 1955:29). This encampment was finally abandoned in August 1782.

As happened at Middlebrook and Pluckemin, local farmers began to reclaim the encampment area once the war was over. This must have been a stupendous task, given that their fields and woodlots had been transformed into a veritable city of wooden huts. Once the huts were torn down and the fields reestablished, the area remained largely agricultural until the 1890s, when wealthy bankers and industrialists from New York City began to purchase the farms and woodlots for country estates. As a result, many components of the encampment escaped the damage that would have been caused by improvements in plowing machinery during the twentieth century (Rutsch and Peters 1977:26).

The first descriptions of the old encampment were published late in the nineteenth century. The Reverend Joseph Tuttle, working with elderly informants, was able to locate the campsites of several units. In 1894 Emory McClintock published *Topography of Washington's Camp of 1780 and Its Neighborhood*, in which he carefully identified and described the brigade sites. Andrew Sherman subsequently photographed many of these same sites in 1916 (Rutsch and Peters 1977:26).

Morristown, like Pluckemin, was the site of some very early archaeological excavations. But whereas a wealthy property owner had funded Max Schrabisch's investigations, the first fieldwork at Morristown was carried out by National Park Service archaeologists, assisted by Civilian Conservation Corps (CCC) labor. The CCC had been established in 1933 as one of President Franklin Roosevelt's New Deal programs to put unemployed young men back to work. Many of the participants worked on projects to develop the nation's park system, including Morristown National Historical Park.

According to Edward Rutsch, who has written extensively on the excavations at Morristown (Rutsch and Peters 1977; Rutsch 1972), before the 1930s few archaeologists had turned their attention or their trowels to historic sites. One noteworthy exception was the Park Service's excavations at Jamestown, Virginia. There archaeologist J. C. Harrington had pioneered excavation techniques at one of the oldest European settlements in North America (Cotter 1993:1). The Park Service shared the results of Harrington's work widely, and some of the techniques employed at Morristown were a direct outgrowth of the excavations at Jamestown. Two are particularly noteworthy: the use of trowels for excavation and cross or slit trenching to find buried structures. According to Rutsch and Peters, in 1935 "Regional Archaeologist Alonzo Pond recommended to Junior Historian Russell Baker the mason's pointing trowel as a hand excavating tool" (1977:28).

The CCC laborers dug linear slit trenches in areas suspected to contain historic structures. Although this technique can be useful for finding the remains of substantial masonry foundations, it is quite destructive and tends to miss less substantial structures, such as log buildings, that lack permanent foundations. Moreover, the archaeologists did not screen the soil they excavated and so likely overlooked small artifacts. Nor is there any evidence that they excavated strati- graphically. Instead they seem to have jumbled together different layers repre- senting distinct time periods. Historian Russell Baker complained that "the greatest difficulty will probably be encountered in attempting to classify the findings chronologically. There is no method yet discovered which brands each article as having belonged to a definite period" (quoted in Rutsch and Peters 1977:28).

The poorly developed field methods did nothing to slow down the excava- tions. The archaeologists and their crews worked at numerous sites connected with the cantonment, including the Wick House, Fort Nonsense, the Ford Man- sion, and campsites associated with the First Maryland, Pennsylvania, and New Jersey Brigades (figures 4.4 and 4.5). The excavations brought to light a large quantity of items illustrative of eighteenth-century life, but these have not yet been intensively examined (figure 4.6). As might be expected, excavation of so many distinct sites by archaeologists with different methods and interests re- sulted in work of varying quality. This situation has been made even worse by the subsequent loss of field notes and other data.

Nonetheless, the excavations of the 1930s provided basic data for ongoing in- terpretations of life in the encampment. Even before any archaeological work had occurred, a single hut had been reconstructed at Jockey Hollow. Although it was later regarded as too conjectural and torn down during the 1930s, three more generations of reconstructions have been erected over some of the ex- cavated archaeological sites. Their locations are based on archaeological evidence, but they have proven detrimental to the long-term survival of ar- chaeological deposits at their sites because they bring increased visitation. Foot traffic at a fragile site like Morristown slowly but surely wears away archaeo- logical remains.

Some of the more recent and careful excavations at Morristown have re- vealed the original earthen floors of soldiers' huts, relict paths, and even the im- pressions left by log foundations. The most interesting insight into the lives of Washington's beleaguered troops at Jockey Hollow comes from the analysis of small fragments of animal bone—food remains—discarded by soldiers in the camp. Stanley Olsen, a zooarchaeologist—a specialist who studies animal bones—has analyzed collections of excavated bones from Morristown and Val- ley Forge. Both assemblages highlight the lack of food available to the troops at these encampments.

Figure 4.4. A 1930s photograph showing CCC excavations at the First Pennsylvania Brigade site. The men are cleaning fireplace stones unearthed during the excavations. Courtesy of Morristown National Historical Park.

Figure 4.5. Cross trenching, a highly destructive archaeological technique employed in some of the early Morristown excavations. This photograph shows the search for a hospital site on the west slope of Sugar Loaf Road. Courtesy of Morristown National Historical Park.

Figure 4.6. Exhibit in the Field Office Museum, 1937, of objects recovered from CCC excavations of hut ruin sites in and around Wick House, Guerin House, and Jockey Hollow. Courtesy of Morristown National Historical Park.

The bones from Morristown, excavated from huts occupied by troops from Connecticut and Pennsylvania, were recovered mostly in or around fireplaces. Almost all of the bone was from cattle and hogs. Olsen was surprised to see that most bones showed evidence of cracking and breaking, that is, attempts to reach the protein-rich marrow. These bones are graphic reminders of the soldiers' efforts to obtain as much nutrition as possible from the scrawny beasts they were provided (Olsen 1964:508). The second surprise was the near total absence of game animals. Soldiers on the brink of starvation might be expected to find ways to supplement their diet through hunting and perhaps fishing. They did not. Apparently, orders prohibiting the firing of weapons in camp were strictly enforced. Thus the occasional white-tailed deer might wander through the camp unharmed. One anonymous soldier noted that in "attempting to catch a doe which had ventured into camp," he was "knocked down and trod upon by the frightened creature in making her escape" (Olsen 1964:507).

From the evidence of the bones, it appears that almost all of the meat consumed by the troops was beef. The most common fragments come from the lower limbs, usually regarded by butchers as scraps. They could have been used to make soups, but were otherwise nearly inedible. At least some of the men must have had other, better cuts of meat, which they roasted on simple grills recycled from barrel-hoop iron. Nonetheless, the overall picture that comes to us from the food remains at Morristown is one of soldiers barely eking out their subsistence.

The Revolutionary War encampments at Morristown have been probed by archaeologists for longer than almost any other sites in the state. During roughly seventy years of excavation, both techniques and research questions have changed. Early archaeologists focused on easily identified foundations of structures and interesting artifacts suitable for display. Modern archaeologists continue to be interested in foundations and artifacts, but they also care about all the little things that once escaped notice: subtle variations in soil texture, fragmentary bones, and even grains of pollen. From these sources archaeologists can put together a revealing picture of the past. One wonders what techniques archaeologists may be using one hundred years from now.

The British Experience in Revolutionary New Jersey

Archaeologists working at Pluckemin, Morristown, and associated sites in the late twentieth century have provided a wealth of new information about Continental soldiers' lives during the trying winters of 1777–1778 and 1779–1780. But what is known of their adversaries, the British regulars, and their Scottish, German, and provincial auxiliaries? They too maintained a presence in New Jersey during the Revolutionary years. In fact, much of northeastern New Jersey, as far west as New Brunswick, was in British hands during 1777. The fact that British encampments have received considerably less attention than those of their American foes is due in part to the patriotic motivations of American historians and archaeologists. Yet several sites associated with the British experience in Revolutionary New Jersey have been examined by archaeologists, including Raritan Landing, which was occupied by the British in 1777 (Howson et al. 1995; Hartwick and Cavallo 1997), and the Old Barracks in Trenton, our subject here.

During the eighteenth century, armies fought in the warm months of the year and spent the winter in garrisons away from the fighting. Sometimes they were billeted in the homes of private citizens—not a popular practice. In an attempt to relieve its citizens of this onerous burden, the colony of New Jersey built barracks where British troops were quartered when not on campaign. Although only one stands today, there once were five barracks in major towns across the colony—Elizabeth, Perth Amboy, Burlington, New Brunswick, and Trenton. The barracks were constructed in the 1750s during the Seven Years' War (1754–1763), better known in North America as the French and Indian War. Although

most of the major battles were fought in Europe, the war spilled over into the
French and British colonies of North America. England's ultimate victory in this
conflict secured its claim to the eastern seaboard and laid the groundwork for
the American Revolution.

The Trenton barracks, completed in 1759, consisted of a two-story, roughly
U-shaped stone building for the soldiers (figure 4.7) and a separate officers' residence attached to the northern wing of the barracks proper (Kardas and
Larrabee 1983:8). Both sections were constructed with rubble stone walls set in
lime mortar. The imposing building would have stood as an impressive symbol
of royal might in the colony.

British troops first moved into the Trenton barracks in 1758, before the building was even completed. In 1765 the troops were withdrawn, the contents of the
barracks auctioned off, and the buildings rented out (Kardas and Larrabee
1983:9). During the Revolutionary War, the structures were again pressed into
service, at first as a recruiting center and supply depot for Continental troops.
But when a series of British victories drove Washington and his army from New

Figure 4.7. The carefully restored Old Barracks in Trenton. Our understanding of this site's
historic appearance was greatly improved thanks to the archaeological excavations performed by Hunter Research, Inc. Photograph by the author.

Jersey in the fall of 1776, the barracks returned to British hands. Trenton was held by "three regiments of Hessian infantry, an artillery detachment, fifty Hessian Yagers, and twenty Light Dragoons of the 16th British Regiment" (Kardas and Larrabee 1983:9). Tory refugees and the Hessian Yagers occupied the barracks. On December 26, 1776, Washington launched a surprise attack on Trenton, routing the slumbering Hessians.

Following the battle, the barracks went largely unused until the fall of 1781, when the building was employed as a convalescent hospital for disabled soldiers from the siege of Yorktown. Roughly one thousand Continental troops were quartered there until the fall of 1782 (Kardas and Larrabee 1983:10). Subsequently, the barracks entered a long period of decline. In the 1790s the structure was remodeled into private homes. Even worse, Front Street was cut directly through the center of the building in 1795! For most of the late nineteenth century, the section of the barracks to the south of Front Street was operated as a home by the Trenton Society for the Relief of Respectable Aged and Indigent Widows and Single Women.

The site's prospects began to look up in 1899, when the Daughters of the American Revolution purchased the southern section. More encouragingly, the Old Barracks Association was formed in 1902. Then, in 1913, the state purchased the section to the north of Front Street. The demolished portion was reconstructed, and by 1917 the structure had been restored—all without benefit of archaeological excavation.

One of the first excavations to take place at the Old Barracks occurred in 1983 under the direction of Susan Kardas and Edward Larrabee. Their work, rather typical contract archaeology, was done in preparation for the installation of a sewer that would cut through the property. They dug several test units and used a backhoe to cut a trench through some very compact rocky soils where Front Street had been. The excavations recovered a small but interesting collection of artifacts and revealed a chronological sequence of soil layers. The deepest levels the archaeologists reached, some five feet below the present ground surface, apparently represented the historic banks of the Delaware River (Kardas and Larrabee 1983:22). Above that was roughly a foot of soil containing artifacts from the eighteenth-century occupation of the barracks, and overlying that was a layer of lime mortar and stucco representing the 1795 demolition. This was overlain by nearly two feet of nineteenth-century deposits, and topped off with more rubble from the now-removed Front Street and modern landscaping soil.

The most interesting deposit is that associated with the eighteenth-century occupation of the barracks. It includes fragments of dark green liquor bottles, as well as shards of glass from a tumbler and a stemmed drinking glass, possibly used by the officers in the garrison. Various eighteenth-century ceramics were recovered, including black basaltware, delft, and scratch-blue stoneware. These artifacts, and the fifty pounds of clam and oyster shells the archaeologists found, clearly relate to the soldiers' day-to-day existence, but few of them are military in nature. One exception is a domed brass button of the type used by both British and French troops between 1726 and 1776 (Kardas and Larrabee 1983). Other items that might be expected on a military site, such as gunflints, musket balls, and gun parts, were surprisingly absent. Apparently the British troops meticulously maintained the area around the barracks. Even more surprising was the presence of Native American artifacts intermixed with the eighteenth- and nineteenth-century finds. They indicate that Native Americans occupied the site for several thousand years before Trenton or the Old Barracks existed.

A second archaeological excavation occurred at the site in 1989, conducted by Hunter Research, Inc. The firm's intensive work at the site has been directed toward evaluating the archaeological potential of the property and helping the state manage this important historic place (Hunter Research Associates 1989: 3–1). Hunter Research's excavations addressed several specific issues: the architectural history of the structure's porches, particularly how and why they were constructed; the evidence for historic modifications to the structure; the location of the original parade grounds; and the general reconstruction of the landscape to its original grade or elevations.

The excavations by Hunter Research, like those by Kardas and Larrabee, found only sparse evidence for the eighteenth-century military occupation of the site. They did, however, reveal the original surface of the parade ground in front of the barracks (Hunter Research Associates 1989:6–12). When first constructed, the barracks were fronted by a paved parade ground at a lower level than the first floor, which was raised on a terrace. The overall effect would have been imposing.

The only artifacts recovered by Hunter Research that clearly relate to the site's military occupation were five broken gunflints, a metal button that may be from a uniform, and a single musket ball. Other colonial artifacts included a hammer and punch and fragments of utilitarian redware plates. Among the more interesting artifacts were two glass trade beads of the type used by colonists trading with Native Americans during the seventeenth and eighteenth centuries. They predate construction of the barracks and highlight the Native American occupation of what would, in the eighteenth century, become Trenton (see Martin 1991).

The archaeologists from Hunter Research also found considerable archaeological evidence for alterations and remodelings of the building. The original building probably had a porch; later, doorways were blocked up and filled in. Moreover, the parade ground went from a manicured space devoted to military exercises to a trash-strewn lot. The restoration activities of the twentieth century added yet another layer to the archaeological deposits on the property. The discoveries made at the Old Barracks are a step toward a better understanding of the eighteenth-century military experience.

Fields of Battle

As well as campsites and fortifications, the battlefields of the Revolution are also beginning to be investigated archaeologically. In some ways they are more challenging to study, because even the longest battles during the eighteenth century—with the exception of sieges—happened in the space of a few hours or, at most, a few days.

The Battle of Monmouth

Although the Battles of Trenton and Princeton resuscitated the flagging hopes for American independence, the situation worsened the following year, when Sir William Howe and his army of twenty thousand British and Hessian troops routed Washington's army at the Battle of Brandywine in Chadds Ford, Pennsylvania, and captured Philadelphia. The Continental Congress hastily evacuated its quarters and headed west toward the security of Lancaster. A week later, Washington attacked the British just outside of Philadelphia, at the Battle of Germantown. Again, his army was defeated. Shortly thereafter, his troops went into winter quarters at Valley Forge.

The British remained ensconced in Philadelphia until the next year, when a new commander, Sir Henry Clinton, decided to consolidate his forces in New York City in preparation for a campaign in the southern colonies (Bill 1964:75). Fearful of attack by a French fleet if he moved his troops by ship, Clinton decided to travel overland to New York through New Jersey. Unknown to Clinton, he and his fifteen thousand troops and three thousand Loyalists and camp followers were headed toward one of the largest military engagements of the Revolutionary War, the Battle of Monmouth.

Clinton left Philadelphia on June 18 and reached Haddonfield, New Jersey, without incident. Shortly after resuming its march, however, Clinton's army was attacked by the local militia. Nonetheless, the long British line continued to snake across the central Jersey countryside, sometimes stretching out for eight or ten miles. On Friday, June 26, the head of the column reached Monmouth Courthouse, today's Freehold. There Clinton allowed his troops to rest, sent out parties to reconnoiter the positions of the Americans who had been harassing him, and replenished his supplies. For his headquarters, Clinton commandeered the substantial farmhouse of William Covenhoven. (This house still stands and is maintained as a museum by the Monmouth County Historical Association.)

As the British juggernaut rolled across New Jersey, Washington met with his senior officers to discuss strategy. Some favored a general action or major battle with the British, while others argued that it would be more prudent to continue to harass them. Eventually, the group decided upon a harassing movement. When General Charles Lee, recently released from British imprisonment, learned that command of the advance force had been given to the young Marquis de Lafayette, he demanded the leadership, and Washington acquiesced. Lee and his force, which totaled approximately fifty-five hundred regulars and New Jersey militia, camped at Englishtown on the evening of June 27, 1778, with orders from Washington to attack the following morning. The main American force, under Washington's direct command, also began moving toward Freehold.

Lee's men passed the Tennent Meetinghouse and marched east toward Freehold. On the road to Middletown, Lee and Anthony Wayne saw what they took to be the rear guard of the British troops. Wayne launched an attack on the roughly five or six hundred men in this detachment. Although they retreated, Lee was surprised to see a new and much larger enemy force of some two thousand men coming into the action. Lee ordered a retreat.

As Lee's troops withdrew, Washington arrived on the scene. After reprimanding Lee, Washington was able to rally the troops and stem the British advance. When evening fell, both armies camped on the battlefield. Under cover of night, the British army moved out of Freehold, toward Middletown, Sandy Hook, and safety. When Washington discovered the flight the next morning, he attempted, unsuccessfully, to overtake the British (Smith 1975:24). Both Washington and Clinton claimed victory after the battle. Although Clinton was able to continue his march across New Jersey, Washington's troops had finally shown that they could stand up to British regulars in a pitched battle.

Historians have studied this pivotal battle exhaustively, yet archaeologists have been able to contribute some new insights to our understanding of it. In particular, two aspects of the battle have been studied with archaeological techniques: the clash during the afternoon of June 28, 1778, between a battalion of New England "Picked men" and the Royal Highlanders of the 42nd Regiment of Foot (Stone et al. 1998); and a campsite on the Neuberger farm, likely associated with the British retreat from the battle (Sivilich and Phillips 1998).

Daniel Sivilich and Ralph Phillips, co-chairmen of the Deep Search Metal Detecting Club's Archaeological Committee, carried out both projects; only the first study is discussed here (figure 4.8).

Many archaeologists look askance at the use of metal detectors. After all, they can be used to pluck from the ground coins, medals, and other easily dated artifacts that can help to identify stratigraphic layers, leaving behind less useful diagnostic items. Nonetheless, skillfully employed metal detectors can provide a considerable amount of useful information, particularly when a site is not amenable to typical archaeological techniques. It would take decades of excavating at a battlefield like Monmouth, which stretches over miles, to generate the sort of data that Sivilich and Phillips have found in a few short years. The methods they employed were based on those pioneered by archaeologists Richard Fox and Douglas Scott at the Little Bighorn Battlefield National Monument in Montana. By using metal detectors to trace the trajectories of bullets, Fox and Scott were able to reconstruct the last moments of George Armstrong Custer's ill-conceived attack (Fox 1993).

Figure 4.8. Dan Sivilich and Ralph Phillips searching for traces of the battle at Monmouth Battlefield State Park. Photograph courtesy of Dan Sivilich.

During the fall of 1990, Garry Wheeler Stone, a historical archaeologist with the New Jersey State Park Service, suggested to the Archaeology Committee of the newly formed Friends of Monmouth Battlefield that they survey the eroded field in front of the eighteenth-century Derick Sutfin House on the battleground (Stone et al. 1998:2). The keen-eyed Phillips rapidly found a musket ball; as time would show, however, the problem was not finding relics but mapping them. With help from talented surveyor Neal Barton, it was possible to map the artifact locations from horizontal control points located around the field margins (Stone et al. 1998:2). Sivilich, an engineer by training, then used FASTCAD, a computer-aided drafting program, to plot the distributions of the artifacts. These included iron grapeshot intended to mow down infantrymen, lead musket balls, cannonballs, musket parts, and all the other detritus of a battlefield (figure 4.9).

The archaeologists found physical evidence of an incident that had occurred

Figure 4.9. The butt plate of a British Brown Bess musket, marked with the Broad Arrow, symbol of royal property, recovered at Monmouth Battlefield. Photograph courtesy of Dan Sivilich.

on the battlefield more than two hundred years earlier—the tactical withdrawal of the Second Battalion of Royal Highlanders as a battalion of carefully picked New England riflemen advanced toward them. Archaeology allows us to trace this single incident in detail because the British and American troops used slightly different munitions, particularly musket balls: the American .58 caliber and the British .69 caliber (Sivilich 1996:103). By plotting their distribution, it is possible to determine where the troops stood and fought during the heat of the battle. The evidence shows both the orderly advance of the Americans and the skillful tactical retreat of the Highlanders under fire.

Sivilich and Phillips have used the same techniques to trace the withdrawal of the British army north through Middletown in the days following the battle (Sivilich and Phillips 1998). Their work highlights how the knowledgeable use of metal detectors by archaeologists can provide valuable new information about the past.

The Baylor Massacre

The discovery of the Baylor Massacre victims is arguably the most spectacular find relating to the American Revolution yet made in New Jersey. As at Monmouth Battlefield, success rewarded the work of avocational archaeologists who maintained a high level of scholarship.

According to traditional accounts of the incident, Lord Cornwallis and some five thousand men were dispatched on a foraging mission into Bergen County in September 1778. Apprised of the situation, Washington believed that the British intended an expedition up the Hudson River. To guard against this possibility, he ordered Colonel George Baylor and the Third Regiment Light Dragoons of Virginia to a post on the Hackensack River (Stryker 1882:4). On the evening of September 27, 1778, Colonel Baylor quartered his dragoons in several barns in the Overkill neighborhood. Baylor and his officers stayed in the farmhouse of Cornelius Haring, with a guard posted at the bridge over the Hackensack (Stryker 1882:6). Baylor was unimpressed when informed that the British were less than ten miles away.

When Loyalists informed Lord Cornwallis of Baylor's whereabouts, the commander decided to seize the opportunity to surprise and capture the dragoons (Stryker 1882:6). He dispatched Major General Grey and a sizable force toward the slumbering Americans. Grey's men easily captured the American sentries guarding the road, and soon thereafter, between one and two o'clock in the morning, arrived at the Haring house and barn where Baylor and his men were sleeping. The British troops burst into the house and brutally bayoneted the sleeping officers. Colonel Baylor and Major Andre Cough sought refuge in the house's large chimney, but were discovered and stabbed, Clough fatally. The British troops then broke into the barn. Although the soldiers cried out for quarter, none was granted. At the end of the grisly evening, 11 of the 116 men in the regiment had been killed, and 17 were left behind so badly wounded they were expected to expire. Thirty-nine dragoons were captured; the rest escaped in the darkness and confusion (Stryker 1882:9).

In many ways, the discovery of the dragoons' burial place is the story of one individual's search for the past. In the years following the massacre, many of the details were forgotten. Local tradition held that the victims "had been buried in three tanning vats on the west side of the Hackensack River, just north of the bridge that leads from River Vale to Old Tappan" (Demarest 1971:70). In 1966 Thomas Demarest began collecting information about the possible location of that burial place. He contacted the U.S. Army and other organizations for assistance, but to no avail (Demarest 1971:71). Then, in 1968, a housing subdivision started to go up on a farm just north of the Hackensack River in Rivervale. The history-minded Demarest read that some college students under the direction of D. Bennett Mazur, a county freeholder, were surveying local historic sites. Demarest asked Mazur if some of them might be assigned to conduct an archaeological excavation at the purported massacre site (Bergen County Historical Society 1968:2). Two weeks of digging during a humid New Jersey summer yielded nothing.

The clue that eventually led to the discovery of the ill-fated dragoons was a visit to the excavation by George Fournier of Westwood, whose father had owned the farm. Based on his recollections, the focus of the excavations shifted (Demarest 1971:73). On the last day of their dig, three students uncovered human bones in what had been a tan vat. Found with this individual, designated Dragoon No. 1, were several silver buttons and an elegant silver buckle bearing the mark, Z.B., used by a noted Boston silversmith, Zachariah Brigden (Demarest 1971:74). The dragoon was buried fully clothed, which may indicate that he was on guard duty and not asleep in the house or barn when he was killed. Even more interesting are the silver buttons and the buckle he wore. All were too costly for the average soldier. Based on extensive research, Demarest believes that this individual was Isaac Howe Davenport of Dorchester, Massachusetts, possibly the sergeant of the guard on the night of the massacre.

With this information in hand, Demarest and Wayne M. Daniels were retained by the Bergen County Board of Chosen Freeholders and the Bergen County Historical Society to carry out a more detailed archaeological study of the site. Working with a team of volunteers, they uncovered the remains of five more dragoons buried in two other tan vats (Demarest 1971:74). Several skeletons showed evidence of considerable trauma, including one skull that appears to have been smashed by a gun butt. When the tannery was in operation, these vats, dug deeply into the soil, held hides soaking in the tanning solution. A hide scraper and an iron hook found in one of the vats provide further corroborating evidence of how they were used (Bergen County Historical Society 1968:3). The tanner, Arie Blauvelt, moved to Rockland County just before the Revolution, and it is likely that the tanyard was abandoned when war began.

Although local tradition maintains that Hessians tossed the bodies into the tan vats, there is no evidence that Hessians participated in the burial. In fact, an affidavit left decades later by a Bergen County militiaman, John Haring, indicates that he and other Continental soldiers buried their dead comrades the morning after the massacre (Demarest 1971:67). The excavations at the Baylor Massacre site provided graphic evidence of the brutality with which the dragoons were slain, but also showed that the dead men were carefully laid to rest there by other Continental soldiers.

If someone should ask, "So what has archaeology told us about the American Revolution that documents could not?" the answer clearly would be, "Quite a lot." At Pluckemin and Morristown, we have physical evidence of how the Continental soldiers lived. Armorers at Pluckemin struggled to produce and repair weapons for the variously equipped troops. The scant scraps of animal bone recovered at Jockey Hollow, often burned and shattered, reinforces our ideas of the brutal conditions the troops suffered. Yet all was not suffering and privation. Sherds of pearlware indicate that at Pluckemin the officers were able to acquire the latest in teawares from England.

The experience of the British troops and their Hessian and Loyalist allies has received less archaeological attention. Yet significant finds have been made, such as the original parade ground at the Old Barracks.

The archaeological remains of an eighteenth-century battlefield are ephemeral when compared with the fortifications and encampments that the troops occupied. Nevertheless, talented avocational archaeologists armed with metal detectors have demonstrated that careful plotting of seemingly nondescript munitions on the field of battle can contribute to a new and better understanding of how a military engagement unfolded. And at the Baylor Massacre site we see the true inhumanity of war graphically revealed through archaeology.

Archaeology has much to tell us about the Revolution. As more sites associated with this war are discovered and excavated, we can anticipate a more nuanced understanding of this defining period in American history.

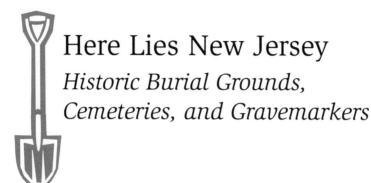

CHAPTER FIVE

Here Lies New Jersey
Historic Burial Grounds, Cemeteries, and Gravemarkers

For many people, cemeteries are scary, spooky places. Looked at in a different light, however, they contain a critical source of information about the lives of past individuals and societies, and it is this aspect that has attracted genealogists, historians, art historians, and, of course, archaeologists. As folklorist Thomas Hannon put it, a cemetery is a "field of artifacts" (Hannon 1983:263).

Historical archaeologists working in New Jersey have devoted as much time to the gravemarkers found in cemeteries as they have to the burials that lie below. Gravemarkers are particularly interesting because they are both artifacts and dated documents specifically designed to convey information to future generations. By examining the changing styles of New Jersey's gravemarkers from the late seventeenth century through the early twentieth century, we can chart the shifting patterns of our state's culture. Changes in religious sensibilities, life expectancy, family relationships, and even attitudes toward death are all represented in the silent markers that populate cemeteries. At the same time, it is possible to trace the arrival and spread of various ethnic groups across the state (see Wacker 1971 and 1975 for a similar approach using architecture).

Archaeologists and forensic anthropologists also conduct excavations in cemeteries—a very direct way to learn about the people buried there. Employing many of the same techniques that are used to understand crime scenes, they can unravel the mysteries of past lives. From the skeleton of a long dead person they can calculate the individual's stature, determine his or her sex and racial background, and often recount the various injuries and ailments the person once suffered. Similarly, objects buried with the dead, whether personal effects, the handles and furniture of long decayed coffins, or even the musket balls that ended a life, can also provide information about people and the society in which they lived.

In this chapter we shall survey a variety of historic cemeteries from many different parts of the state. We start our tour aboveground, looking at New Jersey's historic gravemarkers. Then we shall descend into the earth to examine an archaeological excavation and the surprising discovery of a colonial murder victim underneath Christ Episcopal Church in Shrewsbury. These few examples from the dozens of studies undertaken by archaeologists in New Jersey's cemeteries illustrate the potential of burial grounds to provide new information about the past.

Cemeteries Aboveground

New Jersey is blessed with an abundance of eighteenth-century burial grounds. These graveyards are an important, though often overlooked, part of the historic landscape. They also preserve a rich record of local folk art. Leering skulls, winged cherubs, crossed sabers, wilting tulips, and bold monograms all decorate the state's colonial gravemarkers.

Someone traversing the state from north to south would quickly note the tremendous variability in the state's early gravemarkers. Why in such a small area was there so much diversity? In part, perhaps more so than today, the stone carver was an artist and brought a distinct sensibility to each commission. At the same time, the work of these artisans reflected the beliefs of their communities and cultures.

By 1820 the regional varieties of gravestones, once so notable, had disappeared as though whitewashed away. Plain white marble gravemarkers, carved in the Philadelphia style, became popular throughout New Jersey and, indeed, much of the eastern United States. Later still, middle- and upper-class Victorians erected elaborate marble and granite memorials, and sometimes mausoleums every bit as ornate as the Queen Anne and Second Empire–style houses they lived in. These ostentatious gravemarkers, made possible by new mechanized forms of stonecutting, reflected in a permanent form the social distinctions that characterized late-nineteenth-century America (figure 5.1; McGuire 1988).

Some groups broke free of the mold. Ironworkers in the Pinelands occasionally made and used iron gravemarkers between about 1810 and 1840 (figure 5.2). Although one might expect that iron gravemarkers would corrode, these memorials cast from bog iron survive in very good condition, a tribute both to their makers and to the rust-resistant qualities of bog iron. Glassblowers decorated the graves of their friends and family members with broken shards of green glass, providing a sparkling and durable memorial lawn (Horner 1985). At

Figure 5.1. Victorian mausoleums in Hillside Cemetery, Scotch Plains. These beautifully designed structures illustrate the pinnacle of Victorian mortuary art. Photograph by the author.

Gethsemane Cemetery in Bergen County, archaeologist Joan Geismar found evidence that African Americans decorated their graves with shells and pipes, reminiscent of traditional grave decorations in Africa (Geismar 1995). Later, between the 1870s and 1930s, Danish, Italian, German, Hungarian, and Slovak workers in the terra-cotta industry erected colorful gravemarkers in the cemeteries of Middlesex County's clay district (figure 5.3; Veit 1995).

Even today, gravemarkers provide a permanent record of our changing culture. If memorial parks paved with flat bronze and marble slabs are the product of a late-twentieth-century synergy between lawnmowers and mass production, laser etching and mechanized carving are bringing art and life back into our cemeteries. Interestingly enough, the designs on these new gravemarkers relate as often to the deceased's hobbies and interests as they do to religious beliefs. Once again, our society is changing, and the artifacts called gravestones will provide future archaeologists with a permanent record.

Turning back to the eighteenth century, we find that New Jersey's gravemarkers provide an unparalleled material record of the colony's cultural diver-

3

sity. Three major carving traditions are represented. The northwestern corner, encompassing present-day Warren and Sussex Counties, is home to an unusual collection of German-language gravemarkers dating to the late eighteenth century (Sarapin 1994:92–94; Veit 2000). Heading east, one finds elaborately carved gravemarkers made from fine-grained reddish brown sandstone. Erected by English, Scottish, and Dutch settlers, as well as by transplanted Puritans from New England and Long Island, these stones are concentrated in northeastern New Jersey and date between 1680 and 1820. South Jersey's gravemarkers are also distinct. Suddenly, below an invisible line from Trenton on the Delaware River to Ocean Grove on the Atlantic Ocean, the handsome sandstone gravemarkers of northern New Jersey disappear, replaced by largely unornamented white and gray marble stones. What can these bland stones tell us? A great deal.

First of all, it is important to recognize that gravestones were created to convey information to future generations. Much of this information is genealogical: names, dates, and familial relationships. At the same time, gravemarkers, even

Figure 5.2. Three cast-iron gravemarkers in the Pleasant Mills Cemetery, near historic Batsto Village. These markers highlight the innovative use of a local material by iron-workers in New Jersey's Pinelands. Photograph by the author.

Figure 5.3. A terra-cotta gravemarker made to imitate stone. This carefully produced piece of sculpture marks the grave of Bruno Grandelis and is located in Hillside Cemetery in Metuchen. Photograph by the author.

in public burial grounds and churchyards, were often clustered according to family groupings. Much of this information has since been lost as zealous twentieth-century groundskeepers, blessed with lawnmowers, have moved the stones into more orderly rows to facilitate mowing.

The images carved on the stones—that is, their iconography—also convey messages, aimed particularly at the substantial portion of colonial New Jersey's population that was not literate. Grim death's heads, hourglasses, and crossed bones all served as vivid visual reminders of human mortality. For those who could read, this message was reinforced by poetic epitaphs carved at the base of the gravestones, such as this example from Jane Woodruff's (died 1758) stone in the First Presbyterian Church at Elizabeth:

> As you are now so once was I
> In Health & Strength; tho here I lie
> As I am now so you must be
> Prepare for Death & Follow me

To the modern reader, this seems a distinctly morbid message; but to eighteenth-century readers, many of whom were descendants of Puritans, the rhymed verses rang true. According to Calvinist thinking, humans were depraved, grace was predestined for only a few, and most mortals would suffer eternal damnation, with no earthly hope for redemption (Fischer 1989:112). Moreover, one of the surest signs of damnation was a person's certainty that he or she was saved. What historian David Hackett Fischer has described as a "manic combination of hope and fear about the 'dying time' became a central part of life" (1989:115). This attitude is clearly reflected in northern New Jersey's early-eighteenth-century gravemarkers.

"Stranger Stop and Cast an Eye": East Jersey's Colonial Gravemarkers

Although European settlement of New Jersey began in earnest in the 1660s, the earliest surviving gravemarkers date to the 1680s and 1690s. Concentrated in northeastern New Jersey, they are found in Elizabeth (formerly Elizabethtown), Newark, Perth Amboy, and the Piscatawaytown section of Edison. Most of these very early gravemarkers are large sandstone slabs, more accurately called tombstones, and many mark the graves of prominent early settlers. In Perth Amboy, the tomb of Helen Gordon, wife of East Jersey Proprietor Thomas Gordon, is graced by a carefully inscribed slab. In the cemetery by St. James Episcopal Church in Edison, a slab dated 1693 marks the grave of Charles and Richard Hooper, two unfortunate boys who ate poisoned mushrooms (figure 5.4).

Although particular gravemarkers can provide interesting and sobering glimpses of past lives, the stones as a group allow us to draw broader conclusions about the cultures in which they were produced. Though long of interest to genealogists, gravemarkers were generally ignored by anthropologists and historians until the second half of the twentieth century. One notable exception was Harriet M. Forbes, who published *Gravestones of Early New England* in 1927. Unlike so many of her predecessors, Forbes was interested in more than the genealogical information the stones conveyed.

Figure 5.4. The tombstone of Charles and Richard Hooper (both died 1693). One of New Jersey's oldest surviving tombstones, it is located in St. James Episcopal Churchyard, Edison. Photograph by the author.

In the mid-1960s, archaeologists James Deetz and Edwin Dethlefsen began a study of colonial gravestone iconography in the Boston area. "By treating [gravestones] as archaeological phenomenon," they believed, "one can demonstrate and test methods of inferring diffusion, design evolution, and relationships between a folk art tradition and the culture which produced it" (Dethlefsen and Deetz 1966:502). They further hypothesized that the designs on gravestones and the iconographical variations over time signified a change in the Puritan attitudes toward death. In their study area, mortality images such as winged skulls predominated until the 1770s, which, in their opinion, reflected the strong influence of Puritanism (Deetz and Dethlefsen 1967; Deetz 1977). Then, coinciding with the spread of the Great Awakening, a religious movement stressing a more personal relationship with God, cherubs became the most popular design. The third stage occurred at the end of the eighteenth century, with a transition to urn and willow motifs at the same time as the new Protestant denominations of Unitarianism and Methodism emerged. The designs on these latest gravemarkers stressed memorialization rather than human mortality or heavenly rewards.

At the same time that Deetz and Dethlefsen were beginning their archaeological studies, Allen Ludwig was writing a massive art-historical study of gravemarkers, *Graven Images: New England Stonecarving and Its Symbols, 1650–1815* (1966). Other important large-scale studies also focused on New England's colonial gravemarkers (Tashjian and Tashjian 1974; Benes 1977). Graveyards in New York and New Jersey began to receive considerable scholarly attention as well (see Wasserman 1972; Baugher and Winter 1983; Crowell 1983; Welch 1987; Veit 1996a).

In general, the colonial gravestones of northeastern New Jersey show a similar, though not identical, pattern to the one Deetz and Dethlefsen identified in New England. An examination of fifteen Middlesex County graveyards containing some 634 eighteenth-century markers revealed that the earliest ones were crudely inscribed fieldstones, probably made by family members and friends for deceased loved ones. Simple designs, such as rosettes and circles, were also popular in the early eighteenth century. Winged death's heads, hourglasses, and sometimes skulls and crossbones were also popular, primarily before 1760 (figure 5.5). Most of these more intricate designs were carved in Newark or Elizabethtown (Veit 1996a:81).

Later, as in New England, cherubs appear in Middlesex County's colonial cemeteries. Although some carvers produced them as early as the 1720s, they were most popular between 1740 and 1790. It is worth noting that the faces so carefully carved on the markers are generally not depictions of the individuals

Figure 5.5. The gravestone of Ms. Sarah Woodruff (died 1727), Elizabeth First Presbyterian Church Cemetery. This brown sandstone marker shows the full range of Puritan motifs, including the skull and crossbones representing mortality, the hourglass representing the brevity of life, and flames signifying the torments of Hell. Photograph by the author.

buried below but are generic images of cherubim. In 1661 Thomas Wilson's *Compleate Christian Dictionary* defined cherubim as "Images of men with wings and comely faces" (Tashjian and Tashjian 1974:83).

Two major schools of carving had developed in New Jersey by the mid-eighteenth century. One was centered in Elizabethtown, where Ebenezer Price (1728–1788), a prolific craftsman, produced hundreds of carefully hewn images (figure 5.6). In addition to cherubs, Price also carved tulips and other designs. His stones mark the full flowering of New Jersey carving. Price trained several talented apprentices, among them Jonathan Akin, David Jeffries, and Abner Stewart. A number of other carvers, including Aaron Ross and Elias Darby, employed a very similar carving style and may also have apprenticed under Price. They are generally known as Price imitators (Welch 1987:50).

It is more difficult to trace the evolution of the carving tradition in Newark because that city, unlike Elizabeth, lost its major colonial graveyards to development. We do know that William Grant and Uzal Ward produced numerous

Figure 5.6. The gravestone of Nathaniel Fitzrandolph (died 1780), a veteran of the American Revolution. This stone in the cemetery of the First Presbyterian Church in Woodbridge is an excellent example of Ebenezer Price's carving style. British soldiers reputedly used the stone for target practice during the Revolution, resulting in the pockmarks seen here. Photograph by the author.

cherubs that display pendulous jowls and have rather pear-shaped heads. Their work was popular throughout much of northern New Jersey. Later still, the brothers Jonathan Hand Osborne of Scotch Plains and Henry Osborne of Wood-bridge produced some fine cherubs. They were most active in the 1790s and crafted many of the neatly incised monograms found in late-eighteenth-century graveyards (figure 5.7).

In contrast to the patterns noted by Deetz and Dethlefsen in New England graveyards, the urn and willow motif did not become popular in New Jersey until well into the nineteenth century. More common were monograms, apparently a local design, perhaps popularized by the Osbornes. The message, however, may not have been very different. Monograms, even more clearly than urns and willow trees, reflect the growing importance of the individual rather than the more clearly religious message of the earlier cherubs. Interestingly enough, carvers like Jonathan Hand Osborne began to advertise their handiwork by carving their names in the tympanum—the arched top—of the stones during this period.

These trends in gravestone decoration are best viewed at a regional level, because a single historic graveyard is likely to show a distinctly local pattern. One congregation, for example, may have been opposed to the use of graven images, such as skulls and cherubs, while another may have seen them as entirely appropriate. It is worth noting too that the very use of a gravestone was a mark of

Figure 5.7. The gravemarker of Mary Dunham (died 1794). The stone, located in St. James Episcopal Churchyard, Edison, is decorated with Mary's initials and the name of the carver, Jonathan Hand Osborne. Photograph by the author.

status. Although no stone carvers' account books are known to survive from New Jersey, John Stevens, a Rhode Islander who supplied gravestones to port towns in Middlesex and Monmouth Counties, kept detailed records of his products. His daybook documents that the average cost of an upright gravestone in the first decades of the eighteenth century was between two and three pounds sterling, while large flat tombstones, also known as ledgerstones, cost ten pounds or more—a considerable sum at the time and well beyond the financial means of many settlers.

German-Language Markers in Northwestern New Jersey

The gravemarkers of northwestern New Jersey differ significantly from those in the northeastern part of the state. For much of the eighteenth century, the Delaware River marked the edge of the frontier. Although this part of the state contains some exceptionally fertile farmland, the Kittatinny Ridge, the rugged terrain, and the proximity of Native Americans seem to have limited European settlement. The earliest gravemarkers in the region date only to the years immediately after the Revolutionary War.

It was not until the 1780s that two carvers began to provide for the commemorative needs of this region's settlers. One, John Solomon Teetzel, signed many of his stones and carved in a distinctive style that allows us to identify his work with some degree of surety. The other carver never signed his full name to his works but simply used the initial "D." He may have been Jacob Dodderer. Both the D Carver and Teetzel resided in Hardwick Township, Sussex County (then Warren County), and both had emigrated from what today is Germany, Teetzel from Upper Saxony (Veit 2000:157).

Unlike their contemporaries in East Jersey, the D Carver and Teetzel generally avoided ornamentation and instead used fine calligraphy as the primary decoration on most of their markers. One exception is the ornamented memorial the D Carver produced for John George Windemuth (died 1782), which was initially decorated with a crude face. Surprisingly, the face was later chipped off the stone and replaced with the deceased's initials (figure 5.8). Perhaps members of Windemuth's family, who were likely Lutherans, felt that a graven image was inappropriate.

Unlike the D Carver, Teetzel carved inscriptions in both English and German, employing gray and tan sandstone blanks for his stones. Between 1789 and 1800 he produced at least ninety-nine stones, forty-four of which he signed, in Sussex, Warren, Morris, and Somerset Counties. Almost all of his German-language gravemarkers offer an epitaph or a verse from the Bible in addition to the basic inscription, and most are undecorated. The use of biblical passages,

Figure 5.8. The head-and-shoulder gravestone of John George Windemuth (died 1782) in the Stillwater Cemetery, Sussex County. This unusual German-language marker was produced by the D Carver. Note that a face was once inscribed at the top of the stone but was later defaced. Photograph by the author.

rare on English-language gravemarkers during the eighteenth century, was common on German markers. According to University of Pennsylvania folklorist Donald Yoder, some Pennsylvania German gravemarkers list "the hymn sung at the house, the hymn sung at church, and the hymn sung at the graveside" (Yoder, cited in Graves 1988:93). Teetzel stopped carving gravemarkers in New Jersey and left the state in 1801. After his departure, Abner Stewart, one of Ebenezer Price's apprentices, became the carver of choice in northwestern New Jersey. Teetzel settled in Trafalgar Township, Ontario, Canada, where he continued to produce gravestones in his distinctive style until death overtook him in 1836 (Veit 2000:157).

For a short period at the end of the eighteenth century, these two talented craftsmen, the D Carver and Teetzel, produced beautifully carved German-language markers in northwestern New Jersey. Elsewhere in the area, anonymous artisans carved small flat marble slabs to mark the graves of the Moravian settlers in Hope. As a group, all of these German-language gravemarkers serve to commemorate the early settlers of the region, many of whom were German Americans migrating east from Pennsylvania, and also the unique Anglo-German subculture that flourished in northwestern New Jersey at the end of the eighteenth century.

Missing Motifs in Southern New Jersey

Southern New Jersey's colonial gravemarkers share little in common with those of the northern part of the state. When archaeologist Elizabeth Crowell carried out a detailed study of Cape May County's gravemarkers of the period 1740–1810, she found that undecorated marble markers predominated (Crowell 1983). The symbolically rich images that decorate northern New Jersey's gravemarkers are largely absent, not only in Cape May County but also throughout much of the southern half of the state.

At first glance, Crowell's conclusions are surprising. One might expect to find in Cape May County, an area first settled by transplanted New Englanders, elaborately carved gravemarkers like those in New England and northern New Jersey (Crowell 1983:9). Yet fewer than 10 of the 223 stones Crowell recorded were decorated. Why this difference?

In part, the answer boils down to supply and demand. Procuring a gravestone in southern New Jersey was a challenge. There was no locally available stone from which gravemarkers could be carved, and so wooden markers—or in some cases small, crudely inscribed fieldstones—had to suffice. Someone who wanted a professionally carved gravestone had to import it. According to Crowell, almost all of Cape May's stone colonial markers came from Philadelphia (figure 5.9). Several are even signed by Philadelphia carvers (1983:83).

Not surprisingly, given their source, the Cape May gravestones are identical in material, form, carving, and lack of decoration to contemporary eighteenth-century marble gravemarkers in Philadelphia (Crowell and Mackie 1984:14). Both headstones and large, flat tombstones (ledgerstones) are present, the latter used to mark the graves of high-status individuals. Ironically, the lengthy descriptions of the accomplishments of the deceased that were carved on their flat surfaces catch the rain and become illegible much more quickly than the inscriptions on the upright gravestones of their less wealthy contemporaries.

But why the lack of ornamentation? Crowell argues that the answer lies in the Quaker domination of the Philadelphia area. Quakers eschewed ornate gravemarkers; in fact, many avoided the use of gravemarkers altogether in the belief that all people are equal in the eyes of God. So, even though Quakers were a minority in Cape May County, residents there commemorated their dead with imported markers influenced by the Quaker tradition.

Although most of South Jersey's colonial gravemarkers are undecorated, the shapes of the markers varied over time. The earliest ones, popular in the mid-eighteenth century, have an outline that would have easily accommodated a cherub carved at the top. Also popular at roughly the same time was a stone with a heart-shaped or bipartite top (Crowell 1983:124). In the 1770s and 1780s, four transitional styles emerged. Although each is distinct, they can all be characterized as intermediate between the earlier cherub-form markers and the late-eighteenth-century markers that Crowell terms classical or urn shaped (1983:135–36). This latter form reflects a larger transformation of early American material culture, in which we see classical forms replicated in architecture, furniture, and other decorative arts.

The lack of decoration on gravestones of Cape May County in particular, and southern New Jersey in general, does not mean that they are devoid of useful information for the researcher. In addition to their evolving shapes, many have lengthy and revealing inscriptions. They tell us of ships' captains tragically lost at sea, the accomplishments of ministers, the valor of war veterans, and the personal attributes of upstanding members of society. Epitaphs also provide a glimpse into the religious sensibilities of the time. With or without elaborate decoration, southern New Jersey's gravemarkers still have much to say.

In New Jersey's colonial gravemarkers we can see the cultural landscape preserved in stone. The Quaker-influenced southern half of the state presents few ornately carved markers, while the graveyards of central and northern

Here lies the Body of
WILLIAM CHRISTIE
a Native of Scotland.
and late Merchant of Philad?,
who was cut off in the flower
of his Youth, by falling from
the Stage-coach near Cranberrey
on the 14th of October 1796,
& was killed on the spot.

Figure 5.9. The gravestone of William Christie (died 1796), Cranbury, New Jersey. This is a typical Philadelphia-style marble marker, devoid of ornamentation. Photograph by the author.

New Jersey are rich in folk art. Northwestern New Jersey is home to a unique collection of locally produced German-language markers. As cultural geographer Richard Francaviglia has written, cemeteries can be seen as "miniaturizations and idealizations of larger American settlement patterns, and the world of the dead could be a microcosm of the world of the living" (Francaviglia 1971).

Skeletons of the Past: Excavating Historic Graveyards

Looking under as well as at gravestones, archaeologists have studied the remains of people interred in this state's historic cemeteries to learn, in the most direct manner possible, about their lives. Our example here, the discovery of several early-eighteenth-century burials underneath Christ Episcopal Church in Shrewsbury, is but one of many archaeological investigations undertaken at important New Jersey cemeteries. We shall also look at an excavation by Hunter Research beneath the floor of the Parish House at St. Michael's Episcopal Church in Trenton, which revealed several past congregants (Hunter Research 1998:i), including one whose body had decayed but whose clothes remained remarkably intact. Another important study, by Richard Grubb and Associates, looked at the graveyard of a group of eighteenth-century German immigrants in Somerset County (Lawrence et al. 2001).

One cemetery excavation that did not come to a happy end also bears mentioning. Archaeologists working in Newark attempted to excavate Trinity Cemetery near Military Park. This large middle-class cemetery contained more than eight hundred burials, including the first mayor of Newark (Deborah Fimbel 2000, pers. comm.). Political machinations conspired to sabotage this project. In the end, excavations were abandoned, the remains that had been found were cremated, and the site was bulldozed. If nothing else, this disaster stands as a stark reminder of how flimsy the protections are for New Jersey's cemeteries and graveyards, even when they are well documented.

Anyone who has visited a cemetery is likely to have seen some graves marked with small signs that read "Perpetual Care." For a modest fee, the deceased's loved ones are assured that the grave will be maintained in perpetuity. Unfortunately, despite the best efforts of cemetery caretakers, perpetual care is more a goal than a reality. Maintaining a cemetery is an expensive proposition and a continual battle with the forces of nature, not to mention development and vandalism. Once a cemetery runs out of land to sell for burial plots, it is forced to draw upon its endowment, which rarely suffices to maintain the grounds for more than a few years. Inevitably, the cemetery becomes overgrown. Family graveyards are even more at risk. Generally small and sometimes in secluded locations, they are particularly prone to vandalism and unscrupulous developers. Gravestones tend to "disappear," and with their disappearance the cemetery is lost.

Who Was Buried under Christ Church in Shrewsbury?

Even in a well-maintained cemetery, burial sites can get lost. The restoration of Christ Episcopal Church in Shrewsbury in 1997 led to the chance discovery of several burials, including an unfortunate individual who may have been Monmouth County's first murder victim. Before the remains were reburied, Thomas Crist, a forensic anthropologist, examined them. His study provides an intriguing example of what a skilled investigator can learn from the careful examination of human skeletal remains.

Christ Episcopal Church is a picturesque white frame structure located on the southeastern side of the intersection of Route 35 and Sycamore Avenue in Shrewsbury Borough, Monmouth County (figure 5.10). Despite its great age, it is the second Episcopal meetinghouse to have stood on that spot; an earlier structure graced the corner from 1732 to 1769 (Crist 1998:1). The current

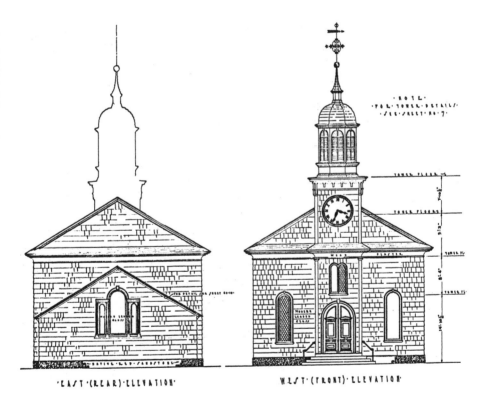

Figure 5.10. Christ Episcopal Church, Shrewsbury. Forensic anthropologist Thomas Crist examined the remains of a colonial murder victim found beneath the church. Library of Congress, Prints and Photographs Division (HABS, NJ, 13-SHREW,1).

building, which is listed on both the New Jersey and the National Register of Historic Places, was designed by Robert Smith (1722–1777), arguably the most famous architect in colonial America. (He designed Carpenters' Hall in Philadelphia and Nassau Hall, the centerpiece of Princeton University's campus.) Christ Church sits just south and across the street from the Shrewsbury Friends Meetinghouse and diagonally across the street from the Allen House, a colonial tavern discussed in Chapter 3. The Shrewsbury Presbyterian Church, also a historic structure, is located just to the east of Christ Church. Surrounding these churches is an impressive and well-maintained colonial cemetery.

The burials under Christ Church were discovered by construction workers who were digging trenches underneath the building prior to installing new mechanical systems (Crist 1998:3). Joseph Hammond, a parishioner who was coordinating the restoration effort, contacted forensic anthropologist Thomas Crist. Three graveshafts were eventually found under the church, along with a group of disarticulated bones buried in a pit, probably a mass reburial associated with previous alterations to the church.

The human remains were photographed in place to document their original positions and then excavated. Crist subjected all of the skeletal remains to a rigorous analysis designed to retrieve as much information as possible about the deceased. All of these data were recorded in a standardized format to facilitate comparison with data from other sites (Crist 1998:4). Crist looked for and found evidence of trauma to the bones and attempted to determine whether it occurred before, around the time of, or after death. He also looked for evidence of disease as reflected in the bones, and assessed the sex, stature, approximate age at death, and ancestry of the deceased.

Although the remains of the first individual were incomplete, they are nonetheless intriguing. Crist describes how this man, age thirty-five to fifty, died:

> The cause of death was a gunshot wound to the head, as indicated by a large circular defect through the right parietal and occipital. This defect, a textbook example of a gunshot exit wound, measured 75 mm transversely, 69 mm in height, and had a maximum diameter of 80 mm. . . . A portion of Individual I's anterior left temporal subsequently recovered from the reburial pit displayed a classic entrance wound caused by a small-caliber projectile. (1998:8)

The entrance wound measured 13 mm in diameter (.52 inches), and staining of the bone in the area around the wound was pronounced and probably caused by the trauma. The projectile itself was not recovered. Although we may never know the identity of this colonial John Doe, the cause of his death, even after nearly three centuries of burial, is gruesomely clear: a bullet to the head. Who shot him? Why? Was the murderer caught and tried? So many questions remain unanswered.

Crist identified the individuals from the two other graveshafts as a young adult male (age twenty-five to thirty-five) and a young adult female, both of European descent (Crist 1998:10). The ages of the two males were calculated from the fusion of the epiphyses, or growth plates, on their long bones; the skeletons were sexed through examination of the sciatic notch of the pelvis and measurement of the femur's head. The woman may have been Elizabeth Ashfield, whose tombstone still lies in the floor of Christ Church. She was thirty-three years old when she died in 1762, an age consistent with the skeletal remains (Crist 1998:14).

The remains found in the reburial pit apparently represent several individuals, including the murder victim buried in Graveshaft I and the woman buried in Graveshaft III. Bones from at least two other individuals are also present (Crist 1998:13).

Crist's work at Christ Church is a model of the application of scientific techniques to the analysis of historic burials. It also highlights an interesting cultural continuity throughout the church's 270 years of existence: respect for the dead. When the current building was erected in 1769, several burials predating the new structure were left in place, and the tombstones commemorating them (Elizabeth Ashfield, Theodosius Bartow, and Henry Leonard) were incorporated into the church floor. In the early twentieth century, when a furnace was installed under the church, historic burials were again affected. In this case the disturbed bones were reburied in a common grave. More recently, the chance discovery of burials under the church led to yet another reburial. Appropriately enough, the ceremony conducted by the Reverend Lisa Mitchell, pastor of Christ Church, drew from the old English burial rite and the 1662 Book of Common Prayer (Crist 1998:16).

The Parish House at St. Michael's Episcopal Church in Trenton

The discovery of a murder victim underneath Christ Church might be unique in the annals of New Jersey archaeology. Yet the recovery of burials from beneath historic structures, especially churches and ancillary buildings, is not uncommon. When the Parish House of St. Michael's Episcopal Church in Trenton was constructed in 1892, it covered much of the old cemetery. Some burials may have been reinterred in Riverview Cemetery, but others were not. As archaeologists from Hunter Research prepared to excavate within the building prior to repair of the Parish House's aged floors, several standing tombstones were clearly visible in the crawl space (Hunter Research 1998:i).

St. Michael's congregation was organized in the early eighteenth century, and the first sanctuary on this site was constructed between 1743 and 1748 (Hunter Research 1998:2–1). As was the case with many Anglican churches, the structure suffered numerous indignities during the Revolutionary War, including its use as a barracks by Hessian troops and later as a hospital by the Continental Army (Hunter Research 1998:2–8). Later still, the building was expanded and remodeled. Part of this remodeling involved the installation of a gothic façade, complete with battlements, making the building vaguely resemble a castle (figure 5.11).

Excavation at the site began after the Parish House's floorboards were removed. Special care had to be taken in the dry, dusty conditions to avoid the hazards of mold spores and bacteria. Another concern for archaeologists working on late-nineteenth-century burials is the toxicity of the various materials once used in embalming, particularly arsenic. All of the archaeologists engaged in this project wore protective gear.

Fifteen sets of remains were discovered, though none of the skeletons was complete, and most of the remains were quite fragmentary. Many of the grave-

Figure 5.11. The façade of St. Michael's Episcopal Church, Trenton. The church, constructed in the eighteenth century, was remodeled in the gothic fashion in the nineteenth century. Note the eighteenth-century marble headstones in the foreground. Courtesy of Hunter Research, Inc.

markers in the crawl space were broken, and, with one exception, it was not possible for the archaeologists to correlate particular markers with the graves. Remains from five of the graves were sent to Dr. Stephen Turkell, a forensic anthropologist and member of New York City's Metropolitan Forensics Anthropology Team. Astonishingly, these five graves turned out to hold the remains of seven individuals: five adult females, one adult whose sex could not be determined, and one child.

One of the graves, that of a woman named Sidney Paul Forman (1809–1891), was especially interesting. Forman's skeleton was too poorly preserved to provide much information, except that a set of dentures made of galvanized rubber with porcelain teeth and a gold palate shows that the octogenarian had lost her teeth. Her clothing and coffin furniture, however, were in excellent condition, thanks to the brick-lined crypt and a wooden outer box that protected her coffin. The plain outer box had been varnished or shellacked before burial (Hunter Research 1998:4–3). A copper plaque found near the headboard of this outer coffin reads:

HEAD

FROM

B.L. DISBROW

UNDERTAKER

TRENTON, N.J.

The plaque apparently served to mark the head end of the outer coffin. Forman may have been buried in the casket's shipping box, complete with the nineteenth-century equivalent of a "this end up" tag (Megan Springate 2001, pers. comm.).

The casket itself was quite nicely made. The woodwork was carefully finished and shaped, and the remains of a pillowed liner were found inside. As the archaeologists noted, this "would have given the interior of the casket an appearance of comfort, an important aspect in presenting the deceased as 'at rest'" (Hunter Research 1998:4–5). A glass viewing plate with a painted border would have allowed visitors at the wake to view the deceased. Her well-preserved burial clothing included square-toed leather boots, a pleated skirt, jacket, and a slip. Not surprisingly, the jacket and skirt were dyed black and made from silk (figure 5.12). The casket's handles, which had become detached in the intervening years, were also found. They were elaborately manufactured, with knobs of pewter or some other base metal and carefully turned wooden handles covered with black fabric (figure 5.13). Nearby, the archaeologists found a metal plate inscribed with Forman's vital statistics (Hunter Research 1998:4–9).

Figure 5.12. The extraordinarily well-preserved funeral dress of Sidney Paul Forman. Made of black silk, it is an unusual example of late-nineteenth-century funeral garb. Photograph by Dawn Turner; reproduced courtesy of Hunter Research, Inc.

Of all the fragmentary sets of remains recovered from the cemetery beneath St. Michael's Parish House, none is as illustrative of late-nineteenth-century attitudes toward death as the grave of Sidney Forman. This elderly woman was carefully prepared for eternity. Like an Egyptian pharaoh, she was buried in casket, which was laid within a coffin and finally entombed in a brick and stone crypt. According to research by the archaeologists, Forman's funeral was held at her home, a common practice, even in urban areas, into the twentieth century (Habenstein and Lamers 1955:260). Family members and friends likely laid out the body. Disbrow, the undertaker, may have embalmed it in the home or at his establishment. Although many people were buried in their best clothing, Forman was attired in what would have been termed a funeral robe. Her casket was likely selected from a catalog or may have been part of Disbrow's stock. As early as the 1870s, caskets were being produced in varieties to suit every budget and social station (Habenstein and Lamers 1955:264). The funeral director would then decorate the home for the funeral and bring in the necessary chairs, stands, and decorations. After a service at home, the funeral procession departed for the cemetery.

Forman died at a time when the funeral industry was undergoing a period of rapid professionalization. The Victorians were deeply concerned both with death and with social appearances. Forman's elaborate burial contrasts sharply with the simple shrouds in which the anonymous colonial settlers of

Figure 5.13. Ornate coffin handles recovered from the grave of Sidney Paul Forman (died 1891). Photograph by Dawn Turner; reproduced courtesy of Hunter Research, Inc.

Shrewsbury were buried. Nonetheless, the remains of each illustrate the changing attitudes toward death in American history.

Cemeteries and graveyards represent rich sources of information about our society's past. In the colonial cemeteries of northeastern New Jersey, carefully carved brown sandstone markers reflect the changing cultural sensibilities of seventeenth- and eighteenth-century settlers. The earliest gravemarkers (ca. 1680–1750) are undecorated or bear gruesome skulls and crossbones, designs that served a didactic function among the Puritan settlers of the region. Later, correlating loosely with the Great Awakening (ca. 1750–1780), cherubs, tulips, and other motifs replaced the grim-visaged skulls. By the end of the eighteenth century, simpler and more personal monograms had become the norm.

In other parts of the state, the gravemarkers are correspondingly distinct. In southern New Jersey, where the influence of Quaker Philadelphia was strong, plain white marble gravemarkers largely devoid of ornamentation were the norm from the early eighteenth century well into the nineteenth. In late-eighteenth-century northwestern New Jersey, a handful of carvers produced German-language gravemarkers for the ethnic group that dominated the region.

The rich regional carving traditions had disappeared by the 1820s, as the Philadelphia white marble gravemarker became the first national style. Later, the Victorians redefined and transformed graveyards into cemeteries. Many served as bucolic sanctuaries from the increasing bustle of urban life. Their gravemarkers are among the most elaborate and present a fossilized picture of Victorian society. In the twentieth century, with the noteworthy exception of ethnic burial places, gravestones became simple and pragmatic, much like suburban tract housing. Today's cemeteries evince an interesting dichotomy between the minimalist memorial parks—full of bronze memorials set flush with the ground—and the elaborate laser-etched memorials that increasingly tell of personal talents and hobbies, and convey no explicitly religious message. Clearly cemeteries and gravestones, like few other artifacts, provide a material record of our changing society.

Obviously, human remains provide another way to learn, sometimes graphically, about life and death in the past. Yet these are not ordinary artifacts, to be studied and filed away during the course of ordinary excavation. Instead, they are our ancestors, teaching us about our past, and must be accorded respect.

CHAPTER SIX

Inclined Planes, Trains, and Automobiles

Transportation in the Garden State

Few physical objects define the cultural landscape of New Jersey as well as the state's roads. Asked where he or she lives, a New Jerseyan is as likely to mention an exit number on the Garden State Parkway or New Jersey Turnpike as a community's name. Musicians like Simon and Garfunkle and Bruce Springsteen have sung about the Turnpike, a postwar engineering colossus that stretches from New York to Philadelphia. Even if too many visitors leave the Garden State believing it to be the space between destinations, and not a destination itself, it is true that New Jersey has been a transportation corridor between the North and South since the seventeenth century. Still earlier, Native American paths and trails, some of which may form the basis for modern roadways, traversed the area (Wacker 1975:70–71; Boyd 2000). By the eighteenth century, an anonymous wit, likely Benjamin Franklin, could characterize New Jersey as a " 'barrel tapped at both ends,' caught between bigger, and better-known, New York and Pennsylvania" (Lurie 1994:1).

This chapter examines some of the transportation modes and routes employed in New Jersey during the past two hundred years. It is by no means comprehensive. Some aspects of transportation that have been particularly important to the state's history, such as aviation, are not represented because they have not yet received enough archaeological attention to be discussed in detail. The carefully selected archaeological examples here range from a simple brown sandstone mile marker on the Trenton and New Brunswick Straight Turnpike, to an inclined plane on the Morris Canal, to the remains of a roundhouse from the Raritan and Delaware Bay Railroad, and to a lighthouse at the Shore (figure 6.1).

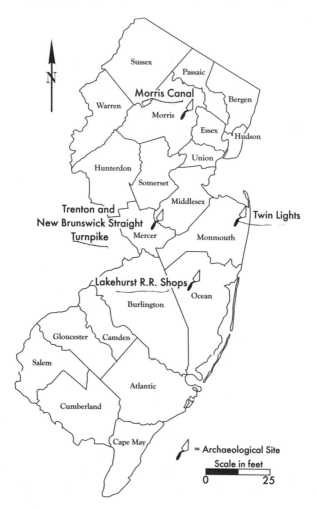

Figure 6.1. Map showing the approximate locations of the Trenton and New Brunswick Straight Turnpike, Morris Canal, Lakehurst Shops, and Twin Lights. Map by Dawn Turner.

Looking for Traces of an Early New Jersey Turnpike

Transportation in colonial New Jersey was either by water—the preferred method for weighty cargoes going any great distance—or overland. Each method had its benefits and liabilities. Waterborne transportation was efficient and, depending upon weather conditions and the skill of the navigator, could be fast. Land transportation was another matter. Peter Kalm, a Swedish botanist who traversed New Jersey in the mid-eighteenth century, described the roads he encountered:

The roads are good or bad according to the difference of the ground. In a sandy soil the roads are dry and good; but in a clayey one they are bad. The people here are likewise very careless in mending them. If a rivulet be not great, they do not make a bridge over it; and travelers may do as well as they can to get over. (Quoted in Cunningham 1966:70)

This situation was by no means unique to New Jersey. Historian Jack Larkin notes that, by the 1830s, dense "crowds of travelers—a continuous procession throughout the day in most weather—could be found on the roads linking Boston, New York, and Philadelphia" (1988:219). Teamsters with their freight wagons and drovers herding cattle and sheep contributed to the congestion.

As Peter Kalm noted, one reason for the abysmal condition of the roads was lack of maintenance. Each community was responsible for the upkeep of the local highways and byways. Landscape historian John Stilgoe put it eloquently when he wrote, "Only a rare Georgia or North Carolina farmer understood the advantages of a turnpike from Massachusetts to Rhode Island, and if he did, he assumed that the citizens of those states ought to pay for it, not him" (1982:112). This attitude began to change around the end of the eighteenth century. Virginia opened the new republic's first toll road in 1785 (Stilgoe 1982:112). It was followed quickly by the Philadelphia and Lancaster Turnpike. Shortly thereafter, in a valiant attempt to make the people who used the roads pay for them, private turnpike companies began building "improved" roads across much of the Northeast. The turnpike mania first hit New Jersey about 1800. Although most of the turnpikes failed to produce the hoped-for profits, they did leave behind a legacy of better and generally straighter roads.

The Trenton and New Brunswick Straight Turnpike was one of fifty-one turnpikes chartered by the New Jersey State Legislature between 1801 and 1829 (Cunningham 1966:131). The name "turnpike" derives from the barriers or "pikes" that were erected across the road to ensure that travelers paid their way. Pedestrians and horseback riders paid the least; wagons and carriages, which were more likely to damage the road's surface, paid proportionately more.

In 1985 a team of archaeologists from the Cultural Resource Consulting Group, led by Charles Bello, was conducting a roadside archaeological survey along a section of U.S. Route 1 between Quaker Bridge Road and Alexander Road in West Windsor Township, Mercer County. As they searched for archaeological traces of the area's history and prehistory, they discovered what is likely the last mile marker to survive from the Trenton and New Brunswick Straight Turnpike (figure 6.2; Bello 1991:55). The turnpike itself had long since been

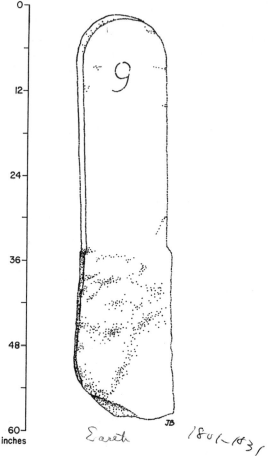

Figure 6.2. Mile marker 9 from the Trenton and New Brunswick Straight Turnpike. Drawn by JoAnn Boscarino; reproduced courtesy of Charles Bello and the Archaeological Society of New Jersey.

forgotten, replaced by Route 1. When improvements were made to the highway in the 1930s, the marker was moved from its original location.

Although exposed to the vicissitudes of weather for 178 years, the marker, fashioned from a single block of brownstone or brown sandstone, was in good condition (Bello 1991:55). According to Bello:

> The weathered surface of the stone is colored a subdued shade of brown to brownish yellow and is stained slightly by the growth of lichen. The object measures 56 inches in overall length of which only a little less than 3 feet stood above ground. The base of the monument was only roughly dressed,

measuring about 13 3/4 inches in width and 7 3/4 inches in thickness, and was anchored 2 feet into the earth. The part of the mile marker which would have been visible to travelers was very nicely finished and evenly proportioned, clearly the result of a skilled craftsman's effort. . . . The number 9 was centered and cut into one face of the stone about 6 inches below its top edge. (Bello 1991:56)

The number 9 referred to the marker's location in miles from New Brunswick along the turnpike's route to Trenton. A detailed survey of the area failed to yield further artifacts that might aid in the interpretation of the marker.

After careful documentation of its placement, the marker was removed from the roadside and delivered to the New Jersey Department of Transportation, where it is now displayed as a reminder of New Jersey's first turnpikes and their importance in determining the routes of the state's modern thoroughfares. This simple sandstone mile marker was a precursor of the huge green signboards that now guide motorists to their destinations along our state's well-traveled highways.

A Canal That Crossed Mountains

By the War of 1812, overuse had "turned the New Brunswick–Trenton roads into 'hopeless ruts and quagmires'" (Cunningham 1966:132). Colonel John Stevens of Hoboken, famous as a promoter of steamships, lobbied for a railroad to solve the state's transportation problem. He was was a man ahead of his time, however. Another idea, canals, caught the eye of the public and the politicians first.

Canals had a strong advocate in Robert Fulton, who argued, correctly, that waterborne transportation would cost far less than hauling freight overland (Stilgoe 1982:116). Although the costs of digging a canal were far greater than those involved in constructing a turnpike or a railroad, canals could carry goods more cheaply. Today, as the 55-mile-per-hour speed limit becomes a thing of the past, it seems hard to believe that mule-hauled canal boats floating across the eastern United States at five miles an hour or less could have created a transportation revolution. Yet at the same pace, on the best macadamized roads, a horse-drawn wagon could carry only about two tons of freight, whereas a canal boat could carry fifty tons or more (Gordon and Malone 1994:133).

Twenty-seven hundred miles of canals had been completed in the United States by 1838 (Stilgoe 1982:116). Two of the canals that contributed to this total were located in New Jersey: the Morris and the Delaware and Raritan. These two artificial waterways helped spur economic development in the northern and central portions of the state and provided an efficient way to ship heavy freight, particularly coal, for relatively long distances.

William Penn is reputed to have authorized a survey of central New Jersey in the seventeenth century to determine the efficacy of building a canal from the Delaware River to New York Bay (Stansfield 1998:88), but nothing came of this plan or of later designs by the engineer Christopher Colles and the Jeffersonian diplomat Albert Gallatin (Veit 1963:12). In fact, New Jersey's first major canal, the Morris Canal, eschewed the obvious central route for a more northerly passage. That project was the brainchild of George MacCulloch, then president of the Morris County Agricultural Society, who envisioned a canal that would bring coal to the flagging ironworks of northern New Jersey and revive the region's tepid economy.

The Morris Canal ran from the coalfields of Pennsylvania to Newark and Jersey City, across ninety miles of the most rugged terrain in the state. According to MacCulloch's estimations, the summit of the canal would be about 185 feet above low tide at Newark and 115 feet above low water in the Delaware. Later surveys showed these estimates to be off by several hundred feet. Nevertheless, the New Jersey State Legislature chartered the Morris Canal in 1824. Construction began the following year and was largely finished by 1831. Following the completion of extensions and feeders, the canal's length totaled just over 109 miles (figure 6.3). While the first boats carried a mere ten tons of freight, by 1860 seventy-ton hinge-boats were common. Passage from one end to the other took about five days.

The major physical difficulty facing the engineers who constructed the Morris Canal was the severe change in elevation along the route. Typically, canals used a series of locks to raise boats from one level to the next. The elevations crossed by the Morris Canal, however, were too great to be efficiently managed with a conventional system of locks. A one-way trip entailed ascending and descending more than 1,672 feet (Veit 1963:32). The solution to this engineering conundrum was the inclined plane, a set of tracks connecting one level of water with another. To proceed from a lower level of the canal to a higher one, the boatmen floated the canal boat onto a submerged cradle. Then, after the boat had been secured, both the cradle and the boat would be dragged up the tracks along the plane. Waterpower from the canal, flowing from the higher level to the lower level, powered turbines that pulled the cables. After reaching the crest of the plane, the cradle would be lowered into the water at the upper level, allowing the boat to float free. It was an ingenious and efficient system.

The Morris Canal, with its inclined planes, was considered an engineering

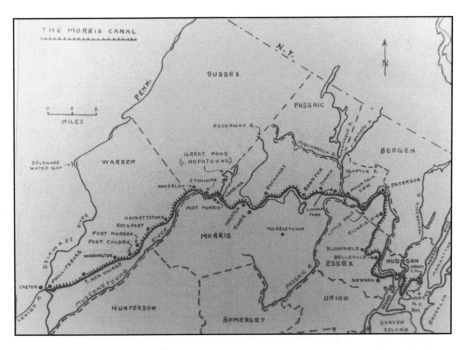

Figure 6.3. The route of the Morris Canal across northern New Jersey. Drawn by Richard F. Veit Sr.; reproduced courtesy of Maryann Veit.

marvel of its day and attracted comments by such notables as Charles Dickens and the indefatigable British traveler and nineteenth-century social commentator Frances Trollope. She wrote: "We spent a delightful day in New Jersey, in visiting . . . the inclined planes, which are used instead of locks on the Morris Canal. . . . [T]his is a very interesting work; it is one among a thousand which prove the people of America to be the most enterprising in the world" (Trollope 1832:308).

Coal was the lifeblood of the Morris Canal. Although many other cargoes were transported, coal for the ironworks of northern New Jersey and the manufacturing hubs of Jersey City and Newark kept the canal profitable until 1871. In that year the Lehigh Valley Railroad began a ninety-nine-year lease on the waterway. The canal never again showed a profit. As early as 1875 the railroad had given up on shipping coal by boat across New Jersey, preferring to load it into railcars (Veit 1963:54). By 1912 officials were describing the canal as "little more than an open sewer" (see figure 6.4). The state acquired the moribund waterway in 1922 and drained it in 1924. An engineering wonder, it had outlived its usefulness and become an eyesore.

Figure 6.4. A 1920s cartoon of the Morris Canal at its abandonment. Note the boat's name, Belle of Newark. *From the author's collection.*

Compared with the Morris Canal, the Delaware and Raritan Canal had an easy passage: it crossed no great elevations, employed no inclined planes, and ran only forty-three miles across the narrow waist of the state. Constructed between 1831 and 1834, the Delaware and Raritan extends from Bordentown on the Delaware River to New Brunswick on the Raritan. In the early twentieth century its finances began to falter, and in 1934 the state of New Jersey acquired the waterway and started selling water from the canal. This practice continues today under the auspices of the New Jersey Water Supply Authority.

One happy byproduct of this situation is that most of the Delaware and Raritan Canal still contains water, although the original locks have, for the most part, been removed. In 1973 the canal was listed on the New Jersey and the National Register of Historic Places, and in 1974 the Delaware and Raritan Canal State Park Law created the Delaware and Raritan Canal Commission, which is charged with reviewing any project that affects the canal's remains. This review power also enables the commission to call for archaeological investigations when a portion of the canal or the immediately surrounding area will be disturbed by new construction. Thanks to this fortuitous combination of events, archaeologists have spent more years excavating along the canal than the Irish workers who originally constructed it spent digging. When a piece of the original canal, be it a lock, culvert, or spillway, decays to the point where it is no longer serviceable, archaeologists, historians, and historic architects document the remains and provide the Canal Commission and the New Jersey Water Supply Authority with the historical data necessary to rebuild it correctly.

The Morris Canal, too, has received its share of archaeological attention. In 1994 and 1995 the Cultural Resource Consulting Group carried out investigations at two locations on the canal in Montville prior to the installation of sewer pipes that would cross the abandoned bed of the canal. At one location, the sewer trench would cut through the canal's prism, the basin-shaped section that held water; at the second, it would bisect what remained of Inclined Plane 9 East. After carrying out extensive background research on the history of the canal in Montville, the archaeologists, under the direction of Charles Bello, James Lee, and myself, began excavating. The goal of the project was a written and photographic record of how the canal and inclined plane had been constructed.

As built in 1831, the Morris Canal's prism was twenty feet wide at the bottom and thirty-two feet wide at the waterline. It measured a mere four feet deep. This depth quickly proved inadequate for carrying a profitable amount of freight, and in 1844–1845 the waterway was enlarged to forty feet wide at the waterline and twenty-five feet wide at its base. The depth was increased to five feet (figure 6.5). A review of historic sources indicated that the canal's prism should be lined with hard-packed clay to prevent water from seeping out of the structure. Despite poring over dozens of nineteenth-century engineering documents, the archaeologists could find no detailed information about the composition of the clay or its prescribed thickness.

The canal itself had largely disappeared from the landscape. Only a slight depression, heavily overgrown with brambles and trees, marked its former route. After clearing away the brush and trees, the team used a backhoe to excavate a four-foot-wide trench perpendicularly across the relict canal (Veit and Bello 1998). Although this method of excavation is more crude than that employed in

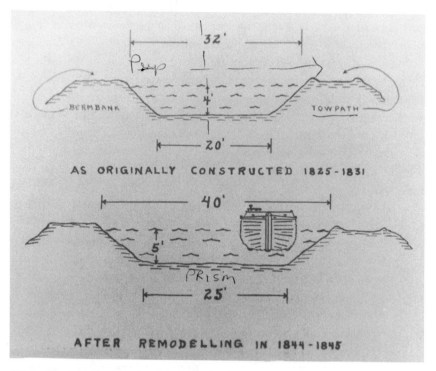

Figure 6.5. A profile view showing an idealized cross section of the Morris Canal. Drawn by Richard F. Veit Sr.; reproduced courtesy of Maryann Veit.

most archaeological settings, the goal here was to salvage information on the construction of the canal. No delicate or easily damaged artifacts were expected.

The backhoe cut enabled the archaeologists to draw a rough cross section of the canal. In this location the canal had run along the side of a hill. The towpath, where mules once pulled the canal boats, was formed from the broken-up stone excavated from the canal's prism. The prism itself was lined with an eighteen-inch-thick layer of clay—but not in all locations. This was puzzling. Were parts of the canal unlined? If so, what kept the water from running out? Perhaps in the seventy years since the structure was abandoned the original lining had eroded away.

Similarly, the cross section revealed that the prism did not match the written specifications. At its base, the canal measured twenty feet wide, and at the top it was approximately forty-four feet wide (Veit and Bello 1998). Overall, it had a depth of six and a half feet. Perhaps local topography necessitated construction that was both narrower and deeper than the canal company's specifications. If variations like this were common all along the canal, they may have seriously affected the waterway's ability to carry freight and accommodate large boats.

The Cultural Resource Consulting Group's second Montville project, Inclined Plane 9 East, proved considerably more challenging than the first. Again, the scarcely visible remains of the Morris Canal would be crossed perpendicularly by a sewer line, this time just west of Plane 9 East's crest. The wisdom of crossing the canal in close proximity to this uncommon historic structure provoked considerable local debate. Could the sewer be located somewhere else, thereby preserving the canal's remains? Despite considerable searching, no other locations were available. Moreover, an archaeological study would provide sufficient information to document what was lost.

In Montville, the canal rose 161 feet with the help of two inclined planes. Although the inclined plane was regarded as a significant engineering feat in the nineteenth century and received considerable attention in books and periodicals, this project showed just how incomplete that documentation is and therefore how important the archaeological data are (Veit and Bello 1998).

Fieldwork at Plane 9 East (it was the ninth plane west of Newark on the eastern half of the canal) consisted of hand excavating a series of twelve carefully spaced shovel tests across what had been the bottom of the canal. These small tests were unable to penetrate what appeared to be stone rubble extending across the canal's entire basin. Again, a backhoe was brought in to provide some additional muscle, and a shallow exploratory trench was excavated along the proposed alignment. Almost immediately, intact structural remains of the inclined plane were encountered.

Just west of the inclined plane's crest an enigmatic feature was found: a deeply buried chain wrapped around a squared timber. Initially, iron chains were used to haul canal boats up the inclined planes. These chains had an unfortunate tendency to break, sending boats careening down the plane. For this reason, they were later replaced by hemp towropes and eventually wire cables. The chain discovered during the Cultural Resource Consulting Group's excavations may have been discarded when towropes were brought in (Veit and Bello 1998).

Upon encountering intact masonry, the archaeologists decided to attempt to find the end of the plane. Although historic maps did not indicate the plane's extent, historic photographs seemed to show canal boats cresting the plane and rapidly descending into the water (figure 6.6). Thus it was assumed that the ramp into the water would be fairly short, perhaps 30 to 50 feet. Surprisingly, however, an exploratory trench dug along the side of the plane using a backhoe revealed that the plane extended well over 120 feet (figure 6.7). To determine

Figure 6.6. A hinge boat cresting an inclined plane. Photograph in the collection of the author.

the width of the structure, a trench exposing the plane's surface and its south side was excavated. At its base, the inclined plane was about eighteen feet wide, while the surface traversed by the canal boats measured roughly fourteen feet wide and was paved with stones. Probing with an iron rod and more shovel tests indicated that the structure's core was compact earthen fill, placed between carefully fitted stone walls. Clearly the workmen charged with building this structure used the most expedient method available. The wood and iron rails that the boat-carrying cradles once rode upon were entirely gone.

At this point, the archaeologists began excavating carefully placed shovel tests along the newly discovered section of inclined plane to determine its length. They found cut stone runners extending at least 220 feet past the plane's crest. Apparently, the plane continued even past this point, but no further excavation was carried out beyond the area where the sewer line might go.

Archaeology is full of mysteries. At Inclined Plane 9 East, a puzzling feature noticed during the initial mapping phase, a stone-lined ramp leading down into the canal basin from the towpath, became the object of intense speculation among the archaeologists and a number of canal aficionados who visited the site. The structure appeared to be old and was constructed of the same rough-cut sandstone as the basin itself. Historic photographs and drawings did not depict it, but their limited value had already been proven. Some visitors and professionals believed that the ramp enabled workmen to service the structure; others hypothesized that it was a means of loading and unloading barges.

These explanations all seemed reasonable enough—until the town engineer described how the ramp had been built in the 1960s to get garbage trucks in and out of the canal bed, which was then being used as a municipal dump!

Just over four miles of the Morris Canal once ran through Montville. Today, this mostly dry section forms a narrow greenway across the suburban terrain. In its heyday, the Morris Canal was regarded as more than a waterway; it was a noteworthy part of the landscape and a famous example of American engineering. Yet, despite numerous written descriptions of the canal and its components, especially the inclined planes, the two archaeological projects clearly showed that investigation of even relatively well-documented structures has

Figure 6.7. A section of Inclined Plane 9 East as revealed by excavations in Montville. The boats would have run along rails laid on top of the massive stone support uncovered by the archaeologists. Courtesy of the Cultural Resource Consulting Group.

the potential to reveal significant new information. The investors and engineers who paid for and built the canal found that their well-laid plans frequently went awry. As the archaeologists found out 160 years later, the canal is still full of surprises.

Who's Been Drinking on the Railroad?

Just as canals revolutionized transportation in early-nineteenth-century America, so too did railroads just a few decades later. In the words of historian Jack Larkin, "In the ten years after 1830, Americans saw the 'Rail Way' as the most striking sign of change in a time filled with changes" (1988:228). Noisy, dirty, and, most of all, fast, railroads brought far-flung communities together, encouraged the growth of cities, and changed the tempo of American life. Even before construction began on the Morris Canal, Colonel John Stevens of Hoboken had petitioned the New Jersey legislature for a railroad charter (Fleming 1984:101). After years of bickering, both the canal and Stevens's railroad, the Camden and Amboy, were chartered in 1830. The next year the state legislature brought them together, creating the Joint Companies and establishing a powerful transportation monopoly across the state's central corridor.

Even so, other lines attempted to compete with the Camden and Amboy. One of these, the Raritan and Delaware Bay Railroad, was chartered in 1854 and constructed by William Torrey of Lakehurst (formerly known as Manchester). It serviced the shore towns of Monmouth and Ocean Counties, providing a rather circuitous connection between New York and Philadelphia. The Raritan and Delaware Bay enjoyed prosperity during the Civil War, when the federal government helped it fend off the powerful Camden and Amboy. This protection disappeared after the war, however, and in 1870 the line became the New Jersey Southern Railway under the leadership of the notorious Jay Gould (Flagg and Schopp 1989:15).

The New Jersey Southern considerably improved the Manchester facilities, which initially consisted of a two-stall roundhouse, a machine shop, a blacksmith shop, and a tin shop (Baer et al. 1994:43). Nevertheless, the New Jersey Southern did not meet with any greater success than its predecessor, and in 1879 it declared bankruptcy (Lane 1939:405). The Jersey Central Company, which acquired the line, undertook further improvements in Manchester.

During the early twentieth century, even as the Jersey Central prospered, the Lakehurst/Manchester facility began to decline. The railroad expanded its main shop complex at Elizabethport in 1915 and reduced the Lakehurst workforce to seventy-five, a 25 percent decrease. Also, the larger locomotives introduced after

1900 were unable to use Lakehurst's relatively small turntable and roundhouse fully (Flagg and Schopp 1989:10), and in 1931 the largely useless roundhouse was demolished. Although passenger trains of the Jersey Central would continue to ride the rails until 1962, the Lakehurst/Manchester shops were no more.

In 1987 and 1988, at the request of the New Jersey Pinelands Commission, the Cultural Resource Consulting Group investigated the site of the Lakehurst Shops to determine whether anything remained from the complex (CRCG 1994:1). Excavations at the site, which was slated for redevelopment, not only revealed the well-preserved remains of a nineteenth-century roundhouse and shops but also uncovered several large caches of early-twentieth-century liquor bottles. That finding particularly surprised the archaeologists, because nearly all railroads banned drinking for the sake of safe and efficient operation (Pennsylvania Railroad System 1927:6–7; Lehigh Valley Railroad Company 1966:5). It is impossible to say whether two or three workers or the majority of the shop's employees drank on the job, yet there is no doubt that workers at the Lakehurst Shops consumed alcoholic beverages and discarded dozens of bottles in little-used and inaccessible places, probably assuming that their transgressions would never be discovered. For seventy-plus years, they were correct.

Archaeological evidence from the Lakehurst Shops excavations contradicts the usual picture of railroaders and alcohol use (Veit and Schopp 1999). The Lakehurst deposits show an increase in drinking through time, not a decrease. Almost all of the bottles were recovered from deposits dating to the early twentieth century, a discovery that may relate to the automation of bottle manufacture. Before the invention of semi-automatic and automatic bottle-making machines in the early twentieth century, bottles were expensive to produce. Automation meant cheaper glass vessels, which translates, archaeologically, into more discarded bottles. Nevertheless, the overwhelming number of twentieth-century bottles in comparison to nineteenth-century ones is striking and likely reflects changes in workplace behavior, not just increased access to disposable bottles.

The archaeological investigations, directed by Philip Perazio, focused on three components of the complex: the roundhouse, turntable, and shops. Testing revealed that substantial remains of the facility survived in an excellent state of preservation. A top priority was investigation of the roundhouse. The structure was composed of eight stalls, each served by a track running from the turntable to the rear wall of the building (figure 6.8). Excavations revealed linear brick foundation walls flanked by wooden beams, which indicated internal divisions between stalls. Most of the stalls contained service pits, which allowed workmen access to the undersides of the locomotives, particularly the running gear.

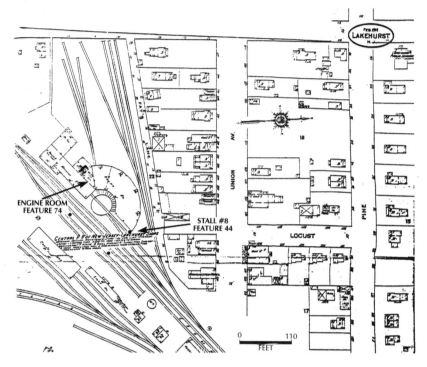

Figure 6.8. A Sanborn Fire Insurance Map (1911) showing the Central Railroad of New Jersey's Lakehurst roundhouse and the two features that contained large quantities of hidden bottles.

Much of the excavation was performed using a backhoe; but the archaeologists excavated exposed features and some structures by hand. They also unearthed a total of 130 historical features, including walls, footings, and fragmentary floors, as well as pits, wells, pipes, and 1,107 artifacts. The number of artifacts was actually small, given the size of the site. Some 556 artifacts—just better than half—were bottles or fragments of bottles. The second largest quantity of artifacts consisted of fasteners such as spikes, nuts, bolts, washers, nails, and tacks—not unexpected at a site where railroad equipment was serviced. Window glass was also common, as were metal fragments, both iron and brass.

Given that glass shatters, it is not surprising that such a large number of bottle fragments was recovered, although many of the bottles were intact. Parts of at least 105 different bottles were found during the excavations, including 71 flasks, 17 soda water and beer bottles, 7 milk bottles, 4 condiment bottles, and 4 prescription or medicine bottles. Although small quantities of bottle glass were recovered from nearly every context at the site, two contexts were particularly noteworthy: Feature 44, a small rectangular area located at the north end of the last service stall (Stall 8); and Feature 74, the flywheel pit in the engine room. From each location roughly 40 bottles—most commonly, whiskey flasks—were recovered (figure 6.9).

A judiciously placed backhoe trench revealed both the structure and the contents of Stall 8 (figure 6.10). Although the work bay of this stall was nearly devoid of artifacts, the area between the bay and the exterior wall of the roundhouse (Feature 44) contained a substantial though shallow deposit of 326 artifacts. Of these, 311 were glass bottle fragments, representing at least 48 bottles. The remaining artifacts were railroad spikes, iron washers and nuts, and machine-cut nails. With only two exceptions, the bottles are half-pint flasks. Based on their manufacturing characteristics, they were probably made during the early twentieth century.

These bottles do not represent a single episode of drinking or the use of the facility as a garbage dump after its abandonment. Instead, the evidence

Figure 6.9. A sample of bottles, primarily liquor bottles, recovered from Stall 8 within the Lakehurst roundhouse. Photograph by the author.

Figure 6.10. Stall 8 after excavation. The narrow area between the boards is where the archaeologists found the whisky bottles. Steam engines would have been serviced in these stalls. Courtesy of the Cultural Resource Consulting Group.

indicates that railroad workers sporadically discarded bottles in a little-used part of the roundhouse. First, the bottles date to the period when the roundhouse was in use, and it is highly unlikely that anyone other than railroad employees would have had access to the roundhouse during its active life. Second, the drinking appears to have been ongoing, as the bottles span a thirty-year range. After the turntable was permanently fastened in place, engines could no longer enter Stall 8; the space would have lost much of its usefulness and may have been an easy and relatively unobtrusive place to drink and discard empty liquor bottles. Moreover, the shop employees did not simply toss the bottles into the stall; they put them in the rear of the stall, probably hiding them in the crawl space under a wooden floor.

Another area of the shops that contained a substantial quantity of bottles was the engine room, a triangular-shaped building wedged between the roundhouse and the machine shop (Sanborn 1911) and located at the opposite end of the complex from Stall 8. In the Lakehurst Shops, as in most late-nineteenth-century factories, all power came from a single central stationary steam engine, which ran a system of overhead shafts. Leather belts and pulleys allowed individual machines to take their power from the shafts (Flagg and Schopp 1989:3). The flywheel turned in a deep trench (flywheel pit) next to the engine. According to Flagg and Schopp, "in March 1930, an electric motor was installed to operate the shafting" (1989:3). The steam engine and boiler would have been rendered obsolete and were presumably taken out of commission.

Excavations in the engine room began by removing the overlying rubble with a backhoe. The bases of three truncated brick walls were rapidly exposed, but no floor level could be identified. As the archaeologists cleared the sand fill, several features were noted. The three most prominent were a massive brick base for the steam engine, the adjacent flywheel pit, and a well. The east side of the stationary engine base and three brick walls formed Feature 74, the flywheel pit. The five-foot-deep pit had no drain, and the soil matrix within it was a tarry black sandy soil, from which sixty-six artifacts were recovered. As was the case with Stall 8, many of these artifacts were intact bottles. At least forty-two bottles were represented, including thirty-one whisky flasks. The bottles originated from J. B. Tilton's Forked River bottling plant, the Lakewood Bottling Company, the Whistle Bottling Company in Allentown, Pennsylvania, and Rubsam and Horrman, a Staten Island brewer. Based on the manufacturing techniques and embossed labels on the bottles, as well as historical information available about this feature, it seems likely that many of the bottles were discarded in 1930 or early 1931, immediately before the structure was torn down. The no longer used flywheel pit became a convenient trash receptacle for the last railroad workers and possibly the demolition crew at the shops. Interestingly, Prohibition was in effect at the time.

Most historians agree that drinking in the workplace was common, if not endemic, in the years before the Civil War. They also concur that this behavior declined in the postbellum period, thanks in large part to the growing prohibition movement and a better disciplined workforce (Pollard 1999:138; Rumbarger 1989:xxi). Increasingly, drinking was associated with leisure time, sobriety with work. There were pockets of resistance, however. Many new immigrants, particularly Catholics, were unsympathetic to the temperance movement foisted upon them by their largely middle-class Protestant employers (Reckner and Brighton 1999:67). In fact, drinking on the job may have been a means of expressing worker independence in the face of onerous rules imposed from above.

The excavation of a railroad roundhouse would be expected to yield all the usual detritus associated with working on locomotives. The features and artifacts are always valuable for what they can tell us about technological change and industrial processes. Other finds, such as hidden bottle caches, also have much to tell us about workplace life and behavior. The bottles recovered at the

Lakehurst Shops highlight the persistence of illicit workplace drinking well into the twentieth century (Veit and Schopp 1999).

The Puzzling Case of the First Twin Lights

Today it is easy to forget the perils faced by mariners heading out to sea, coming into port, or transporting cargo along the coast. J. H. Merryman, writing in 1880, explains why the New Jersey coast was so widely feared:

> No portion of the ten thousand and more miles of the sea and lake coast-line of the United States, extending through every variety of climate and containing every feature of coast danger to the mariner can exhibit a more terrible record of shipwreck than the long stretch of sandy beaches lying between Cape Cod and Cape Hatteras. Of this region the New Jersey coast is notoriously the worst. It has been said that if all the skeletons of vessels lying upon or imbedded in the sand between Sandy Hook and Barnegat could be ranged in line, the ghastly array would reach from one point to the other. (1880:7)

Although estimates vary and records have been kept only since the eighteenth century, it is clear that many hundreds of boats have wrecked along the Jersey shore. Here we shall examine the remains of a famous Monmouth County lighthouse built by the federal government in an effort to make the approaches to New York Harbor safer.

Sandy Hook peninsula extends northward toward New York Harbor like a giant finger pointing mariners to their port of call, but perhaps also cautioning them, for the entrance to the harbor can be extremely treacherous. In an effort to better guide sailors, a group of New York City merchants raised money, through a lottery, to erect a lighthouse on Sandy Hook in 1764 (Smith 1765:492). The Sandy Hook Light still stands, the oldest surviving lighthouse in the United States (Holland 1988:75).

In the 1820s, because the volume of ships entering and departing the port of New York had become enormous, the federal government acquired just over two acres of land in northeastern Monmouth County for a new lighthouse. Jonathan Thompson, superintendent of lighthouses, purchased the property from Nimrod Woodward and his wife, Ann. He also contracted Charles H. Smith of Stonington, Connecticut, to build two lighthouses and a keeper's dwelling. (Two lights were needed on the Navesink Highlands to prevent confusion with the nearby Sandy Hook Lighthouse.) Smith completed the lighthouses in 1828, and they guided ships into New York Harbor until 1861, when they were replaced by the current Twin Lights, an imposing pair of conjoined castle-like lighthouses.

In 1998 Tom Laverty, Principal Historic Preservationist Specialist at Twin Lights State Park, contacted the Department of History and Archaeology at Monmouth University. As part of his ongoing efforts to interpret the park for visitors, Laverty wanted to locate site of the original lighthouses. In the summer of 1999 nearly twenty Monmouth University undergraduates excavating in the shadow of the Twin Lights found the remains of both earlier lighthouses and even came across some clues about their demise.

Before beginning their excavations, the young archaeologists reviewed an extensive collection of documents relating to the lighthouses. This information provided a historical baseline for interpreting their discoveries and also helped them to locate the earlier lights. One of the most important documents was the lighthouse builder's contract. It noted that Charles Smith was to "well and faithfully construct, erect, build, and in every respect completely finish two lighthouses and a dwelling house and sink and shore up a well near the house (if practicable) on the Highlands of Navesink" (Thompson 1826). The lights were to be octagonal in form and constructed of blue split stone (granite) using "the best quick lime and sand mortar" (Thompson 1826). The contract further specified that the buildings were to be forty feet tall from the water table to the deck of the lantern. To help mariners orient themselves, the northern light was to be fixed, while the southern one would revolve. The two towers stood roughly three hundred feet apart (figure 6.11).

In 1828 Captain Henry Cahoone of the revenue cutter *Alert* certified that "the materials furnished and work has been done according to the contract. Being now completed, I have this day particularly examined them and find them

Figure 6.11. "Light House Establishment at Highlands of Navesink," from Frank Leslie's Illustrated Newspaper, *October 4, 1856. This view shows the two lighthouses of the original Navesink Light Station and a variety of ancillary structures.*

finished in a good and workmanlike manner affecting much credit to the builders" (Cahoone 1828). In less than a year the mechanism for rotating the southern light was out of order. In 1838, when the Twin Lights were only ten years old, a major inspection of all lighthouses in the United States noted further deterioration: "the works slightly out of repair; the window-sills and many of the beams rotten; silver burnt off the reflectors. The Highland stationary light burns six lamps with parabolic reflectors; the beams under the floors rotten; tower leaks in many places; the light shows badly to the north" (Fifth Auditor's Report 1838). Perhaps in response to this criticism, Stephen Pleasonton, general superintendent of lighthouses, persuaded Congress to approve the purchase of a pair of Fresnel lenses. Installed at the Navesink Twin Lights, these were the first Fresnel lenses ever used in the United States. An undated account from the 1840s declared that the "Navesink lights are justly esteemed by intelligent navigators and others, who have compared them, as the best lights on the coast of the United States" (U.S. Light-House Establishment 1871:598).

Structural problems continued to plague the lights, however. Their walls were cracking, and the southern lighthouse was settling at an ominous angle. In 1851 an anonymous inspector noted that a "common black-lead pencil was run into the wall six inches; mortar exceedingly poor—lime gone entirely, leaving nothing but sand" (Light-House Board 1852:170). It is not surprising, then, that in 1862, in the midst of the Civil War, the troublesome towers were demolished and a new pair raised at a cost of $74,000. Joseph Lederle designed the new lighthouses, which stand a hundred yards apart (Roberts and Youmans 1997:240). The north tower is octagonal and the south one square, with a central fortress-like keeper's dwelling connecting them. Constructed of brown sandstone quarried in Belleville, New Jersey, they rise fifty-three feet from their bases to their lights. Both lanterns were equipped with the most powerful type of lenses available, visible for more than twenty-two nautical miles (Leonard 1923:78). In 1898 the south tower was wired for electricity, and a powerhouse was constructed to its rear. By 1949, however, the lights were decommissioned, rendered obsolete by newer navigational equipment (Gately 1998:35), and they became a New Jersey state historic site in 1960 (Roberts and Youmans 1997:242).

In light of what they learned from their historical researches, the Monmouth University students pursued two major archaeological goals: to determine where the original lights once stood and, if possible, to understand why the towers had fared so badly. The extremely dry weather of the summer of 1999 proved to be a blessing when a ring of dead grass appeared in the approximate location of the southernmost lighthouse. Using this clue and the information from historic maps, the students excavated two lines of shovel tests across the spot, one running north to south and the other running east to west. All of the shovel tests in the east-west line contained artifacts, most quite recent, including wire nails, fragments of modern beer bottles, and sherds from ceramic drainpipes. The site was also littered with small sandstone fragments, apparently debris from the construction of the current lighthouses.

In the third shovel test excavated on the first day, the base of the 1828 lighthouse was encountered only four inches underground. It consisted of squared granite blocks bonded together with a brown mortar, which crumbled to powder when touched. The next test fell, as later became clear, within the lighthouse proper. The stratigraphy within the structure was distinct. A dark brown sandy soil, roughly eight inches deep, overlay extremely dense and mottled brown and white clay. The clay was apparently an original construction feature, perhaps used to impart stability to the foundation. It was also very hard and difficult to excavate with hand tools.

Based on the results of the shovel tests, nine excavation units were laid out around the southern tower, seven to investigate the remains of the lighthouse itself and two to excavate the remains of an ancillary structure, possibly a fuel storage shed. The lowest levels of soil within the secondary building contained large chunks of coal, providing a clue to the structure's function.

The excavation units exposed the uppermost surface of the lighthouse foundation and parts of the outer edge of its southern, southeastern, and eastern walls. The exterior of the lighthouse's foundation was composed of carefully shaped granite blocks. The core of the wall was made of irregular granite, sandstone, and ironstone blocks. About 50 percent of the fill was granite, with 30 percent ironstone, and 20 percent sandstone. The largely intact octagonal foundation extends at least four feet underground, and each of the octagon's sides is roughly ten feet long. The lighthouse itself would have measured roughly twenty feet across at its widest point.

After identifying the south tower, the crew concentrated on finding the northern one. Eighteen shovel tests were excavated on two lines bisecting the likely location. The tests revealed the lighthouse's wall, along with a variety of twentieth-century artifacts, including bottle glass, wire nails, electrical wire, nuts, and bolts. In order to determine the condition of the northern foundation, three three-foot-square excavation units were placed over the structure. They showed that, while the interior of the foundation was carefully finished and plastered, the foundation's core was filled with irregular pieces of sandstone, ironstone, and granite. Where the center of the southern foundation had been filled with hard-packed clay, the northern one was filled with a brown sandy

Figure 6.12. Archaeological remains of the original south tower at the Navesink Light Station, as revealed by Monmouth University's excavations. Photograph by the author.

soil. After drawing and photographing the units, the student archaeologists ended their excavations and began the hard work of washing and cataloging the artifacts.

The team succeeded in its primary goal of discovering the locations of the earlier lighthouses. Its work also revealed the probable reason for the towers' demise: their foundation walls were constructed with rubble-filled cores (figure 6.12). The rubble, primarily granite and sandstone, was laid in a lime-based mortar, and the sand in that mortar appears to be similar in consistency to the sand on nearby beaches. Beach sand is not suitable for construction because the salt it contains leads to rapid mortar failure. Built on and with a foundation of sand, the lighthouses had rapidly crumbled away.

Nevertheless, in their brief lifetimes the original Twin Lights saved numerous lives as they guided ships to harbor. Today, the site is a popular tourist destination. The excavations at the Navesink Light Station enhance our appreciation of this important part of our state's history.

New Jersey's self-image, landscape, and continuing economic vitality all depend to varying degrees on its position as a transportation nexus. In this chapter we looked at some of the turnpikes, canals, railroads, and lighthouses that have shaped the state's history. In some cases the archaeological sites serve simply to provide a more detailed understanding of the past. A turnpike mile marker from the New Brunswick and Trenton Straight Turnpike is literally a touchstone to that road's history. Excavations along the state's canals are providing a wealth of new information about how these waterways were constructed and functioned. The excavations at the Lakehurst Shops of the Raritan and Delaware Bay Railroad revealed a surprising aspect of workers' lives in the early twentieth century. Monmouth University's dig at Twin Lights State Park unearthed new information about the fate of the original lights. Each archaeological vignette enriches our understanding of a state on the move.

CHAPTER SEVEN

From Potteries to Pipelines
What New Jersey Makes, the World Takes

Since the early twentieth century, a large illuminated sign on a bridge over the Delaware River has greeted visitors approaching Trenton from the south with the phrase, "What Trenton Makes the World Takes." What is true of Trenton also holds for the rest of the state. New Jersey has always welcomed industries. At first they were small-scale affairs: saw and gristmills, potteries, and brickyards. By the end of the eighteenth century, the state was home to several ironworks and the first commercially successful glassworks in North America. Nineteenth- and twentieth-century New Jersey manufacturers made everything from Samuel Colt's first revolvers to rickshaws destined for Asian markets.

The study of the places and processes whereby these and other items were manufactured is a special subfield of archaeology known as *industrial archaeology*. According to R. A. Buchanan, "Industrial archaeology is a field of study concerned with investigating, surveying, recording, and in some cases with preserving industrial monuments. It aims, moreover, at assessing the significance of these monuments in the context of social and technological history" (Buchanan 1972). Certainly, industry has reshaped America's landscapes in ways unimagined three centuries ago, while at the same time changing "the entire social fabric [of our nation] with its religious, educational, and political institutions as well as economic system" (Kemp 1996:1). Nor were industrial archaeologists the first to notice the importance of different forms of production; social thinkers from Karl Marx to Lewis Mumford have commented on the interrelationship between society and technology. Although many archaeologists are disdainful of industrial sites, regarding them as too recent and their study as too particularistic, few sites are more important or interesting than the often rusty reminders of our manufacturing past.

Often the information gained from industrial archaeological studies is available nowhere else. Many artisans and factory workers lacked the time, skill, or incentive to write about their work (Gordon and Malone 1994:13). In other cases, mechanics may have accurately described their tasks but in terms so arcane that today we are unsure of what they actually meant. Sometimes writing about manufacturing processes was actively discouraged and seen as tantamount to industrial espionage. On the other hand, when factory owners put pen to paper, they often succumbed to boosterism and purveyed inaccurate and bombastic accounts of their successes. Artifacts and sites can provide physical evidence for past manufacturing techniques, processes, successes, and even failures. When this information is combined with written sources and available oral histories, a much richer and more accurate description of the past results.

Industrial sites, like all other archaeological sites, are finite resources. Although many communities have had the foresight to preserve a surviving colonial farmstead as a reminder of simpler times, few recognize a dilapidated factory building from the 1890s as something worthy of preservation or study. All too often, industrial sites fall prey to the voracious wrecker's ball in the name of urban redevelopment. Although the Historic American Engineering Record (HAER), founded in 1969 as a National Park Service program, has documented thousands of important structures through large-format photographs, careful line drawings, and meticulous written descriptions, many sites have been lost. In New Jersey, industrial archaeologists, both professional and amateur, have succeeded in documenting the remains of ironworks, glassworks, potteries, mills, and even munitions factories (Mounier 1990).

In this chapter we shall examine five archaeological sites that reflect the state's varied industrial history (figure 7.1). They range from small-scale rural industries, such as a colonial potter's kiln and colliers' pits in the Pinelands, to the massive Long Pond Ironworks and the Batsto Window Light Factory. We shall also trace the first major petroleum pipeline system in the United States.

Other industrial sites in New Jersey, most notably America's first planned industrial community at Paterson, have been the subject of extensive archaeological study (see Brady 1981; Morrell 1975; Rutsch 1975; Wilson 1975; DeCunzo 1983, 1987). The wealth of information relating to the locomotive shops, silk mills, and other industries there is too formidable to summarize here. Interested readers are referred to the above sources and others sure to follow.

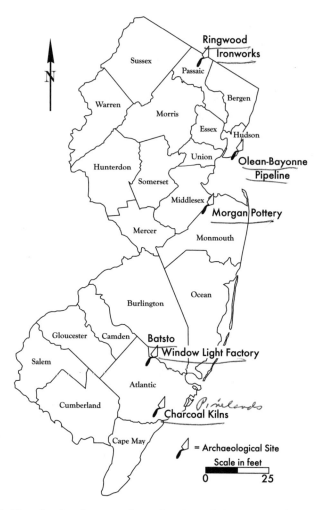

Figure 7.1. Map showing the approximate locations of the Morgan Pottery, Long Pond Ironworks, Batsto Window Light Factory, Pinelands charcoal kilns, and Olean-Bayonne Pipeline. Map by Dawn Turner.

Shards of the Past: Excavating New Jersey's Potteries

Potteries and brickworks were among the first industries established in New Jersey. As early as 1679, John Ogden of Elizabethtown was described as a stonemason and brick maker (Weiss and Weiss 1966:29). In 1685 Thomas Budd, author of a pamphlet promoting settlement in New Jersey, wrote encouragingly, "There are several sorts of good clay, of which Bricks, Earthen-Ware, and Tobacco-Pipes are made" (Budd 1685:8). Most early potteries were small-scale family affairs producing for a local, or at best regional, market. In colonial New Jersey two types of pottery were commonly produced: earthenware and stoneware.

Earthenwares were made from common glacial or alluvial clays fired at a temperature of roughly 1100° centigrade (Turnbaugh 1985:11). Minerals in the clay, particularly iron oxide, impart a reddish or brown hue to the fired pieces, leading to the descriptive label "redware." In colonial America these vessels would have been thrown on a potter's wheel and glazed with lead to give them a fine lustrous sheen and make them watertight. Color could be added to the glaze with metallic oxides. Sometimes slips (liquid suspensions of clay and water) were also applied as a form of decoration.

Stoneware differs from earthenware in that it is fired at a higher temperature, between 1200° and 1400° centigrade, and it is made with different varieties of clay, which are blue or white before firing (Ketchum 1983:18). The resulting vessels, generally gray, buff, or brown in color, are waterproof, hard, and need no glaze. Nonetheless, salt glazes were commonly applied, lending the vessels a characteristically pebbled surface resembling an orange peel (Ketchum 1983:10). Sometimes the vessels were decorated with incised or impressed designs or splashes of blue cobalt.

Antiquarians and archaeologists have been searching for the remains of New Jersey's first potteries since the early twentieth century (Sim and Clement 1944). In part, this fascination stems from the value of their products as collectibles—when whole. Archaeologists are less interested in the potsherds for what they are worth to antique dealers than for what they may reveal about cultural traditions and patterns of consumption, production, and trade. Ceramics are, after all, an archaeologist's best friend. Having little value once broken, vessels seem always to have been readily discarded, becoming part of the archaeological record. The sherds are nearly indestructible and often can be dated with some measure of accuracy. Moreover, potters sometimes marked their wares, allowing archaeologists to identify some makers.

Historical archaeologists in New Jersey have undertaken extensive investigations of the state's ceramic history. Brenda Springsted searched for an early delft manufactory in Burlington (1985, 1999). Archaeologists from the New Jersey Department of Transportation conducting a roadside survey in Mannington Township, Salem County, found a deposit of redware wasters (fragments of vessels that broke during firing) dating between 1767 and 1780 (Zmoda 1990:26–28). The sherds seemed to indicate that local potters were attempting to emulate fashionable creamware plates imported from England. In 1981 archaeologist Richard Hunter excavated the nineteenth-century Boozer Pottery, a redware manufactory on

Sourland Mountain in Hunterdon County (Hunter 1985:229–48). More recently, his firm has carried out extensive research on Trenton's nineteenth-century potteries.

Similarly, the gray and brown salt-glazed pieces produced by eighteenth- and nineteenth-century New Jersey stoneware potteries have been studied by antiquarians, art historians, and archaeologists for decades (Sims and Clement 1944; NJSM 1972; Mitchell 1972; Branin 1988). In recent years, some important pottery sites have been found, and several previously known sites have been more intensively studied, resulting in an improved understanding of New Jersey's stoneware potting tradition. Archaeologists from the firm Louis Berger and Associates found archaeological remains, particularly wasters and kiln furniture (ceramic pieces used to keep vessels separate in the kiln), from the Price Pottery in Sayreville and the Morgan–Van Wickle Pottery in Old Bridge (Louis Berger and Associates 1990, 2000a). Sites associated with the Morgan and the Warne and Letts Potteries in Cheesequake and the Richards Pottery in Trenton have been studied by archaeologists from Hunter Research, working for the New Jersey Department of Transportation, Bureau of Environmental Analysis, funded by the Federal Highway Administration (Hunter et al. 1996; Hunter 2000).

The Morgan Pottery is arguably the most important of those found so far in New Jersey. Its story begins in 1710, when Charles Morgan acquired a tract of land rich in stoneware clay near Cheesequake Creek on the south shore of Raritan Bay. Although Morgan himself was probably not a potter, he may have mined the clay and supplied it to potters in the region. As early as the 1720s, several émigré potters from Germany, most notably William Crolius and Johannes Remmey, had introduced into the greater New York City region the German tradition of wheel-thrown, gray-bodied salt-glazed stoneware, sometimes accented with cobalt blue.

James Morgan inherited his father's clay-bearing lands in 1764 (Branin 1988:34). Perhaps tired of his position as a clay broker, he began manufacturing stoneware vessels on his own. Although it is impossible to say for sure whether Morgan actually threw pots or simply owned the pottery and employed other potters, the Morgan Pottery was actively turning out pots in Cheesequake during the late eighteenth century. James may have learned the trade in New York, as his pottery's vessels strongly resemble those produced at the Crolius and Remmey Pottery there.

The Morgan Pottery experienced a significant setback in 1779, when a British raiding party razed the facility. Given Morgan's service as a captain in the Continental Army, it is not surprising that the British targeted his pottery for destruction. Three years later, in 1782, Morgan filed a claim for war damages, including "1 kiln of stoneware not burnt" (Branin 1988:37). Undeterred, Morgan continued to manufacture his distinctive gray-bodied stoneware. A watch-spring motif in cobalt blue decorates some of his pieces.

After James Morgan's death in 1784, his son, also named James, inherited the pottery. The younger James Morgan had diverse business and political interests, and may not have had time to work in the pottery himself. The ceramics historian M. Lelyn Branin believes that Morgan brought in a skilled potter to run the pottery for him (1988:35). That person may well have been William Crolius, a member of the well-known New York City family of potters, who lived in South Amboy in the late 1780s. Another potter who may have worked at the Morgan Pottery was Thomas Warne, James Morgan's brother-in-law. In the 1790s Warne established his own pottery in Cheesequake. What information we have about the Morgan Pottery indicates that it had stopped producing by 1800, whereas Warne continued throwing pots at his nearby establishment between about 1800 and 1827 (Hunter et al. 1996:7–10).

Although nothing remains aboveground to alert the casual passerby to the presence of the Morgan Pottery, the buried fragments of pottery found there provide a glimpse of the formative years of one of New Jersey's great industries. In the 1940s historians Robert J. Sim and Arthur W. Clement found and excavated what they believed to be the site, revealing a deep deposit of potsherds. "To judge from the fragments," they wrote, "the articles produced in the greatest numbers were jugs, two handled jars, chamber pots, and beer mugs—each in several sizes. There were shallow and deep bowls with curved sides, flat-rimmed plates, soup plates, colanders, spouted field jugs, and thin cups with handles" (Sim and Clement 1944:122). All in all, it was a veritable emporium of broken crockery.

More recent, and considerably more exacting, excavations conducted by Hunter Research for the New Jersey Department of Transportation relocated the site of the Morgan Pottery. (A pottery dump associated with the Warne and Letts Pottery was also discovered nearby.) A typical roadside survey yielded several fragments of stoneware. This in itself was not particularly surprising; however, more intensive testing uncovered a rich deposit of "pottery wasters, items of kiln furniture and fragments of kiln debris" (Hunter et al. 1996:5–12). Further excavation revealed that these fragments were associated with a substantially intact, though buried, kiln. The archaeologists who directed the excavation, Richard Hunter, William Liebeknecht, and Michael Tompkins, described their find (see figure 7.2):

Figure 7.2. (overleaf) The remains of the Morgan Pottery kiln as revealed in excavations conducted by Hunter Research, Inc. The drawing combines profile or cross-section drawings and a plan view showing the excavated portions of the kiln, as well as unexcavated areas. Unfired vessels would have been stacked around the walls near the center of the kiln. Courtesy of the New Jersey Department of Transportation, Bureau of Environmental Analysis, and Hunter Research, Inc.

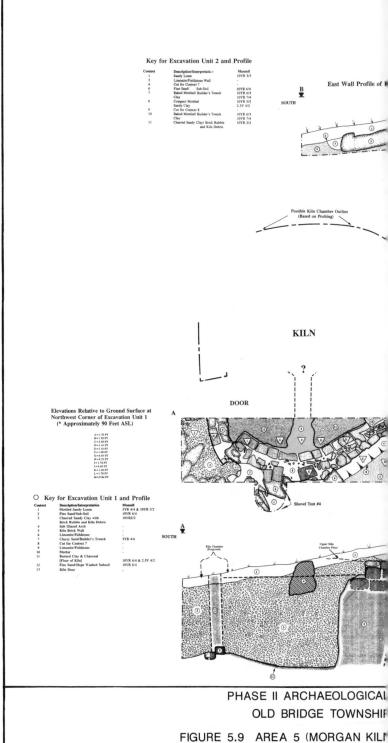

Key for Excavation Unit 2 and Profile

Context	Description/Interpretation	Munsell
1	Sandy Loam	10YR 3/3
3	Limonite/Fieldstone Wall	-
4	Cut for Context 7	-
6	Fine Sand/ Sub-Soil	10YR 6/4
7	Baked Mottled/ Builder's Trench	10YR 6/3
	Clay	10YR 7/4
8	Compact Mottled	10YR 5/2
	Sandy Clay	2.5Y 4/2
9	Cut for Context 8	-
10	Baked Mottled/ Builder's Trench	10YR 6/3
	Clay	10YR 7/4
11	Charred Sandy Clay/ Brick Rubble and Kiln Debris	10YR 2/2

East Wall Profile of

B

SOUTH

Possible Kiln Chamber Outline
(Based on Probing)

KILN

?

DOOR

Elevations Relative to Ground Surface at Northwest Corner of Excavation Unit 1 (* Approximately 90 Feet ASL)

A = 1.70 FT
B = 1.50 FT
C = 2.30 FT
D = 1.41 FT
E = 5.10 FT
F = 1.00 FT
G = 4.95 FT
H = 4.25 FT
I = 1.74 FT
J = 4.60 FT
K = 1.20 FT
L = 1.70 FT
M = 0.84 FT

A

SOUTH

Key for Excavation Unit 1 and Profile

Context	Description/Interpretation	Munsell
1	Mottled Sandy Loam	5YR 4/4 & 10YR 3/2
2	Fine Sand/Sub-Soil	10YR 6/4
3	Charred Sandy Clay with Brick Rubble and Kiln Debris	10YR2/2
4	Salt Glazed Arch	-
5	Kiln Brick Wall	-
6	Limonite/Fieldstone	-
7	Clayey Sand/Builder's Trench	5YR 4/6
8	Cut for Context 7	-
9	Limonite/Fieldstone	-
10	Mortar	-
11	Burned Clay & Charcoal [Floor of Kiln]	10YR 6/4 & 2.5Y 4/2
12	Fine Sand/Slope Washed Subsoil	10YR 6/4
13	Kiln Door	-

Shovel Test #4

Kiln Chamber (Projected)

Upper Kiln Chamber Floor

PHASE II ARCHAEOLOGICAL

OLD BRIDGE TOWNSHIP

FIGURE 5.9 AREA 5 (MORGAN KILN

PLAN VIEW AND WEST PROFILE, AND

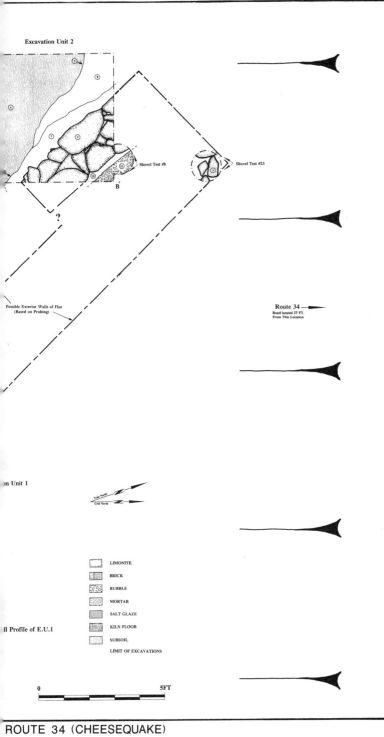

Excavation Unit 2

Shovel Test #8

Shovel Test #23

B

?

Possible Exterior Walls of Flue
(Based on Probing)

Route 34
Road located 27 FT.
From This Location

on Unit 1

True North
Grid North

LIMONITE

BRICK

RUBBLE

MORTAR

SALT GLAZE

ll Profile of E.U.1   KILN FLOOR

SUBSOIL

LIMIT OF EXCAVATIONS

0   5FT

ROUTE 34 (CHEESEQUAKE)
COUNTY, NEW JERSEY
LED SITE PLAN, EXCAVATION UNIT 1,
NIT 2, PLAN VIEW AND EAST PROFILE

As excavation proceeded downwards, a massive, three- to four-foot-thick deposit of charred sandy clay with brick rubble and kiln debris was removed from above and inside the curving perimeter wall of the kiln. . . . The interior surface of the kiln was very heavily salt-glazed, while the outside surface appeared to have been encased in limonite fieldstone. . . . Removal of all the debris from within the lower chamber (or firebox) of the kiln revealed an intensely burned clay floor impregnated with charcoal. (1996:5–14)

The archaeologists had found a portion of the kiln's firebox, where wood was burned to heat the green (unfired) ware stacked above in the upper chamber. Some 493 fragments of kiln furniture were also recovered from the Morgan Pottery site. These included a variety of items used to separate and assist in stacking, such as kiln pads and wads, wedges, saddles, and other pieces used to load the vessels (figure 7.3). These pieces were often dipped in sand to prevent them from sticking to the ware. Many of them were quickly made, probably used once, and then discarded.

The artifacts indicate that the Cheesequake potters specialized in the manufacture of storage vessels, such as jugs and jars (figure 7.4). In terms of decoration and surface treatment, both the Morgan and the Warne and Letts Potteries used brushed-on slip decoration, often in blue, though sometimes in green and brown. A watch-spring motif, poured in cobalt slip, was also noted on sherds from the Morgan site. In contrast, the Warne and Letts Pottery made considerably more use of stamped and rouletted, embossed decoration, an expedient that may represent a step toward industrialized production (Hunter et al. 1996:6–8). The Warne and Letts name was also stamped on some sherds.

Hunter Research's excavations at the Morgan Pottery and the Warne and Letts Pottery sites demonstrate the sort of information skilled historical archaeologists can deduce from a site and the associated written records. From the detritus of two early American potteries, they were able to reconstruct both the vessels once produced there and examine them in the larger context of stoneware potting in colonial New Jersey (Hunter et al. 1996). As they and other archaeologists further explore New Jersey's potteries, we are likely to develop a much better understanding of the transition from craft to industrial production in what once was one of the state's most important industries.

Long Pond Ironworks

Scattered throughout the Pinelands of southern New Jersey and the Highlands of northern New Jersey are the remains of dozens of ironworks. Although

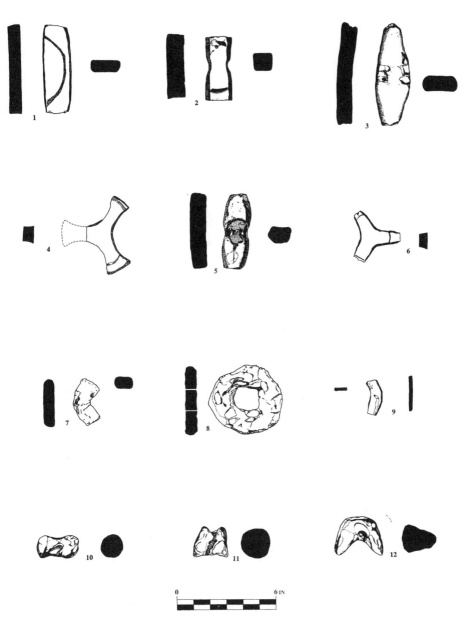

Figure 7.3. Select pieces of kiln furniture recovered from the Morgan Pottery site. The items include pads in the first row, trivets and pads in the second row, wads and pads in the third row, and wads in the fourth row. These roughly formed pieces of clay, often dipped in sand, would have supported unfired ware in the kiln and ensured that the pieces did not fuse to each other during firing. Courtesy of the New Jersey Department of Transportation, Bureau of Environmental Analysis, and Hunter Research, Inc.

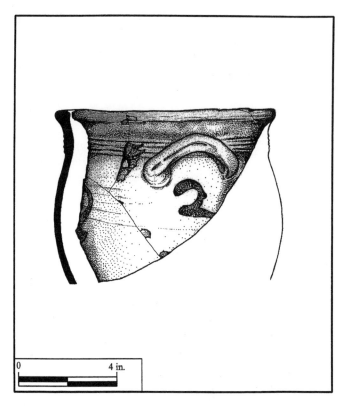

Figure 7.4. A stoneware vessel reconstructed from fragments recovered at the Morgan Pottery site. Courtesy of the New Jersey Department of Transportation, Bureau of Environmental Analysis, and Hunter Research, Inc.

silent and crumbling today, their ruins are vivid reminders of a once-great industry. Iron ore was one of North America's first economically exploitable resources, and many iron products came from New Jersey, a state blessed with the ingredients needed for their successful manufacture: ore, charcoal, and flux.

Three types of iron ore are found in New Jersey: magnetite, red hematite, and limonite (also known as bog or meadow ore) (Boyer 1931:2). Magnetite and hematite are present only in northern New Jersey and must be mined from underground. In contrast, bog ore precipitates out of iron-rich soils to be deposited on leaves, trees, and other forms of vegetation. The result is a bed of iron, often rather thin, that can be dug out of swamplands, dried, and eventually used to make iron.

In addition to ore, a successful iron manufacturer needed access to large stands of timber. Most New Jersey furnaces owned 5,000–10,000 acres of woodland (Mudge 1986:35) for the production of charcoal. Colliers labored day and night to produce enough charcoal to keep a furnace "in blast" (lit) through a "campaign," a period that could extend months. A third key ingredient used in blast furnaces was a flux of calcined lime that helped remove impurities from the molten iron.

During the eighteenth century, there were two basic ways of making iron: bloomery forges and blast furnaces. The earliest technique employed a bloomery forge, where iron ore was mixed with charcoal and heated with the help of a bellows. "The carbon reacted with the oxygen in the air blast to form carbon monoxide gas, which in turn reacted with the oxide ore to remove the oxygen and leave metallic iron" (Chard 1995:2). The spongy, impure iron left behind was then beaten under a waterpowered trip hammer to remove impurities (Rutsch 1974:12). Blacksmiths could easily forge the bloomery iron produced this way.

A small bloomery forge required very little capital to establish and might be operated by a handful of individuals as a part-time enterprise (Heite 1974:18). In contrast, a blast furnace was a large-scale means of manufacturing pig or cast iron. Often these furnaces served as the nucleus of small, mostly self-sufficient communities. The furnace itself was "a massive stone structure with a much larger production capacity than the forge" (Rutsch 1974:12). Standing about twenty-five feet high, the furnace was often situated at the base of a hillside, which helped the ironworkers to "charge" the furnace, that is, to load it with raw materials—ore, charcoal, and flux. A waterwheel powered a large bellows and forced air into the bottom of the furnace through a blower or tuyere. When the furnace was tapped, the melted iron and slag ran out the bottom and onto a sand-covered floor where the iron was cast into pigs. Once a furnace was in blast, it would be tapped every nine or ten hours so that the molten iron could flow out (Rutsch 1974:12). The resulting pig iron contained significant amounts of carbon and was too brittle for a blacksmith to work by hammering. Often it was reheated in a finery forge, "a small charcoal-fired hearth with bellows," to remove the extra carbon, and then it was hammered into a useful shape (Chard 1995:7).

Artisans and capitalists established New Jersey as an important center for the manufacture of iron almost from the beginning. The colony was home to a seventeenth-century ironworks (Smith 1983) and even one of North America's first steel manufactories (Hunter Research Associates 1989). Our focus here is on the Long Pond Ironworks, one of northern New Jersey's best-known furnaces. Today, its remains, designated a National Register Historic District, are located within Ringwood Manor State Park.

At various points in its history, Long Pond Ironworks operated blast furnaces fueled by charcoal and later by coal, a bloomery forge, and a finery forge. Few other sites contain such a variety of archaeological resources related to iron making. The location was particularly advantageous. Not only were there rich deposits of magnetite, but the heavily wooded region provided the raw material for charcoal, while nearby Greenwood Lake was an excellent water source.

Peter Hasenclever established the Long Pond Ironworks in the 1760s (see Boyer 1931:24; Ransom 1966:78; Rutsch and Morrell 1992). An enthusiastic booster of the iron industry, he came to New Jersey in 1764, working "on behalf of a group of investors from London known as the American Company" (Rutsch and Morrell 1992:42). After purchasing a run-down ironworks at Ringwood from members of the Ogden and Gouvernour families, he began to build an empire of iron. Along with Long Pond, generally regarded as one of the smaller works, he also managed furnaces at Ringwood and Charlotteburg. By 1768 the Long Pond furnace was in blast. It could produce twenty to twenty-five tons of pig iron a week (Ransom 1966:78). Although the industrious Hasenclever laid the groundwork for several productive ironworks in the wilderness, his English backers lost faith in his abilities. In 1767 Jeston Humfray was the first of several managers to replace him. During the Revolutionary War, Robert Erskine, surveyor-general for the Continental Army, also served as manager. Erskine died in 1783, and operations at Long Pond were discontinued.

After a roughly twenty-year hiatus, the Long Pond Ironworks again buzzed with activity, this time under the direction of Martin Ryerson, "whose holdings included an iron furnace at nearby Pompton, and also forges at Bloomingdale and Wynockie" (Rutsch and Morrell 1992:43). Ryerson appears to have operated only a bloomery forge at the site. A third phase in Long Pond's history began in 1853, when Peter Cooper, Edward Cooper, and Abram Hewitt, purchased the tract (Ransom 1966:81). Their company, Cooper and Hewitt, used the iron manufactured in the expanded bloomery to make wire.

During the Civil War, demand for iron increased greatly. In response, a new charcoal furnace was built at Long Pond in 1862 (Rutsch and Morrell 1992:43). The new furnace was a success, and a second charcoal blast furnace was erected in the 1860s. Although many other manufacturers had switched from charcoal to anthracite by this date, Cooper and Hewitt did not. According to industrial archaeologists Edward Rutsch and Brian Morrell, they believed "charcoal-made wrought iron was a better iron for some uses, especially general blacksmithing, traditional iron manufacturing, producing railroad wheels, and of course making guns" (1992:44).

During the 1870s, Cooper and Hewitt again redeveloped the site, rebuilding one furnace for anthracite and beginning to rebuild the second. A new water raceway was also cut. The planned rebuilding was never completed, however, and by 1882 the furnace was out of operation. After nearly 120 years of making iron, the scarred landscape of Long Pond began to return to nature.

It seems fitting that the first archaeologist to excavate at Long Pond was Roland Wells Robbins, an individual as colorful and controversial as Peter Hasenclever. Known to his admirers as "the pick and shovel historian" and to his detractors as "a charlatan of the first order" (Linebaugh 2000:5), Robbins was a self-taught historical, archaeologist active from the 1940s through the 1980s (figure 7.5). His first excavation, in the fall of 1945, uncovered the re- mains of Henry David Thoreau's home on Walden Pond. After this foray into the material culture of past poets, he developed considerable skill at locating, excavating, and assisting in the restoration of historic ironworks. Between 1948 and 1983 he investigated the remains of nineteen ironworks from Massachusetts south to New Jersey (Linebaugh 2000:6). When in 1962 he began excavating at Long Pond, the results were impressive.

On a visit to the site with noted ironworks historian James Ransom, Robbins stumbled upon the exposed bottom of the blast furnace's bosh, the lowest area

Figure 7.5. Ironworks savant Roland Wells Robbins (on the right) and archaeologist Edward Lenik discussing the excavations at Long Pond Ironworks. Photograph by W. Mead Stapler; reproduced courtesy of Edward J. Lenik.

in the furnace where the molten iron is held before flowing out. A small amount of excavating revealed the crucible pit and hearth, literally the heart of the blast furnace. These finds in turn showed the direction in which the molten iron flowed and thus the site of the casting room (Robbins 1982:26).

Identifying the location of the eighteenth-century blast furnace turned out to be the first of many answers that Robbins provided to longstanding questions. After securing permission from the park superintendent and the Department of Conservation and Economic Development, Robbins began a preliminary survey. Probing with iron rods and excavating small test pits, he determined that the furnace once stood twenty-six feet square. In some areas of the furnace he found that as much as four feet of stonework survived intact and in excellent condition. Surprisingly, no slag refuse was found in the hearth.

Robbins noted, correctly, that iron furnaces are unusual among archaeological sites in that they tend to preserve themselves:

> Once a furnace begins to disintegrate and topple, the process continues through the years, until the spilled rubble builds to a height that reaches the crumbling descent of the top of the furnace. Then the furnace disintegration ceases, and the buried ruins lie dormant, until disturbed at a later generation by seekers of stones, with which they plan to build walls and foundations for new homes and industries. (1982:35)

The eighteenth-century site was exceptionally well preserved and may well be the remains of Peter Hasenclever's furnace (figure 7.6). Nearby stand the remnants of the Cooper and Hewitt Company's furnaces. Together, "the two ruins represent the beginning and ending of more than a century of an industrial way-of-life in the Ramapo Mountains" (Robbins 1982:46).

At the close of his initial survey, Robbins recommended further excavations and the establishment of an outdoor history museum to interpret the remains of the furnace. His suggestions found a sympathetic listener in the state park system, and in 1967 Robbins returned to excavate the site. When he began, the structures were buried under as much as eight feet of rubble fill from a variety of sources, including the collapse of the furnace, erosion down a nearby embankment, and dumping from the nineteenth-century operations (Robbins 1982:51). Although two centuries of ironmaking had considerably altered the landscape, Robbins was able to expose the blast furnace, wheel pit, tailrace, bellows house, and casting house. He also found a subterranean drainage system designed to keep the furnace and casting house dry (Robbins 1982:54).

The furnace Robbins excavated stood only twenty-six feet square, placing it within the smaller range of furnaces. It closely parallels a 1640s blast furnace in

Figure 7.6. The possible remains of Peter Hasenclever's Long Pond furnace, as revealed by Roland W. Robbins's excavations. The wheel pit is at the left and the bellows arch at the center. Photograph by W. Mead Stapler; reproduced courtesy of Edward J. Lenik.

Saugus, Massachusetts, and perhaps represents both the effectiveness of this technology and the conservatism of eighteenth-century ironworkers. Although Robbins's excavation methods would not meet today's professional standards, particularly his decision to ignore nineteenth-century remains as he searched for the original Long Pond furnace, his maps, his concise and well-written site report, and his clear photographs amply document his excavations.

Robbins advocated reburying the ruins he had uncovered, but this crucial final step was not taken at Long Pond, and the structures once again fell prey to erosion and decay (Rutsch and Morrell 1992:52). In 1981–1982, industrial archaeologists Edward Rutsch and Brian Morrell revisited the site (1992:41). Unlike Robbins, they were not solely interested in the eighteenth-century remnants of what is probably Peter Hasenclever's furnace, and they documented other ruins from the eighteenth century, along with some from the Federal era, the Civil War era, and the anthracite conversion era.

The remains of the charcoal blast furnaces built by Cooper and Hewitt at Long Pond during the Civil War are particularly impressive. Although similar in form to the earlier eighteenth-century blast furnace, they are much larger and made with worked stones tied together with wrought iron reinforcing rods (Rutsch and Morrell 1992:53). Two twenty-five-foot-diameter wooden waterwheels designed to provide blasts of air for the furnaces were arranged so that the air blast was "continuous rather than intermittent" (Rutsch and Morrell 1992:56). Unfortunately, the waterwheels had been badly damaged by fire.

Despite their superficial similarity to the eighteenth-century blast furnace, the Cooper and Hewitt furnaces at Long Pond were technologically superior. Even more interesting, "the northern charcoal blast furnace was reworked to be fueled with anthracite coal, and the southern furnace was dismantled in preparation for a similar conversion" (Rutsch and Morrell 1992:57). This transition from charcoal to fossil fuel represents an important transition in blast furnace design. At Long Pond, archaeological deposits may survive that could allow this poorly understood technological development to be understood.

Rutsch and Morrell successfully documented the aboveground remains of one of New Jersey's great historic ironworks. If the state follows their recommendations to stabilize the site and carry out additional investigations, a new generation of archaeologists will be able to learn about and interpret the history of iron making in the north Jersey Highlands.

"Black and Dirty Work": Making Charcoal in the Pine Barrens

Charcoal plays such a minor role in our lives that it is easy to forget how critical it was to many early American industries. The manufacture of iron, for example, depended entirely upon the availability of charcoal to fuel furnaces; it was also a key ingredient in the manufacture of gunpowder. Today it is used primarily to cook backyard barbecues and as a key ingredient in medicines and water filters. Archaeologist R. Alan Mounier, through meticulous excavations in the Pine Barrens of southern New Jersey, has traced the sooty trail of the "black and dirty work" that produced this largely forgotten commodity (Mounier 1997).

Charcoal making flourished in southern New Jersey from the eighteenth century until as late as about 1970 (figure 7.7; Moonsammy et al. 1987:75). Though simple in principle, the manufacture of charcoal is complicated in practice. The primary ingredient is wood, and Mounier's excavations have shown that pitch pine (*Pinus rigida*) was the wood of choice in the Pinelands. Colliers chopped the wood to the desired length, generally three or four feet, and stacked it in a pit (or aboveground around a guide pole). The collier then covered the pit with blocks of sod known as floats, which in turn were covered by a thick layer of sand, forming an airtight seal. The layers of sod and sand controlled the combustion process and prevented the wood from bursting into

Figure 7.7. A charcoal kiln and collier's camp. Reproduced from Kobbé 1889.

flames and immediately burning to ash. Mounier notes that charcoal pits were generally twelve to forty feet in diameter and stood six to ten feet high (Mounier 1997:55).

Much of the collier's skill involved knowing how to stack and seal the charcoal kiln, as well as understanding how to regulate the air supply to ensure that wood charred without burning. This was a twenty-four-hour-a-day job that, depending upon the size of the kiln, could last from eight to fourteen days. During this period, the collier relied on the color of the smoke venting from the kiln to determine whether the wood was carbonizing: white steam indicated progress; blue smoke meant a fire—and the loss of the collier's labors and perhaps a conflagration in the woods (Moonsammy et al. 1987:77). Once the wood had turned to charcoal, the sand-covered mound would settle. After a cooling period, the sand was raked off, and the charcoal was broken up and bagged for sale. According to Robert Sim and Harry Weiss, a pit would yield between 7,200 and 18,000 pounds of charcoal (1955:41, 43).

Only rarely did New Jersey's colliers employ permanent structures for their work. Therefore, it is only with the most careful archaeological excavation that relict charcoal kilns can be identified (figure 7.8). The charcoal making sites that Mounier has excavated show two distinct types of deposits: the blackened impressions of the kilns themselves and small scatters of domestic debris—bottles, ceramics, tobacco pipes, and the like—discarded by the colliers during their lengthy vigils. According to Mounier, "When discovered archaeologically in the Pine Barrens, relict charcoal kilns appear as low circular mounds of stained soil

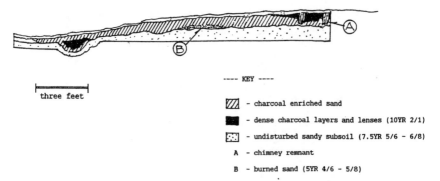

Figure 7.8. *A cross-section view of a relict charcoal kiln near Whitesville, Ocean County. Reproduced courtesy of R. Alan Mounier and the Archaeological Society of New Jersey.*

interspersed with pieces of charcoal and partially carbonized wood. Typically, the diameters can be expected to range from approximately 20 to 40 feet" (1997:56). The mounds rarely exceed one-and-one-half feet in height. Sometimes the archaeologists have noted a ditch or ring dug around the perimeter of the mound.

Usually, the kilns are found clustered, with several located about two hundred to three hundred feet from each other (Mounier 1997:57). Their stratigraphy typically consists of charcoal-enriched soil and patches of pure charcoal. During his investigations, Mounier recovered samples of charred wood and examined them to determine the size and species of trees represented and how the wood was cut. All of the wood that showed clear evidence of cutting had been chopped with an axe. Pitch pine was the predominant species, and generally young trees of fairly small diameter had been used. An increment borer (see Chapter 1), enabled Mounier to determine the ages of trees growing at the kiln sites today and thereby estimate that most sites had been abandoned sixty to eighty years ago (Mounier 1997:57).

More work might yield further insights into this forgotten industry, and perhaps reveal how the production of charcoal changed through time. For now, Mounier's careful study has breathed some life back into the cold embers of southern New Jersey's charcoal industry.

From Sand to Glass in Southern New Jersey

Another early industry located in the southern part of the state was glassmaking. Caspar Wistar, a former manufacturer of buttons in Philadelphia, established New Jersey's first glassworks in 1739 on Alloways Creek, Salem County.

Wistar himself did not know how to make glass, and so he recruited four talented glassblowers from Rotterdam, Holland, to come to America. He provided them with money for the passage and expenses, as well as "land, fuel, servants, food and material for a glassworks" (McKearin and Wilson 1978:32). They in turn were expected to teach him and his son, Richard, how to make glass. The endeavor was a success, and the glassworks flourished from the 1740s until the 1780s (Louis Berger and Associates 2000b:18). Many of the glassmakers who learned their skill there subsequently went on to found other glass manufactories in southern New Jersey.

Today, the products of the Wistarburg glassworks are quite rare, and until recently the exact location of the glassworks was a mystery. Investigations at the Wistarburg Glassworks site by Hunter Research, Inc., may provide valuable new information on one of North America's first successful glassworks. Archaeologists digging in Glassboro have also found deposits that may be associated with the Stanger Glassworks (1780–ca. 1824), a successor firm to the Wistarburg works (Louis Berger and Associates 2000b).

Here we focus on a less famous, but nonetheless important, New Jersey glassworks, the Batsto Window Light Factory. Batsto, a New Jersey State Historic Site, is perhaps best known for the important ironworks established there by Charles Read in the 1760s. By the 1840s, southern New Jersey's bog iron industry was faltering, due in part to competition from Pennsylvania's ironworks and perhaps in part to exhaustion of the bog ore deposits. Jesse Richards, the last ironmaster at Batsto, determined to salvage the future of his village by building a glass factory (Wilson 1971, 1972).

In 1846, on a site located behind the ironworkers' houses, Richards constructed a factory consisting of several distinct structures: furnace, flattening house, cutting house, lime shed, and pothouse. Richards, like Wistar before him, employed émigré glassmakers from Germany, Belgium, and England. Making glass was a dangerous job that required exceptional skill and entailed considerable training; hence, "glassblowers were well paid and always in demand" (Moonsammy et al. 1987:108). Although Richards was able to attract glassblowers to Batsto with promises of "free rent and free transportation," these workers proved a footloose lot, and there was considerable turnover among employees (Wilson 1971:11).

Glass is manufactured primarily from silica mixed with an alkali to lower the melting temperature and serve as a flux. Generally lead or lime was added to the batch as a stabilizer (Jones and Sullivan 1989:10). In addition to sand, ash, lime, and wood to fuel fires for melting, a successful glassworks needed access to fine clay for making crucibles (melting pots) and to supplies of cullet (old broken glass), which could be added to the raw materials to improve the final product (Starbuck 1986:6). The raw materials were mixed and heated in a calcining or fritting oven before being transferred to a crucible and placed in the melting furnace. There the mixture was heated to between 1800° and 2300° Fahrenheit (Starbuck 1986:7), at which temperature it could be worked.

The primary product of the Batsto factory was window glass, or windowlight as it was known. Glassblowers used two different techniques to make windowlight: crown and cylinder. In the crown method, "[t]he blower took a pear-shaped globule of melted glass from the oven and twirled it into a disk about 36 inches in diameter. After it was slowly cooled in an annealing oven, small panes were cut from the disks" (Moonsammy et al. 1987:108). The resulting panes were often wavy, and sometimes displayed a rounded boss or pontil mark in the center.

Sometime before 1820, a more efficient way to manufacture glass was developed. This cylinder method was the technique employed at Batsto (figure 7.9). To make a cylinder, a glassblower

gathered 80 to 100 pounds of melted glass in two or three stages and turned it into a hemispherical shape. Then the blower blew the glass into a balloon shape several feet long and took it to a pit. Swinging his blowpipe like a pendulum, the blower stretched the glass into a six-foot length. After the glass was cooled, the ends were cracked off, leaving a glass cylinder which was grooved, split, and then flattened into sheets which were cut into windowpanes. (Moonsammy et al. 1987:108)

According to archaeologist Budd Wilson, the Batsto lights came in sizes from six by eight inches to twenty-six by thirty-six inches and were produced in several different grades. Some 19,550 boxes of window light were produced in 1850 (Wilson 1971:27). By this time, a second glasshouse was in operation at Batsto. Although some of the glass was used locally, most was shipped to New York and Philadelphia.

During its twenty years of operation (1846–1866), the Batsto Window Light Factory was plagued by many of the problems endemic to the industry. The factory burned to the ground in 1847 and again in 1850. Nor was the combustible nature of its buildings the factory's only problem. The glass it made was sometimes criticized as inferior; the workmen repeatedly struck for better wages; and shipping the glass to market entailed its own dangers. Although the company's ledgers survive in the state archives, little was known about the old glassworks' physical plant, production methods, or products.

In 1960 Wilson conducted some initial testing at the site, which had been left

Figure 7.9. The cylinder method of blowing glass as depicted in Harper's Weekly, *1871. Courtesy of Budd Wilson and the Archaeological Society of New Jersey.*

undisturbed since the factory's demise, and more intensive fieldwork was carried out between 1965 and 1967 (Wilson 1971:13). During three years of concerted effort, Wilson and his crew found the remains of the flattening factory, melting furnaces, lime shed, cutting house, oven, pot house, a wood storage area, and cellar hole (figure 7.10; Wilson 1971:13).

The artifacts Wilson unearthed are quite revealing. Of course, there were thousands of broken windowpanes, as well as amorphous pieces of once molten glass, fragments of broken cylinders, and cuttings from the cutting house. Also unearthed were fragments of the crucibles used to melt the batch. Wilson even found a tobacco pipe made from the same clay that was used in the crucibles (Wilson 1972:29). In their off hours, glassworkers are known to have made fancy canes, walking sticks, and paperweights from glass. These pieces, which are rare today, were known as whimsies, or tempo work, after the vernacular for a break at the factory. They provide colorful reminders of the glassblowers' skills. Although the drab tobacco pipe is nowhere near as elaborate as the glasswork, it too highlights the resourcefulness of the workers.

The most evocative artifacts Wilson recovered are the heads of seven blowpipes and a pewter bebee (blowpipe mouthpiece). Using these very tools,

Figure 7.10. A flattening oven used in the flattening of cylinder glass. Excavated by Budd Wilson at the Batsto Window Light Factory. Courtesy of Budd Wilson and the Archaeological Society of New Jersey.

Batsto's glassblowers once turned the fine sand of the Pinelands into windows for the growing metropolises of New York and Philadelphia.

Why the Batsto Window Light Factory failed in 1867 remains a subject for investigation. Was the lack of a railway connection for shipping its products a factor? Did the fires prove too great a strain on the finances of the owners? Were the techniques employed at Batsto outmoded? With the passing of Jesse Richards in 1854, was there simply no motivating force to keep the factory in operation? Although we may never know the answer, the artifacts excavated by Wilson and his team provide a glimpse of an important industry in nineteenth-century New Jersey. Our next site, a pipeline constructed only thirteen years after the Batsto Window Light Factory failed, shows just how rapidly American life and technology were changing in the decades after the Civil War.

Standard Oil's Olean-Bayonne Pipeline

That New Jersey has no naturally occurring fossil fuels may come as a surprise to visitors who have seen the enormous refineries around Linden, Woodbridge, and Elizabeth. We live in a world fueled, quite literally, by petroleum products. This was not always the case. Native Americans occasionally employed petroleum for medicinal purposes; physicians used it in medical preparations; and teamsters lubricated their wagons with it. Then, in 1859, Edwin Drake drilled the nation's first oil well at Titusville in northwestern Pennsylvania. By the early twentieth century, the possible uses for petroleum products had exploded. America's cars and industries, which today guzzle oil with apparent abandon, took their first tentative sips in the 1880s.

Archaeologist Edward Lenik is one of the few scholars who has tracked down the relics of what might be termed the early petroleum era. Among his finds are the remains of the Olean-Bayonne Pipeline, the nation's first major pipeline system, constructed by the Standard Oil Company (figure 7.11; Lenik 1976). From several small Pennsylvania oil refineries, John D. Rockefeller cobbled together Standard Oil and an enormous industrial empire that controlled "85 percent of the American oil industry" (Johnson 1987:188). Most of the oil at the time was used to produce kerosene and lubricants—gasoline and automobiles were things of the future. Rockefeller selected Bayonne as the site of his

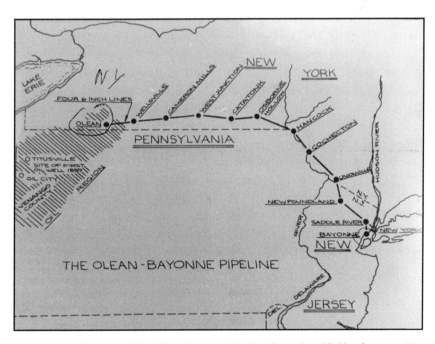

Figure 7.11. The route of the Olean-Bayonne Pipeline from the oilfields of western New York to Bayonne, New Jersey. Courtesy of Edward J. Lenik and the Society for Industrial Archaeology.

company's new refinery because of the city's easy access to New York City and its excellent port facilities. Standard Oil's was actually the second refinery in Bayonne; the first, built in 1875, belonged to the Prentice Refining Company (Johnson 1987:188). By the turn of the century, Bayonne had become one of the world's major refining centers.

Construction on the pipeline began in 1880 and was completed by 1882. By today's standards, the line was minuscule, measuring a mere six inches in diameter and running some 315 miles from Olean, New York, to Bayonne (Lenik 1976:29). Eventually three additional pipes were laid, quadrupling the flow of oil to New Jersey. The line ran as straight as possible, crossing "fourteen rivers, twenty creeks, and eight mountains' peaks" (Lenik 1976:29). Wherever possible, the pipes were buried underground in trenches; where the rock was impenetrable, the iron pipes were simply laid on the ground surface.

Standard Oil constructed a series of pumping stations at regular intervals along the line. Each pumping station became something of a miniature community, with the pump house, a small office, storage tanks, and houses for oil company employees (Lenik 1976:32). For forty-five years the Olean-Bayonne Pipeline supplied oil to New York. Eventually, new oil fields in Texas, combined with cheaper and faster transportation by water, spelled the end of this pioneering pipeline. In 1927 the pumps were permanently shut down.

In the mid-1970s archaeologist Lenik carried out a survey of the Olean-Bayonne Pipeline route with the goal of "locat[ing] and record[ing] existing sites relating to the oil pipeline" (Lenik 1976:32). Like the pipewalkers once employed by Standard Oil and its subsidiaries, Lenik hiked along the former route. He found that six of the eleven pumping stations have disappeared—victims of progress—and that sections of the pipeline have been removed. One of the rare spots where the pipe was still visible was in the bed of the Pequannock River, where the twin iron pipes lie submerged, silent reminders of an important engineering accomplishment (figure 7.12).

The Olean-Bayonne Pipeline, though toylike in comparison to today's massive transcontinental pipelines, pointed the way toward a new means of transporting oil to the thirsty metropolis. Although archaeologist Lenik did no excavating, his careful aboveground survey is a good example of industrial archaeology.

As any visitor who has cruised the New Jersey Turnpike can attest, the state has a powerful industrial heritage. Factories producing anything and everything from whoopee cushions to the ceramic cladding of skyscrapers have called New Jersey home. Industrial archaeology, the study of the places where these products were made and the processes that created them, is a special subfield of historical archaeology. It is no surprise that industrial archaeology first developed in Great Britain, home of the Industrial Revolution. It is also appropriate that New Jersey has been an important American center for industrial archaeology. Many of the individuals who excavated the sites discussed in this chapter—Edward Rutsch, Edward Lenik, Richard Hunter, Budd Wilson, and even the black sheep of the bunch, Roland Wells Robbins—made important contributions to our understanding of the state's and the nation's industrial heritage.

The sites we examined range from the ephemeral remains of colliers' huts in the Pine Barrens to the massive stone stacks of forgotten ironworks in the Highlands, with stops at the Batsto Window Light Factory, the Morgan Pottery, and

Figure 7.12. A rare glimpse of the Olean-Bayonne Pipeline as it passes under the Pequannock River. Courtesy of Edward J. Lenik and the Society for Industrial Archaeology.

the Olean-Bayonne Pipeline. Each represents a different facet of the New Jersey's industrial heritage. Undoubtedly, future generations of archaeologists will continue to investigate the remains of local industrial sites for what they can tell us about how we made and did things in the past. Perhaps the industrial archaeologists of the twenty-second century will find the ruins of today's refineries and gas stations as odd and compelling as we find the ironworks of the nineteenth century.

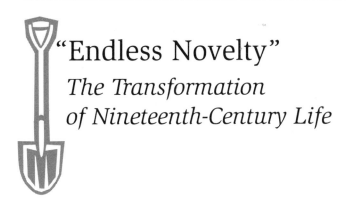

CHAPTER EIGHT

"Endless Novelty"
The Transformation
of Nineteenth-Century Life

The nineteenth century was a time of phenomenal change—endless novelty—
in the lives of Americans (Scranton 1997). The Industrial Revolution transformed the way objects were made, from chamber pots to steam engines.
Urbanization was inextricably linked to industrialization, and by the century's
end more Americans lived in cities than ever before. The often crowded living
conditions made sanitation and hygiene important priorities. Improvements in
transportation early in the century, such as canals, turnpikes, and railroads,
helped to bind the growing nation together. Then slavery split it apart. Only
after four years of bloody warfare were North and South forcibly reunited. New
religious and utopian movements sought to provide individuals with an alternative to an increasingly impersonal society marked not by the natural rhythms
of life but by the constant ticking of the time clock. At the same time, the Industrial Revolution offered unprecedented opportunities for the accumulation of
wealth and the exploitation of many by a few. To feed the voracious appetite of
America's industries for laborers, thousands of immigrants, particularly from
eastern and southern Europe, came to the United States. Many of them settled
in New Jersey, not far from the docks at Castle Garden or Ellis Island where they
disembarked. For them, as for the descendants of earlier generations of settlers,
America truly was a new world, if not the promised land.

In this chapter, we shall look at New Jersey's nineteenth-century experiences
with slavery, health care, and the company town. New Jersey was the last of the
northern states to outlaw slavery. It did so in 1804 by means of a fundamentally
flawed gradual emancipation act that left some African Americans still enslaved as late as 1860. Free African Americans faced considerable prejudice as
they strove to build successful lives, and they sometimes created self-sufficient
communities apart from white society. Archaeologist Joan Geismar's work at

Skunk Hollow, a little-known community of free African Americans in the Palisades of northeastern New Jersey, is briefly reviewed in this chapter.

Located between the burgeoning metropolises of New York and Philadelphia, New Jersey was at the center of the changes in industry, transportation, and social life. As several important smaller cities grew up during the nineteenth century—Newark, Trenton, Camden, Perth Amboy, Jersey City, and Paterson—they gained unenviable reputations as places where sickness was widespread. One historian has even characterized Newark as America's unhealthiest city (Galishoff 1988)! Here we shall look at the pioneering work of Clifford Morrogh, a physician in New Brunswick, whose discarded medical implements testify to his efforts to improve health and relieve suffering in the city.

Suburbanization, often thought of as a twentieth-century phenomenon, followed closely upon urbanization in New Jersey, aided in part by improvements to the transportation network, and especially by the growth of railroads. Some of the first suburbs in the United States were located in northern New Jersey, forming a ring around Manhattan. In recent years archaeologists have begun to study the origins and dynamics of these important American communities (Yamin and Bridges 1996).

Dreamers and idealists established a variety of communities inspired by utopian visions of the future. These included the North American Phalanx, the Raritan Bay Union, and what might be termed the paternalist utopias of the industrialists Hezekiah Smith, who built Smithville in Burlington County, and David Felt, who created Feltville, a paper manufacturing town nestled in the Watchung Mountains. The latter has been the site of several years of intensive excavations by Montclair State University.

These three sites—Skunk Hollow, New Brunswick, and Feltville—are of course just the tip of the historical iceberg when it comes to what archaeology can tell us about nineteenth-century America. They serve to illustrate the important themes of slavery and freedom, health and hygiene, and utopia and paternalism (figure 8.1).

A Free Community in a Slave State

Despite the presence of a vocal abolitionist community, the sad fact is that slavery remained legal in New Jersey until the end of the Civil War. Archaeologists have only just begun to explore the lives of the state's enslaved African Americans. At the site of the eighteenth-century Beverwyck estate in Morris County, shackles and other stark reminders of enslavement have been excavated (see Chapter 3). In Middlesex and Union Counties, a handful of early nineteenth-

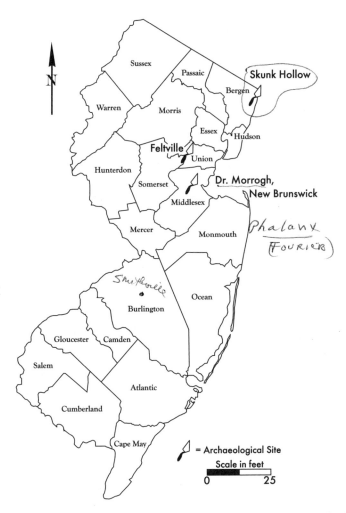

Figure 8.1. Map showing the locations of Skunk Hollow, New Brunswick, and Feltville. Map by Dawn Turner.

century gravemarkers commemorates the lives of slaves and freed slaves (Veit 1992). Some of the names on the stones, such as Ambo, harken back to African roots; others, such as Caesar, show the historical interests of the slaveowners (figure 8.2). Incredibly, given slaves' living conditions, several of the stones declare that the individuals they memorialize reached one hundred years of age, though we cannot know whether that was simply a guess. Archaeology can be a valuable source of information about the lives, successes, and sufferings of people who all too often were unable to write about their experiences.

Figure 8.2. The gravemarker of Ambo, a servant of the Terrill family, in the Rahway Cemetery, Rahway. This is one of the few gravemarkers for slaves and freed slaves that survive in New Jersey cemeteries. Photograph by the author.

Undoubtedly, as time goes on, more and more sites with links to African Americans will be discovered and investigated.

The first concerted study of an African American community in New Jersey began in 1978, when archaeologist Joan Geismar undertook a detailed examination of Skunk Hollow, a nineteenth-century African American community in New Jersey's Palisades (Geismar 1982:63). Skunk Hollow, which probably took its name from the skunk cabbage that grows in the area, was established around 1806 and survived just over one hundred years (Geismar 1982:65). Initially settled by freed slaves and the descendants of freed slaves, the community was sixty years old before New Jersey fully abolished slavery (Calligaro 1967:170). Geismar was particularly interested in testing theories regarding the community's decline and abandonment. Equally important are the reasons for its survival and what they can tell us about African American life during this time.

Geismar's research began with a meticulous analysis of the scanty surviving records relating to the community. These included tax records, census enumerations, land records, and oral histories. Her work documented the first land purchase in Skunk Hollow by Jack Earnest, a freed slave, in 1806 and the eventual acquisition of his property by William Thompson, an African American Methodist preacher and day laborer (Geismar 1982:23). Thompson and his wife, Betsy, as well as several other families, including the Olivers, Siscos, Cartwrights, and Whiteheads, all called Skunk Hollow home.

Geismar and her team examined a twenty-eight-acre area that contained some twenty-one archaeological features, including ten cellar holes, seven foundations, two wells, and other structures. All of the features were mapped and described, test excavations were performed in two of them, and a systematic surface survey was carried out across the rest of the site. This investigation yielded 11,892 artifacts, a fair sample from which to generalize about life in the community (Geismar 1982:105). Geismar concluded that the artifact assemblage indicated a relatively affluent community, particularly when compared with other African American sites from the same period (Geismar 1982:170).

To determine the factors leading to the community's decline, Geismar compared the artifact assemblages from the various cellar holes where houses once stood. She found a relative decline in the wealth of the community's inhabitants after the death of the Reverend Thompson. Apparently, his leadership helped to attract and keep individuals in the community. After his death, some of the more prosperous inhabitants left.

Geismar's survey is important on several levels. First, it documents a poorly understood chapter of New Jersey's history. On a social level, it highlights the importance of certain individuals to the overall health of a small community. Furthermore, her historical research disputes the notion held by some scholars that African American families are generally unstable, dominated by the female members, and characterized by absent males (Moynihan 1965:63). The available documents indicate that, despite their relative poverty compared with whites, Skunk Hollow's inhabitants typically lived in stable households with both men and women present. This isolated community was a place of refuge and community for African Americans during the challenging years before and after emancipation.

No Pain, No Gain

If the archaeological work at Skunk Hollow shows us how a community survived during a time of intense social change, an archaeological deposit excavated from a New Brunswick privy tells us about changes in medical and health-related practices at about the same time. The late nineteenth century was, quite simply, a watershed in medical innovation, witnessing everything from the the introduction of anesthesia and antiseptics to the development of a wide range of diagnostic instruments, including the stethoscope and thermometer. Historians of medicine and science have done an excellent job of documenting the specific changes that occurred in medical practice during the nineteenth century and the accomplishments of innovative physicians. Only rarely do archaeological sites yield data that can augment that work, but one exceptional site in New Brunswick did just that.

In December 1986 a team of archaeologists from the Cultural Resource Consulting Group began an intensive study of Block 44 in the city of New Brunswick. Present-day George, Washington, and Albany Streets bound the site in the central commercial district of the city, a neighborhood first laid out in the early nineteenth century. Many of the properties in the area were owned by prominent local families, including physicians, merchants, and attorneys. One of the physicians, Dr. Clifford Morrogh, was a self-made man who by the 1860s had come to be regarded as one of the best surgeons in the state (figure 8.3).

Morrogh arrived in New Brunswick in 1847, having recently received his medical degree from the City University of New York. Despite his excellent credentials, Morrogh found himself the object of discrimination and contempt, not just for his ethnic origins (he had emigrated from County Cork, Ireland) and religion (Roman Catholic), but also for his attempts to use anesthesia during operations. It was believed that pain indicated healing; therefore painless medicine would lead to improper healing. Unable to find paying patients, Morrogh and

1847

Figure 8.3. Pioneering anesthesiologist Dr. Clifford Morrogh of New Brunswick, ca. 1882.

another local physician, Dr. Augustus F. Taylor, performed leg amputations on two African American men from the local poorhouse who had suffered badly broken legs in a wagon accident. The surgeries were successful, and soon paying patients recognized the benefits of anesthesia and the skill of Dr. Morrogh.

Apparently, Morrogh was the first physician in the state—and one of the first in the United States—to make use of chloroform, an inhaled anesthetic. Later he employed a variety of injected anestethics. Although there are several claimants when it comes to the title of inventor of anesthesia—Dr. Crawford Williamson Long of Danielsville, Georgia (1842) (Marks and Beatty 1973:168), Dr. Horace Wells, a dentist from Hartford, Connecticut (1844), and Charles T. Jackson and T. G. Morton at the Massachusetts General Hospital in 1846 (Shyrock 1960:133)—Morrogh and Taylor appear to be true pioneers.

In 1851 Morrogh established his practice at the home he built on Albany Street. During the Civil War, his skills came to the attention of the federal government, and he worked at the battlefields on the Peninsula and at Fredericksburg, Chancellorsville, and Gettysburg (Veit 1996b:38). One of many laudatory contemporary accounts described his relationship with patients: "In the sickroom he was like a ray of sunshine. There seemed to be healing in his very presence. There was something about him that inspired implicit confidence" (Veit 1996b:38). Morrogh excelled at the treatment of hard-to-cure maladies and appears to have become a physician of last resort, turned to when other treatments had failed (Wall and Pickersgill 1921:264). Personally modest, he was widely involved in philanthropic ventures, including the founding of an orphanage and the establishment of New Brunswick's first hospital, St. Peter's, in 1872 (Clayton 1882:5).

After Morrogh's death in 1882 at the age of sixty-two, his assistant, Dr. Frank Donahue, assumed his practice. Donohue purchased the Albany Street property in 1890 from Morrogh's widow, Cornelia, and maintained the practice there until he died of a heart attack in 1919.

When archaeologists began excavating the block where Morrogh once lived, they discovered dozens of nineteenth-century features, particularly privies, wells, and cisterns, many of which contained rich deposits of glass and ceramics. Disappointingly, bottle collectors had already dug through one of the features, a rectangular stone-lined foundation that may have been a privy. Broken bottles and glassware sat on the ground where the collectors had dropped them. Although it seemed unlikely that anything of archaeological value could have survived the looting, the archaeologists decided to re-excavate the feature.

Much to their surprise, more than two hundred artifacts were salvaged— syringes, test tubes, graduated cylinders, beakers, a crucible, eye droppers, thermometers, a toothbrush, nail brush, test tubes, and ninety-eight pharmaceutical bottles. Although the bottle collectors had tumbled and obscured the original stratigraphy, it seems likely that the artifacts were all discarded at the same time, possibly at the end of Dr. Morrogh's, Cornelia Morrogh's, or Frank Donahue's tenure.

The artifacts recovered from what was likely a privy provide a unique, and at times disturbing, glimpse of nineteenth-century medical practice. Both Clifford Morrogh and Frank Donahue were highly regarded as skillful surgeons, and several fragmentary tortoiseshell-handled scalpels reflect this aspect of their profession. Yet these scapels, though clearly of high quality, could not be sterilized. Ironically, Morrogh's early and innovative use of anesthesia enabled him to perform more complicated operations than would otherwise have been possible, which in turn greatly increased the chance of infection (Pernick 1985:7).

Interestingly, one small graduated syringe and fragments of at least twelve large ungraduated syringes were recovered from the feature (figure 8.4). The latter may have been used to administer anesthetics, although each injection would have been an experiment, because there was no easy way to measure the material being dispensed. Alternatively, these large syringes could have been used to drain wounds or to administer enemas (Adams 1952:125).

A good sample of pharmaceutical glassware was also recovered from the feature, including eleven test tubes, twelve graduated cylinders, and four glass funnel fragments. Two of the funnel fragments are embossed with patent dates of 1880; therefore, the medical artifacts, which appear to have been deposited as a group, must have been discarded after 1880. Presumably, Dr. Morrogh used these funnels, test tubes, and so on in the preparation of medicines. Certainly, the artifacts show that he kept a well-stocked medicine cabinet and so may have dispensed medications to his patients. The ninety-eight medicine bottles recovered from the feature included six morphine vials, as well as bottles for quinine

Figure 8.4. The artifact collection recovered from Dr. Clifford Morrogh's privy. Note that, although there are many bottles, none is a patent medicine bottle. Plungers from several large syringes are at the bottom center. To the right are funnels and graduated cylinders, and in the center are handles from scalpels, pessaries, a smelling salt ampule, and thermometers. Courtesy of the Cultural Resource Consulting Group.

(a treatment for malaria) and strychnine (a stimulant for the nervous system), which is poisonous in high doses.

The most surprising discovery in the privy assemblage was a pair of fragmentary pessaries and a vaginal syringe. Although gynecology was literally in its infancy during the late nineteenth century, Morrogh seems to have been treating women's illnesses. Pessaries—objects made from hard rubber that were used to reposition a prolapsed uterus—were very popular in the 1860s (Speert 1958:543). The vaginal syringe could have been used as part of what was called the water cure, the controversial use of water injections both during pregnancy and following delivery as a means of relieving pain and preventing hemorrhaging and uterine collapse (Donegan 1986:126).

The collection of artifacts recovered from the Morrogh-Donahue privy shows that these two well-respected surgeons also maintained what might be termed a "general practice." Although several of the artifacts relate to surgery and anesthesia, the archaeologists also found gynecological or obstetric items unmentioned by prudish Victorian authors. The fascinating collection highlights the uneven development of medical techniques in the nineteenth century as physicians strove to improve the practice of medicine.

Feltville: Utopia for Whom?

While physicians like Clifford Morrogh worked to alleviate the pain of individuals, other men and women sought to reform society's ills. In Lincroft, near Red Bank, a group of forward-thinking idealists, influenced by the philosophy of Charles Fourier, established a model self-supporting community known as the Phalanx. Their utopian experiment, begun in 1843, lasted just over a decade, its end hastened by a disastrous fire that destroyed the community's mills. Rutgers University professor Michael Ester carried out limited excavations at the site in the 1970s. Although his work was never fully reported, his preliminary statements note an intensely ordered community, with trash carefully disposed of in inconspicuous locations (Kirchmann 1980:17).

In 1845, just a few years after the Phalanx was established, David Felt, a successful printer and stationery dealer from New York City, purchased a secluded 760-acre tract in the Watchung Mountains. There he established Feltville, a mill town dedicated to the manufacture of paper and books and, if contemporary sources are to be believed, to the improvement of workers' lives (figure 8.5). Since 1996, Montclair State University has been excavating Feltville, which is now situated in the Watchung Reservation, a Union County park. These exca-

Figure 8.5. The Feltville church store, social hub of David Felt's papermaking town in the Watchung Mountains. The restored building, which served as both church and store, was modified in the late nineteenth century with the addition of rustic Adirondacks-style porches. Photograph by the author.

vations, directed by Professors Matthew Tomaso, Stanley Walling, and myself, have revealed a carefully laid out community influenced by nineteenth-century ideas about social improvement, and yet considerably different from our modern concepts of utopia (Tomaso et al. 2001).

During the eighteenth century two families from Long Island, the Willcockses and the Badgleys, had carved farmsteads out of the forest and constructed a sawmill and gristmill in what was known as the Blue Brook Valley (Hawley 1964). W. Woodford Clayton, a nineteenth-century historian, described Felt's motivations for later selecting this site for his company town: "those who were employed here by being situated in a village free of any demoralizing tendencies, they would be free, and in this once happy busy place, he endeavored to cultivate their minds as well as their moral tendencies, having a circulating library, a good school, the church and in no way that their means should be wasted, but saved to themselves and families" (Clayton 1882:354). Like many of his industrialist contemporaries who established their own towns along mill-streams in New England—Lowell, Massachusetts, is perhaps the most famous

(Mrozowski et al. 1996)—Felt built everything he considered needful: workers' cottages and dormitories, a three-story mill, a smaller gristmill, an office, black-smith shop, school, combination church and store, and possibly a mansion.

Felt was also deeply interested in religion, and contemporary sources describe him as one of New York City's leading Unitarians (Harwood 1908:68). He worked hard to ensure that his employees were regularly served by ministers or priests in an attempt to promote benevolence, righteousness, and strong family values. In 1850, close to the community's apex, Felt hired Austin Craig, a rising young Unitarian minister. Craig stayed at Feltville for just under a year, leaving to become pastor of a church in Orange County, New York. (He later founded Antioch College in Ohio.) In his resignation letter, Craig highlighted Felt's central importance for this town:

> I need not tell you that you, yourself, are, pecuniary at least, the "Society" of this place. The permanence of my situation here, is, then, at the utmost identical with the continuance of a single life. Some time it might be expected, should I live, that your withdrawal from the village, by death, or otherwise would end the enterprise of the Free Religious Society, which your liberality has hitherto sustained. (Quoted in Harwood 1908:115)

Craig's observation was prescient: the lifespan of Feltville was measured by the length of David Felt's interest in the place.

For fifteen years Feltville flourished as a hive of industry. A. Van Doren Honeyman, writing in the 1920s, noted: "In 1845 the community was as large as Westfield. There were thirty-five houses, a church, a school, and a paper mill" (1923:530). The paper or book factory, as it is noted on nineteenth-century maps, was apparently successful, though only a single book and two tracts published in the town are known to survive today.

In 1860, for reasons that have never been satisfactorily explained, David Felt sold Feltville to Amasa Foster and abandoned the town. Some sources suggest that Felt closed his factory because of increasing sectional tensions and the importance of the southern market to his business (Dolkart 1985). Another possibility is that the sixty-year-old Felt had simply tired of running both the mill village and his retail operation in New York. Moreover, his waterpowered factory was likely becoming outmoded as larger and more successful manufacturers were making the switch to steam power (Dolkart 1985:169). His brother and sometime business partner, Willard, died in 1862. Perhaps a lingering illness preceded Willard's death and demanded David Felt's attention.

Local legend has it that, when leaving the village for the last time, David Felt said to his driver, "Well, King David is gone and the village will go to hell!"

1845-60 feet
1860-64 Foster
1864-82 Townsend
1882-1920's Ackerman, Glenside Park
Union County Park system

"ENDLESS NOVELTY"   179

(Hawley 1964:18). Despite this ominous prediction, the town did not die out completely. In 1864 Foster sold the land and buildings to a New York City manufacturer of patent medicines, Samuel P. Townsend, known as the "Sarsaparilla King." Townsend tried to replicate his success in Feltville, but failed. In 1882 he sold the property to Warren Ackerman, an industrialist from Scotch Plains, who turned the community into a successful summer resort called Glenside Park. Instead of tearing down the old structures and starting anew, he remodeled them by adding rustic Adirondack-style porches and dormer roofs. The resort drew vacationers until the 1920s, when improved roads and automobiles opened up more distant resort destinations. The property was broken up, sold off, and eventually acquired by the Union County park system during the 1930s. Today, there are ten extant structures in the village, which has a total population of seven. The park is currently undergoing extensive restoration and serves a variety of recreational and educational goals. It is also the site of Operation Archaeology, an award-winning Union County program designed to bring historical archaeology into primary schools.

Montclair State's excavations at Feltville have been carried out with several goals in mind: to gather physical evidence about the arrangement of the community; to examine the lives of the workers who lived there; to explore Felt's utopian model for the community; and to trace the evolution of the village through time. Here we shall concentrate on several archaeological features—two privies and a carefully constructed brick-lined well—and consider what they can tell us about the community.

During the second season's excavations, the archaeologists focused on a feature located behind the former mill office, now the home of the park superintendent. A shallow depression there seemed like a likely location for a privy. Testing almost immediately uncovered a thick layer of coal ash and cinder, which was used to fill in the abandoned outhouse early in the twentieth century. This privy, associated with a building that probably served as Feltville's office, differed considerably from the privies behind the workers' cottages. Although it probably was used by a smaller number of individuals, it was larger, measuring four feet square and just over three-and-a-half feet deep, and could have contained a considerably greater quantity of refuse. Moreover, it was better made, with carefully fitted cut stone walls of sandstone. In contrast, the workers' privy was crude, shallow, and poorly constructed. From these construction differences it can be inferred that if Feltville was indeed utopian, it was not egalitarian.

The deposit found in the privy related not to Felt's occupation of the town, but to the later resort era (1882–1916). Near the bottom, the excavators found a rich deposit of plates, teacups, pitchers, and at least thirty-nine beverage bottles, many of which were still intact (figures 8.6 and 8.7). They were primarily from beer and soda bottlers in Newark, Plainfield, the Oranges, and Bernardsville. One bottle for Bromo Seltzer, a popular antacid, was also found. Also present were an ironstone wash basin, a chamber pot, nails, window glass fragments, and chimneys from kerosene lamps. The most surprising find was a tin can containing a crumpled wad of newspaper. Amazingly, the newspaper, partially covered in red paint, was still legible. It was the January 30, 1915, issue of the *World Magazine*. Presumably it was disposed of soon after being read. In fact, if it were not for the paint that covered much of it, we might speculate that it was the early-twentieth-century equivalent of toilet paper.

Based on the evidence of these artifacts, and particularly the newspaper, the archaeologists concluded that the privy was likely filled during the second decade of the twentieth century, near the end of the Glenside Park era. The bottles were probably discarded when the privy was still in use. Then the washbasin, chamber pot, and tin can filled with newspaper were tossed in. Cinders and ash followed them to fill the privy shaft.

The artifacts from this privy provided useful information about where the va-

Figure 8.6. Teacups and a water pitcher dating from the Glenside Park era at Feltville. Photograph by the author.

Figure 8.7. Soda and beer bottles recovered from a deposit representing the Glenside Park era (ca. 1915) of Feltville's history. Most of these bottles came from local bottlers in Newark or the Oranges. Photograph by the author.

cationers at Glenside Park acquired their goods and what sorts of beverages they were consuming. Clearly, David Felt's temperance rules had been long forgotten. The absence of nineteenth-century deposits may indicate regular cleaning episodes that removed earlier artifacts and maintained a modicum of sanitation, in contrast to the privies at the workers' cottages.

Montclair State's third season of work focused on the lower road, a residential area of the community where several intact workers' cottages survive (figure 8.8). Testing revealed some subsurface features, including a privy, a well, and a gravel walkway, which probably date to Felt's construction of the community. Although the archaeologists expected to find features like these, their locations, construction, and fill provided new data about the lives of the men and women who lived and worked in Feltville. Census records show that many of these individuals were Irish and German immigrants, often of limited financial means. The records also indicate that several families, sometimes as many as four, were crowded into a single house. Excavations showed further that as many as two and possible three houses shared a single shallow privy.

The privy excavated during the third season was a crude rectangular structure, lined with rough-cut stone blocks. Although only three feet deep, it contained an extensive deposit of artifacts dating from the Felt (1845–1860) and
Townsend (1864–1882) eras (figure 8.9). Particularly impressive was the large
number of small octagonal paneled medicine bottles, all of which fall into a few
standard shapes and sizes. Found with them was a small collection of animal
bones representing various wild game, including deer, turkeys, fish, and even
turtles.

The assemblage is intriguing. Were the residents of Feltville living in such a
state of poverty that they were forced to live off the land? Does the collection of
medicine bottles indicate that one or two individuals were attempting to treat a
particular ailment with a now unknown medication? Could it be that they
were taking the medicine, which may have been made with an alcohol base, in
an effort to sidestep Felt's prohibition rules? Alternatively, we might posit that
the workers were forced to buy all their goods at a company store, using scrip
currency, thereby limiting the types of goods available for purchase.

Also found near the workers' cottages were carefully constructed gravel
paths connecting one house to the next, and between the houses were well-

*Figure 8.8. Several of the workers' cottages at Feltville during the 1870s. Photograph from
the author's collection.*

Workers privy

Figure 8.9. A box privy dating from the 1840s excavated at Feltville by Montclair State University's field school. Photograph by the author.

made brick wells. The gravel paths contained pipe fragments typical of the mid-nineteenth century and were probably laid out during Felt's ownership of the community. They show an attention to detail and order unexpected in this rural location, yet perhaps not surprising in a utopian community.

Artifacts like the ones found around the workers' cottages provide a material counterpoint to the written documentation concerning the site. By examining the material and written sources together, we can come to a better understanding of life in the company town.

This handful of sites and collections—a forgotten African American community, an early anesthesiologist's discarded instruments, and a company town in the Watchung Mountains—offers glimpses of the past that are not always reassuring. For instance, we must face the persistence of slavery in New Jersey until the very end of the Civil War. In other cases, the findings are heartening, such as the hard work and perseverance of Clifford Morrogh as he struggled to introduce the concept of painless medicine. Feltville is important because it highlights the contrast between present-day interpretations of utopia and those of a nineteenth-century industrialist, David Felt. His was a community of temperance and religion, where hard work brought education and other benefits to his employees, but not equality or independence. Later, in the 1890s, Feltville became a vacation spot, a middle-class Adirondacks-like resort near the emerging suburban communities of Summit, Fanwood, and Plainfield. We might almost see it as a different sort of utopia, a respite from the workaday world for a few days or weeks.

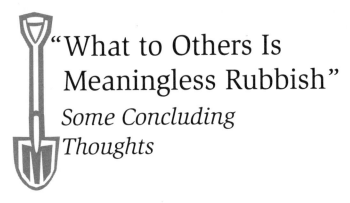"What to Others Is Meaningless Rubbish"
Some Concluding Thoughts

Historical archaeology in New Jersey has come a long way since Charles Conrad Abbott probed the ruins of a Dutch house on Burlington Island. In a little more than one hundred years, historical archaeology has evolved from an enthusiast's avocation to an increasingly regimented and professionalized field. Abbott coyly described his finds on Burlington Island as "what to others is meaningless rubbish" (Abbott 1898:171). Today, with the benefit of hindsight, we can say that Abbott's "meaningless rubbish" is anything but meaningless. Instead, it is a valuable source of unedited information about our past. Ironically, in what must be a unique instance of meta-archaeology, excavators have since dug the site of Abbott's home, "Three Beeches," near Trenton (Stanzeski 1974). The coins, projectile points, and charred books recovered from the cellar hole of Abbott's burned-out house provide a unique glimpse of this pioneering archaeologist's life and work.

As you have read, historical archaeologists have turned their trowels, databases, and powers of analysis to sites associated with the colonial settlers of the state, eighteenth-century life, and the brutality of the Revolutionary War. They have also examined graveyards and cemeteries and deciphered what the silent markers and crumbling bones have to say about changing patterns of religious and cultural beliefs. New Jersey's importance as a manufacturing hub and a transportation nexus are other topics that historical archaeologists have examined. We looked at turnpike roads, canals, a railroad roundhouse, and darkened lighthouses. Each of these discoveries represents a different part of the growing nineteenth-century transportation network.

Industries have thrived in New Jersey from the beginning. We visited eighteenth- and nineteenth-century ironworks in the North Jersey Highlands, potteries by Raritan Bay, a glassworks, and the ephemeral remains of charcoal kilns in the Pine Barrens. The nineteenth century also saw emancipation, massive immigration, and stunning developments in medical instruments, health, and sanitation. At the same time, some individuals, like David Felt, established utopian communities in an attempt to cure the real and perceived ills of the new industrial world.

Archaeologists have studied these and other ways in which daily life was radically altered over the course of the nineteenth century. In fact, it might seem that historical archaeologists have looked at everything in New Jersey's past that is worth studying. Not so. In comparison with parts of New England and the Chesapeake Bay region, the map of New Jersey's historical landscape shows much uncharted territory. In this last, brief chapter, we shall touch upon some of the topics that have so far eluded New Jersey's historical archaeologists, the challenges and possibilities posed by new technologies, and the changing social climate within which archaeology occurs.

Time for a Closer Look

So what pieces are missing from New Jersey's archaeological puzzle? The answer is: several important topics that could help round out our understanding of the peoples and cultures who helped make this state. Subjects that immediately come to mind are: early colonial life, especially during the seventeenth century, when Native Americans and Europeans first encountered one another; the lives of African Americans, particularly in the poorly documented years before emancipation; the experiences of nineteenth-century immigrants from eastern and southern European; invention and industrial development; and women's lives.

The Early Years

Surprisingly, the first century of European settlement in New Jersey is a period that has received relatively little archaeological study. Although a few important seventeenth-century sites located along the Delaware River have felt the probe of the spade, other areas of the state that were settled in the seventeenth century remain archaeological unknowns. In Newark, Elizabeth, Perth Amboy, Woodbridge, Piscataway, Middletown, Shrewsbury, and many other early communities, archaeologists have yet to excavate and conclusively date a seventeenth-century site. Although archaeologist Marshall Becker has identified the capital of New Sweden on Tinicum Island, Pennsylvania, near Philadelphia International Airport (Becker 1979, 1999), Swedish settlements along the Jersey side of the Delaware River remain, so far as archaeology is concerned, enigmatic (see Liebeknecht 1986 and Becker 1988). There are some obvious reasons why. First, urban development has probably destroyed or deeply buried the earliest sites in many towns. Moreover, early sites are often ephemeral and hard to find. Nonetheless, archaeologists in nearby New York City have shown great skill in locating and excavating deeply buried seventeenth-century sites in the megalopolis. Who knows what diligent archaeologists may yet unearth in Burlington, Elizabeth, or Perth Amboy?

African American Life in Slavery and Freedom

In Chapter 8 we noted Joan Geismar's excavations at Skunk Hollow. Since that model study, published in 1982, there has been only one other large-scale examination of a site with a significant African American component. It was performed for the New Jersey Department of Transportation, Bureau of Environmental Analysis, at Beverwyck, once the lavish estate of Lucas von Beverhoudt in the eighteenth century and a plantation maintained with slave labor (Silber and Catts 2001). There are probably other sites that also contain archaeological deposits relating to this critical phase of our history. Why New Jersey archaeologists have not sought them out for study is puzzling. While archaeologists in states from Massachusetts to Florida have made the discovery of the material remains of African American life a top priority, archaeologists in the Garden State seem to have overlooked the topic. African American life is both an important and likely a fruitful area for further research.

Immigrants' Lives

Of course, African Americans are not the only group of immigrants who left behind archaeological remains. In Chapter 3 we visited Dutch and English sites. During the nineteenth and twentieth centuries, settlers from Germany, Ireland, Italy, Russia, and, particularly, from eastern and southern Europe poured into the state. Some were Jewish, others Catholic, and still others Greek Orthodox. Many established their own communities, with churches, synagogues, cemeteries, and fraternal halls. In some places they re-created a life reminiscent of what they had known in the Old World. Towns like Brotmanville in Salem County (established by Jewish émigrés), Egg Harbor City in Atlantic County (settled by Germans), and Cassville in Ocean County (a Russian community) may well contain archaeological remains that speak to the lives of their founders.

The creation and maintenance of ethnicity is an important topic in historical archaeology. New Jersey, a state more diverse than most, is a perfect laboratory for studying these processes, which continue to shape our communities and lives.

Invention and Innovation

Industrial archaeologists have conducted outstanding studies of the state's iron, glass, and ceramics industries. Yet, one important aspect of the industrialization process in New Jersey has been largely overlooked: invention. From John Stevens and his pioneering railroads and steamboats to Bell Laboratories, this small state has been a hotbed of invention and technical innovation. During the early nineteenth century, Colonel John Stevens demonstrated his "steam waggon," a precursor of the railroad, on his Hoboken estate. Later, in the 1830s, his son Robert L. Stevens built New Jersey's first railroad, the Camden and Amboy. Alfred Vail and Samuel F. B. Morse developed the magnetic telegraph at Vail's Speedwell Ironworks near Morristown in 1837, sparking a communications revolution. Their simple invention was the direct precursor of today's Internet. Later still, Thomas Edison established labs in Newark, Menlo Park/Edison, and West Orange, where he cranked out thousands of new inventions, including the first commercially successful incandescent lamp, phonograph, and motion picture. Edison's Menlo Park laboratory is generally credited as the world's first research laboratory. Guglielmo Marconi, inventor of the wireless telegraph, set up his receiving mast by the Twin Lights in Monmouth County. Innovative ceramicists working for the Atlantic Terra Cotta Company made the terra-cotta sheathing for some of America's first skyscrapers.

The list of innovations is nearly endless, and the sites associated with early inventors are potentially revealing. They may pose new challenges to archaeologists, however, particularly because of the hazardous materials that were employed at some of these sites. Yet, careful and thoughtful examination might provide some surprising insights into the process of invention.

Women's Lives

Although women made and continue to make important contributions to New Jersey, they are, so far as archaeology is concerned, a silent majority. To the best of my knowledge, no historical archaeologist working in the state has developed a research project that focuses primarily on the contributions of women or looks at the life, property, or possessions of a woman. Ironically, it must be noted that many of the artifacts that archaeologists recover—broken bits of crockery, shattered bottles, rusted kitchen kettles—were used by women. Children too are often overlooked by traditional histories. Archaeology has the potential to reveal new information about their lives.

As these examples show, many important areas of research await historical archaeologists in New Jersey. We can hope that in the next decades at least some of these sites and topics will receive the attention they deserve.

Challenges Facing Archaeology Today

As the new millennium begins, and with roughly a century of archaeological fieldwork under our belts, it is a good time to take stock of where we are, what we have learned, and where we might go in the future. Several challenges face archaeology at this critical juncture. First and foremost is site destruction. Other significant challenges include the lack of communication among archaeologists, historians, educators, and the interested public. A final stumbling block that is sure to haunt our successor archaeologists and those who hope to make use of the collections currently being unearthed is what might be termed the curatorial crisis. What happens to all those artifacts after they emerge from the ground?

Site Destruction

Of the tens of thousands of archaeological sites in New Jersey, existing local, state, and federal statutes protect only a small percentage. Although state agencies, such as the State Historic Preservation Office, have done significant work as the designated protectors of historic resources, there are many archaeological sites—the majority, in fact—over which they have no control. As development continues in this, the most densely populated of states, New Jersey's heritage is being rapidly bulldozed away. Obviously, it is impossible to protect every site forever; yet we must recognize that archaeological sites, whether privately or publicly held, are finite resources. Their loss is no less significant than the loss of a unique species due to overpredation or human encroachment in the Amazon Basin.

Nor is development the only threat to our state's archaeological heritage. Sites are being lost to uninformed and poorly documented excavation. What separates archaeologists from pot hunters and looters is not a piece of parchment bearing the imprimatur of a prestigious educational institution—though that should indicate a certain familiarity with basic archaeological methods and theories. Rather, archaeologists, whether amateur or professional, are committed to documenting how they excavate and to recording what they find and where they found it so that others might understand what the artifacts mean. The difference between arrowheads for sale at a flea market and those stored in a cabinet drawer at a museum is provenience. Though also removed from the ground, the arrowheads in the museum were documented in such a way that their context has not been lost. In other words, we know who found them, when they were found, where they were found, and what other objects were found with them. That information allows us to move beyond the artifacts and toward an understanding of the people who once used them.

The best defense for our fragile archaeological heritage is an educated public that is involved in and aware of the uses and importance of archaeology and preservation for their communities. This awareness should start in elementary schools. All too many individuals complete their education without a clear understanding of the differences between archaeology, paleontology, and geology. If you don't know what archaeology is, it's hard to care about it.

Another important step toward saving our archaeological heritage might be a stewardship program, such as that recently proposed by Matthew Tomaso, an archaeologist at Montclair State University. Knowledgeable and interested local individuals would act as volunteer stewards for sites in their communities, helping local, state, and federal authorities know when they are endangered so that they might be protected from destruction.

Local preservation ordinances, which often focus exclusively on the built landscape—houses, streetscapes, places of worship, and the like—should also start to take into account, wherever possible, archaeological sites. They too are part of our shared heritage worth preserving and saving for the future.

Another problem hampering the development of historical archaeology, and of archaeology in general in the state, is a lack of coordination. Reports on excavations are filed at the State Historic Preservation Office in Trenton, but sites are registered at the State Museum, halfway across town. Archaeological collections are scattered in various museums and repositories, many of which are understaffed and poorly funded. Movie buffs may recall how at the end of *Raiders of the Lost Ark* the Ark of the Covenant is shipped off to an enormous warehouse and shelved with thousands of other nondescript boxes. Although New Jersey has no single repository on this scale, many artifacts are more deeply buried and in greater danger of destruction or loss after excavation than before. A well-funded and fully staffed archaeological research lab and curatorial facility could help to make the archaeologically recovered past much more accessible to academic researchers and the general public alike.

The Archaeological Society of New Jersey, an important voice for local archaeology, helps ameliorate some of these problems and provides a crucial forum for presenting and publishing research. However, historical archaeology specifically, and archaeology in general, remains underfunded and uncoordinated in New Jersey.

What Type of Archaeologist Are You?

Within the archaeological community itself, not all relations are harmonious. New Jersey's first archaeologists were amateurs or avocationalists who made a hobby of collecting artifacts. Later, academics at colleges and universities, such as Dorothy Cross Jensen at Hunter College, got involved. Since the passage of the National Historic Preservation Act in 1966, a new generation of archaeologist— the contract archaeologist—has developed. As the title implies, these are hired experts whose livelihood is based on searching for and excavating archaeological sites in the context of bureaucratic regulation. Many of the senior personnel are dedicated scholars and researchers in their own right. Working with them are the excavators—officially known as the field crew, unofficially called "field techs" or "shovel bums." Theirs is often a nomadic life. They are peripatetic wanderers drawn here and there by the lure of an interesting project or a few consecutive paychecks. Rewards generally come in the form of knowledge rather than money.

These three groups—the avocationalists, the academics, and the professionals—though sharing the same love for the past, are often at odds with each other. Professors decry nonacademic professionals for their lack of research interests and their dedication to Mammon rather than devotion to Clio. Avocationalists often feel that they are more dedicated than either academics or contract archaeologists because they are motivated solely by their interest in the past. Contract archaeologists see academics as unrealistic purists who are unaware of the realities imposed by legislation, budgets, and construction schedules. At the same time, contract archaeologists sometimes perceive avocationalists as useful, but not totally initiated, members of the fraternity. All in all, the archaeological family could be described as dysfunctional.

Each camp needs the others. By working together, comparing ideas, and sharing knowledge, techniques, and information, archaeologists could be more productive and present a more united front than at present.

Why Excavate?

There are many good reasons to excavate an archaeological site: to test scientific hypotheses, to explore a particular anthropological theory, to gather data about a historical problem, to teach excavation methods, to interpret the remains to the public, and to salvage information before a site is lost to construction. We must be careful, however, not to fall into the fallacy that simply by excavating a site we are saving it. Deciding to excavate an archaeological site is like making a commitment to any long-term relationship. To succeed, you must possess the skills to take care of the site and must realize that the commitment is not something to be undertaken lightly. To quote the noted Rutgers University anthropologist Carmel Schrire:

A site is like a lover. Early on, you fool around, testing, probing, seeing other sites, but eventually you either dig it or you don't. If you do, it costs money, it takes time. There is a bond between you, and it's yours for the duration. . . . After the first season the excitement fades a little and things become familiar. . . . And, finally, when all the digging is over, there remain the last rites. There are rules and laws, and most agree that there is a moral obligation to protect, but some fill in the holes, some shore up the sides, and others simply walk away and leave the deposit to collapse. The site may be described in full, or briefly, or even not at all. The finds may be packed in velvet, highlighted in a museum or gallery, or they may be boxed and lost. It all depends. It's up to you. (Schrire 1995:92)

Although Schrire's "lover analogy" may seem far-fetched, it is accurate. Excavating a site properly requires forethought, planning, and follow-through, not to mention the acceptance of responsibility to deal properly with the consequences.

The Future of Historical Archaeology

"Put Your Future in Ruins." So read a catchy poster at Drew University's Museum of Archaeology in the early 1980s. Despite the challenges of site destruction, the curatorial crisis, and a lack of coordination among various archaeological entities in New Jersey, the future of historical archaeology looks bright. Many important topics have yet to be studied, and some that have been revisited, such as canals, are providing new and often surprising insights into our past. With new technologies, better training, and greater coordination among historical archaeologists, historians, architectural historians, geographers, and, of course, anthropologists, historical archaeology can rewrite history from the bottom up—recording and sharing the experiences of everyday people like ourselves who lived in generations past. We can come to understand better the people who settled this state, the landscapes they lived in, and the struggles they endured—military, political, and social.

Technologies such as the Internet and digital photography make it easier than ever to share the results of archaeological research. Scientific techniques such as pollen analysis may reveal the crops that once covered a field, while dendrochronology can tell us when the woodsman's axe bit into the bark of the oak that contributed the beams and sills for his house on the frontier. Parisitology can tell us what illnesses plagued our predecessors; Geographic Information Systems can be used to map distributions of artifacts and sites with an efficiency previously undreamed of; and improved surveying techniques and Global Positioning Satellites make it easier for archaeologists to find and record sites.

Of course, nothing can, or ever will, replace the hard work and sweat of excavation, the tedious hours spent poring over old documents reluctant to share their secrets, and the thrill of discovery, be it in the field, in the library, or in the kitchen when an elderly informant's fragile memory delivers just the clue you need to interpret what you are finding in the ground. Thomas Edison is famous for saying that invention is 99 percent perspiration and 1 percent inspiration. What held true for invention is certainly the case in archaeology. Let's keep digging.

Bibliography

Abbott, Charles Conrad. 1898. *Travels in a Tree Top*. Philadelphia: J. B. Lippincott.

———. 1899. *Recent Rambles; or, In Touch with Nature*. Philadelphia and London: J. B. Lippincott.

Adams, George Worthington. 1952. *The Medical History of the Union Army in the Civil War*. New York: Henry Schuman.

Aiello, Lucy. 1967. "Charles Conrad Abbott, M.D., Discoverer of Ancient Man in the Delaware Valley." *Bulletin of the New Jersey Academy of Science* 12(2):3–6.

Baer, Christopher T., William J. Coxey, and Paul W. Schopp. 1994. *The Trail of the Blue Comet: A History of the Jersey Central's New Jersey Southern Division*. Palmyra, N.J.: West Jersey Chapter of the National Railway Historical Society.

Bahn, Paul G., ed. 1996. *The Cambridge Illustrated History of Archaeology*. New York: Cambridge University Press.

Bailey, Rosalie Fellows. 1968. *Pre-Revolutionary Dutch Houses and Families in Northern New Jersey and Southern New York*. New York: Dover.

Batinski, Michael C. 1982. "Jonathan Belcher." In *The Governors of New Jersey: 1664–1974*, ed. Paul A. Stellhorn and Michael J. Birkner, 58–62. Trenton: New Jersey Historical Commission.

Baugher, Sherene, and Frederick A. Winter. 1983. "Early American Gravestones: Archaeological Perspectives on Three Cemeteries of Old New York." *Archaeology* 36(5):46–54.

Baurmeister, Carl Leopold. 1973. *Revolution in America: Confidential Letters and Journals 1776–1784 of Adjutant General Major Baurmeister of the Hessian Forces*. Translated and annotated by Bernard A. Uhlendorf. Westport, Conn.: Greenwood Press.

Beaudry, Mary C. 1996. "Reinventing Historical Archaeology." In *Historical Archaeology and the Study of American Culture*, ed. Lu Ann De Cunzo and Bernard L. Herman, 473–97. Winterthur, Del.: Henry Francis du Pont Winterthur Museum.

Becker, Marshall J. 1979. "Ethnohistory and Archaeology in Search of the Printzhof: The 17th-Century Residence of Swedish Colonial Governor Johan Printz." *Ethnohistory* 26(1):15–44.

———. 1983. "The Boundary Line between the Lenape and the Munsee: The Forks of Delaware as a Buffer Zone." *Man in the Northeast* 26:1–20.

———. 1986. "Cultural Diversity in the Lower Delaware River Valley: An Ethnohistorical Perspective." In *Late Woodland Socio-Cultural Evolution in the Middle Atlantic*, ed. Jay Custer, 90–101. Newark, Del.: University of Delaware Press.

———. 1988. "Swedish Colonial Sites in New Jersey: Needle in a Haystack/Spoon in a Dune." *Bulletin of the Archaeological Society of New Jersey* 43:17–18.

———. 1993. "Lenape Shelters: Possible Examples from the Contact Period." *Pennsylvania Archaeologist* 63(2):64–76.

———. 1999. "Archaeology at the Printzhof (36DE3): The Only Documented Early 17th-Century Swedish Colonial Site in the Delaware Valley." *Journal of Middle Atlantic Archaeology* 15:77–94.

Bello, Charles A. 1991. "The Trenton and New Brunswick Straight Turnpike: Mile Marker No. 9." *Bulletin of the Archaeological Society of New Jersey* 46:55–56.

Benes, Peter. 1977. *The Masks of Orthodoxy: Folk Gravestone Carvings in Plymouth County Massachusetts 1689–1805*. Amherst: University of Massachusetts Press.

Bergen County Historical Society. 1968. "The Baylor Massacre Dig." *In Bergen's Attic: A Sometime Publication for Members and Friends of the Bergen County Historical Society* 3(1):1–8.

Bertland, Dennis. 1998. *Merchants and Drovers Tavern, Rahway, New Jersey: A Historical Study of a New Jersey Tavern during the Early American Period*. Report submitted to the Rahway Historical Society, Rahway.

Bill, Alfred Hoyt. 1964. *New Jersey and the Revolutionary War*. Princeton: D. Van Nostrand.

Bill, Alfred Hoyt, W. E. Edge, C. M. Greiff, and B. F. Schwartz. 1978. *A House Called Morven: Its Role in American History*. Rev. ed. Princeton: Princeton University Press.

Binford, Lewis R. 1962. "A New Method of Calculating Dates from Kaolin Pipe Stem Fragments." *Southeastern Archaeological Conference Newsletter* 9(1):19–21.

Bisbee, Henry. 1972. *Burlington Island: The Best and Largest on the South River, 1624–1972*. Burlington, N.J.: Heidelberg Press.

Boyd, Paul D. 2000. "Settlers, or Summer Shore Trekkers: Lenape Life Evidence in Coastal New Jersey." Paper presented at the 65th Annual Meeting of the Society for American Archaeology, Philadelphia.

Boyer, Charles S. 1931. *Early Forges and Furnaces in New Jersey*. Philadelphia: University of Pennsylvania Press.

Brady, Barry. 1981. "Paterson, New Jersey: Birthplace of the American Industrial Revolution." *Archaeology* 34(5):22–29.

Branin, M. Lelyn. 1988. *The Early Makers of Handcrafted Earthenware and Stoneware in Central and Southern New Jersey*. Madison, N.J.: Fairleigh Dickinson University Press.

Buchanon, R. A. 1972. *Industrial Archaeology in Britain*. London: Penguin Books.

Budd, Thomas. [1685] 1966. *Good Order Established in Pennsilvania & New-Jersey*. Reprint. Readex Microprint Corporation.

Cahoone, Henry. 1828. Letter to Jonathan Thompson, 9 May 1828. Navesink Light Station/Twin Lights Papers. Twin Lights Historic Site.

Calligaro, Lee. 1967. "The Negro's Legal Status in Pre–Civil War New Jersey." *New Jersey History* 85:167–80.

Chard, Jack. 1995. *Making Iron and Steel: The Historic Processes, 1700–1900*. Ringwood, N.J.: North Jersey Highlands Historical Society.

Clayton, W. Woodford. 1882. *History of Union and Middlesex Counties, New Jersey*. Philadelphia: Everts and Peck.

Cosans-Zebooker, Betty. 1992. *A Cultural Resource Survey of the Burr/Haines Mill Site (Site 28 BU 414), Tabernacle Township, Burlington County, New Jersey*. New Jersey Pinelands Development Application #89-1099.02. Report on file at the New Jersey Pinelands Commission, New Lisbon.

Cosans-Zebooker, Betty, and Ronald A. Thomas. 1993. "Excavations at the Burr/Haines

Site, Burlington County, New Jersey." *Bulletin of the Archaeological Society of New Jersey* 48:13–20.

Cotter, John L. 1993. "Historical Archaeology before 1967." *Historical Archaeology* 27(1):4–10.

Crist, Thomas A. J. 1998. *Report on the Bioarchaeological Excavation and Analysis of Human Remains Discovered Beneath Christ Episcopal Church, Shrewsbury Borough, Monmouth County, New Jersey.* Report prepared for Christ Episcopal Church, Shrewsbury.

Cross, Dorothy. 1941. *Archaeology of New Jersey.* Vol. 1. Trenton: Archaeological Society of New Jersey and New Jersey State Museum.

Crowell, Elizabeth A. 1983. "Migratory Monuments and Missing Motifs: Archaeological Analysis of Mortuary Art in Cape May County, New Jersey, 1740–1810." Ph.D. diss., University of Pennsylvania.

Crowell, Elizabeth A., and Norman V. Mackie III. 1984. "'Depart from Hence and Keep This Thought in Mind': The Importance of Comparative Analysis in Gravestone Research." *Northeast Historical Archaeology* 13:9–16.

Cultural Resource Consulting Group [CRCG]. 1994. *Lupaldi Project-Block 70-Lakehurst Railroad Shops, Stage II Management Summary and Stage III Proposal.* Manuscript on file. Highland Park, N.J.: Cultural Resource Consulting Group.

Cunningham, John T. 1966. *New Jersey: America's Main Road.* Garden City, N.J.: Doubleday.

Daniel, Glyn. 1967. *The Origins and Growth of Archaeology.* New York: Thomas Y. Crowell.

Deagan, Kathleen. 1991. "Historical Archaeology's Contributions to Our Understanding of Early America." In *Historical Archaeology in Global Perspective,* ed. Lisa Falk, 97–112. Washington, D.C.: Smithsonian Institution Press.

DeCunzo, Lu Ann. 1983. "Economics and Ethnicity: An Archaeological Perspective on Nineteenth-Century Paterson, New Jersey." Ph.D. dissertation, University of Pennsylvania.

———. 1987. "Adapting to Factory and City: Illustrations from the Industrialization and Urbanization of Paterson, New Jersey." In *Consumer Choice in Historical Archaeology,* ed. Suzanne M. Spencer-Wood, 261–96. New York: Plenum Press.

Deetz, James. 1977. *In Small Things Forgotten.* New York: Anchor Books.

Deetz, James, and Edwin S. Dethlefsen. 1967. "Death's Head, Cherub, Urn and Willow." *Natural History* 76(3):29–37.

Demarest, Thomas. 1971. "The Baylor Massacre—Some Assorted Notes and Information." *Bergen County History,* 29–94.

Dethlefsen, Edwin, and James Deetz. 1966. "Deaths Heads, Cherubs, and Willow Trees: Experimental Archaeology in Colonial Cemeteries." *American Antiquity* 31(4):502–10.

Dolkart, Andrew S. 1985. *David Felt and Stationers' Hall Press.* Princeton, N.J.: Historic Sites Research.

Donegan, Jane B. 1986. *"Hydropathic Highway to Health": Women and the Water-Cure in Antebellum America.* New York: Greenwood.

Epperson, Terrence W. 1992. *Archaeological Assessment for the N.J. Route 18 Freeway Extension, N.J. Route 138 to the Brielle Circle, Wall Township, Monmouth County, New Jersey.* Report prepared for the Federal Highway Administration and New Jersey Department of Transportation, Bureau of Environmental Analysis. Trenton: Hunter Research, Inc.

Ewald. Johann. 1979. *Diary of the American War: A Hessian Journal.* Translated by Joseph Tustin. New Haven: Yale University Press.

Fifth Auditor's Report. 1838. *Report of the Fifth Auditor, in relation to the execution of the act of 7th July last, for Building Light-Houses, Light-boats, & c.* Washington, D.C.: U.S. Department of the Treasury.

Fischer, David Hackett. 1989. *Albion's Seed: Four British Folkways in America.* New York and Oxford: Oxford University Press.

Flagg, Thomas R., and Paul W. Schopp. 1989. *Description of the Lakehurst Shops of the Raritan and Delaware Bay Railroad.* Revised. Manuscript on file. Highland Park, N.J.: Cultural Resource Consulting Group.

Fleming, Thomas J. 1973. *The Forgotten Victory: The Battle for New Jersey, 1780.* New York: Dutton.

———. 1984. *New Jersey: A History.* New York: W. W. Norton.

Forbes, Harriet M. 1927. *Gravestones of Early New England.* Boston: Houghton Mifflin.

Fox, Richard Allan, Jr. 1993. *Archaeology, History, and Custer's Last Battle.* Norman: University of Oklahoma Press.

Francaviglia, Richard V. 1971. "The Cemetery as an Evolving Cultural Landscape." *Annals of the American Association of Geographers* 61(3):501–9.

Galishoff, Stuart. 1988. *Newark, the Nation's Unhealthiest City.* New Brunswick: Rutgers University Press.

Gately, Bill. 1998. *Sentinels of the Shore: A Guide to the Lighthouses and Lightships of New Jersey.* Harvey Cedars, N.J.: Down the Shore Publishing.

Geismar, Joan H. 1982. *The Archaeology of Social Disintegration in Skunk Hollow, a Nineteenth-Century Rural Black Community.* New York: Academic Press.

———. 1995. *Gethsemane Cemetery in Death and Life: A Bergen County Historic Site in an Archaeological Perspective.* Hackensack, N.J.: Bergen County Department of Parks, Division of Cultural and Historic Affairs.

Goddard, Ives. 1978. "Delaware." In *Handbook of the North American Indians,* vol. 15, *Northeast,* ed. Bruce G. Trigger, 213–39. Washington, D.C.: Smithsonian Institution Press.

Goodwin, Conrad McCall, Karen Bescherer Metheny, Judson M. Kratzer, and Anne Yentsch. 1995. "Recovering the Lost Landscapes of the Stockton Gardens at Morven, Princeton, New Jersey." *Historical Archaeology* 29(1):35–61.

Gordon, Robert B., and Patrick M. Malone. 1994. *The Texture of Industry: An Archaeological View of the Industrialization of North America.* New York: Oxford University Press.

Graves, Thomas E. 1988. "Pennsylvania German Gravestones: An Introduction." *Markers V: The Journal of the Association for Gravestone Studies,* 60–95.

Grossman, Joel W. 1982. *Raritan Landing: The Archaeology of a Buried Port.* Report prepared for Charles J. Kupper, Inc. New Brunswick: Rutgers Archaeological Survey Office, Cook College, Rutgers University.

Grossman, Joel W., and Richard L. Porter. 1979. *Raritan Landing Archaeological District.* National Register of Historic Places nomination form. On file, New Jersey Historic Preservation Office, Trenton.

Grumet, Robert S. 1995. *Historic Contact: Indian People and Colonists in Today's Northeastern United States in the Sixteenth through Eighteenth Centuries.* Norman: University of Oklahoma Press.

Grummere, Amelia M. 1884. *Friends in Burlington.* Philadelphia: Collins.

Habenstein, Robert W., and William M. Lamers. 1955. *The History of American Funeral Directing.* Milwaukee: Bulfin.

Hammond, Joseph W. 1998. *The Luyster Farm in Middletown, New Jersey: A Land Title History.* Typescript. Monmouth County Historical Association, Freehold.

Hannon, Thomas J. 1983. "The Cemetery: A Field of Artifacts." In *Forgotten Places and Things: Archaeological Perspectives on American History,* ed. Albert E. Ward. Albuquerque, N.M.: Center for Anthropological Studies.

Harrington, J. C. 1954. "Dating Stem Fragments of Seventeenth- and Eighteenth-Century Clay Tobacco Pipes." *Quarterly Bulletin of the Archaeological Society of Virginia* 9(1):220–29.

Harris, Edward C. 1989. *The Principles of Archaeological Stratigraphy.* 2d ed. London: Academic Press.

Hartwick, Carolyn L., and John A. Cavallo. 1997. *A Cultural Resource Survey and Archaeological Data Recovery Completed in Connection with the Route 18 Extension and Interim Improvements Project, Piscataway Township, Middlesex County, New Jersey.* Vol. 1. Report prepared for the New Jersey Department of Transportation, Bureau of Environmental Analysis. New Brunswick: Rutgers University Center for Public Archaeology.

Harwood, W. S. 1908. *Life and Letters of Austin Craig.* New York: Fleming H. Revell.

Hawley, W. S. 1964. *The Deserted Village and the Blue Brook Valley.* Mountainside, N.J.: Trailside Museum Association.

Heite, Edward F. 1974. "The Delmarva Bog Iron Industry." *Northeast Historical Archaeology* 3(2):18–33.

Henry, Susan L. 1979. "Terra-cotta Tobacco Pipes in Seventeenth-Century Maryland and Virginia: A Preliminary Study." *Historical Archaeology* 13:14–37.

Heye, George G., and George H. Pepper. 1915. *Explorations of a Munsee Cemetery Near Montague, New Jersey.* Heye Foundation, Contributions 2(1). New York: Museum of the American Indian.

Hinsley, C. M., Jr. 1985. *Savages and Scientists: The Smithsonian Institution and the Development of American Anthropology 1846–1910.* Washington, D.C.: Smithsonian Institution Press.

Holland, Francis Ross, Jr. 1988. *America's Lighthouses: An Illustrated History.* New York: Dover.

Honeyman, A. Van Doren. 1923. *History of Union County, New Jersey, 1664–1923.* New York: Lewis Historical Publishing Company.

Horner, Roy C. 1985. *Tempo: The Glass Folks of South Jersey.* Woodbury, N.J.: Gloucester County Historical Society.

Howson, Jean, Leonard G. Bianchi, and Richard L. Porter. 1995. *Pre-Data Recovery Archaeological Investigations at Raritan Landing, N.J. Route 18 Extension Project, Piscataway Township, Middlesex County, New Jersey.* Report prepared for the New Jersey Department of Transportation, Bureau of Environmental Analysis. New Brunswick: Rutgers University Center for Public Archaeology.

Huey, Paul. 1991. "The Dutch at Fort Orange." In *Historical Archaeology in Global Perspective,* ed. Lisa Falk, 21–68. Washington, D.C.: Smithsonian Institution Press.

Hunter, Richard. 1985. "The Demise of Traditional Pottery Manufacture on Sourland Mountain, New Jersey, during the Industrial Revolution." In *Domestic Pottery of the*

Northeastern United States, 1625–1850, ed. Sarah Peabody Turnbaugh, 229–48. New York: Academic Press.

———. 2000. "William Richards' Stoneware Pottery Discovered!" *Trenton Potteries, Newsletter of the Potteries of Trenton Society* 1(3):1–3.

Hunter, Richard, William Liebeknecht, and Michael Tomkins. 1996. *Phase II Archaeological Survey N.J. Route 34 (Cheesequake) Old Bridge Township, Middlesex County, New Jersey.* 2 vols. Prepared for the Federal Highway Administration and New Jersey Department of Transportation, Bureau of Environmental Analysis. Trenton: Hunter Research, Inc.

Hunter Research Associates. 1989. *Intensive Test Excavations at the Old Barracks, City of Trenton, Mercer County, New Jersey.* Prepared for Mendel, Mesick, Cohen, Waite, Hall Architects, Albany, N.Y. Trenton.

Hunter Research, Inc. 1998. *Archaeological Investigations in Connection with the St. Michael's Parish House Restoration and Rehabilitation, City of Trenton, Mercer County, New Jersey.* Report to the New Jersey Historic Trust, Trenton.

Hurry, Silas D., and Robert W. Keeler. 1991. "A Descriptive Analysis of the White Clay Tobacco Pipes from the St. John's Site in St. Mary's City, Maryland." In *The Archaeology of the Clay Tobacco Pipe,* vol. 12, *Chesapeake Bay,* ed. Peter Davey and Dennis J. Pogue, 73–88. Monographs in Archaeology and Oriental Studies no. 14, International Series 566. Liverpool: British Archaeological Reports.

James, Bartlett Burleigh, and J. Franklin Jameson, eds. 1959. *Journal of Jasper Danckaerts, 1679–1680.* New York: Barnes and Noble.

Johnson, James P. 1987. *New Jersey: History of Ingenuity and Industry.* Northridge, Calif.: Windsor Publications.

Jones, Olive R., and Catherine Sullivan. 1989. *The Parks Canada Glass Glossary.* Studies in Archaeology, Architecture, and History. Ottawa: National Historic Parks and Sites Branch, Parks Canada.

Kammler, Henry. 1995. "J.F.H. Autenrieth's 'Description of a Short Walking Tour in the Province of New Jersey . . . ' [A Report from 1795 about the Brotherton Reservation]." *Bulletin of the Archaeological Society of New Jersey* 51:34–41.

Kardas, Susan, and Edward McM. Larrabee. 1983. *Archaeological Survey of the Old Barracks Area for the Trenton District Heating Project, Trenton, New Jersey.* Report prepared for the Cogeneration Development Corporation. Princeton: Historic Sites Research.

Kemp, Emory L. 1996. *Industrial Archaeology: Techniques.* Malabar, Fla.: Krieger Publishing Company.

Ketchum, William C., Jr. 1983. *Pottery and Porcelain.* New York: Alfred A. Knopf.

Kirchmann, George. 1980. "Why Did They Stay? Communal Life at the North American Phalanx." In *Planned and Utopian Experiments: Four New Jersey Towns,* ed. Paul A. Stellhorn, 11–28. Newark: New Jersey Historical Commission.

Kobbé, Gustav. 1889. *The Jersey Coast and Pines.* New York: De Leeuw and Oppenheimer.

Kraft, Herbert C. 1975. *The Archaeology of the Tocks Island Area.* South Orange, N.J.: Archaeological Research Center, Seton Hall University Museum.

———. 1986. *The Lenape: Archaeology, History, and Ethnography.* Newark: New Jersey Historical Society.

———. 1993. "Dr. Charles Conrad Abbott, New Jersey's Pioneer Archaeologist." *Bulletin of the Archaeological Society of New Jersey* 48:1–2.

Kryder-Reid, Elizabeth. 1995. "Living Landscapes: Formal Gardens and the Ideology of Order." In *Invisible America: Unearthing Our Hidden Heritage*, ed. Mark P. Leone and Neil Asher Silberman, 104–6. New York: Henry Holt.

Landsman, Ned C. 1985. *Scotland and Its First American Colony, 1683–1765*. Princeton: Princeton University Press.

Lane, Wheaton J. 1939. *From Indian Trail to Iron Horse*. Princeton: Princeton University Press.

Larkin, Jack. 1988. *The Reshaping of Everyday Life, 1790–1840*. New York: Harper and Row.

Lawrence, John, Paul W. Schopp, and Robert Lore. 2001. "Raritan in the Hills: Salvage Archaeology of a Pre-Revolutionary German Lutheran Cemetery, Bernards Township, Somerset County, New Jersey." Paper presented at the May meeting of the Archaeological Society of New Jersey.

Leaming, Aaron, and Jacob Spicer. 1758. *The Grants, Concessions, and Original Constitutions of the Province of New Jersey*. Philadelphia.

Lehigh Valley Railroad Company. 1966. *Lehigh Valley Railroad Company Book of Rules*. Privately printed.

Leiby, Adrian C. 1962. *The Revolutionary War in the Hackensack Valley*. New Brunswick: Rutgers University Press.

———. 1964. *The Early Dutch and Swedish Settlers of New Jersey*. New Jersey Historical Series, 10. Princeton: D. Van Nostrand.

Lenik, Edward J. 1976. "The Olean-Bayonne Pipeline: A Preliminary Survey." *IA: The Journal of the Society for Industrial Archaeology* 2(1):29–35.

———. 1989. "New Evidence on the Contact Period in Northeastern New Jersey and Southeastern New York." *Journal of Middle Atlantic Archaeology* 5:103–20.

———. 1998. *Max Schrabisch, Rockshelter Archaeologist*. Wayne, N.J.: Wayne Township Historical Commission.

Leonard, Thomas H. 1923. *From Indian Trail to Electric Rail: History of the Atlantic Highlands, Sandy Hook, and Original Portland Poynt, One of the First Three Settlements of New Jersey*. Atlantic Highlands, N.J.: Atlantic Highlands Journal.

Leone, Mark. 1988. "The Georgian Order as the Order of Merchant Capitalism in Annapolis, Maryland." In *The Recovery of Meaning: Historical Archaeology in the Eastern United States*, ed. Mark P. Leone and Parker B. Potter Jr., 235–62. Washington, D.C.: Smithsonian Institution Press.

———. 1996. "Interpreting Ideology in Historical Archaeology: Using the Rules of Perspective in the William Paca Garden in Annapolis, Maryland." In *Images of the Recent Past: Readings in Historical Archaeology*, ed. Charles E. Orser Jr., 371–91. Mountainview, Calif.: Altamira Press.

Leone, Mark P., and Parker B. Potter Jr. 1994. "Historical Archaeology of Capitalism." *Bulletin of the Society for American Archaeology* 12(4):14–15.

Liebeknecht, William B. 1986. "The Fort Elfsborg Spoon, 1643–1653." *Bulletin of the Archaeological Society of New Jersey* 40:45–46.

Light-House Board. 1852. *Report of the Officers Constituting the Light-House Board, Convened under Instructions from the Secretary of the Treasury to Inquire into the Condition of the Light-House Establishment of the United States, under the Act of March 3, 1851*. Washington, D.C.: A. Boyd Hamilton.

Linebaugh, Donald W. 2000. "Forging a Career: Roland W. Robbins and Iron Industry Sites in the Northeastern U.S." *IA: Journal of the Society for Industrial Archaeology* 26(1):5–36.

Louis Berger and Associates, Inc. 1990. *Archaeological Investigations at the Sayre & Fisher Brickworks and Price Pottery Site.* Report prepared for Coastal Group, Inc., Colts Neck, N.J. On file with the New Jersey State Historic Preservation Office, Trenton.

———. 1998. *Historic Sites. Trenton Complex Archaeology: Report 12.* Report prepared for the Federal Highway Administration and the New Jersey Department of Transportation, East Orange, N.J.: Cultural Resource Group, Louis Berger and Associates, Inc.

———. 2000a. *Report of Archaeological Monitoring, Route 18: Sections 4E and 6E, Bridge Replacement, Route 18 Bridge over South River, Conrail, and Main Street, Townships of East Brunswick and Old Bridge, Middlesex County, New Jersey.* Report prepared for the New Jersey Department of Transportation, Bureau of Environmental Analysis. East Orange, N.J.: Cultural Resource Group, Louis Berger and Associates, Inc.

———. 2000b. *Route 47 Improvements, Glassboro, Gloucester County, New Jersey, Draft Archaeological and Historic Architectural Study.* Report prepared for the Federal Highway Administration and the New Jersey Department of Transportation. Bureau of Environmental Analysis. East Orange, N.J.: Cultural Resource Group, Louis Berger and Associates, Inc.

Ludwig, Allen I. 1966. *Graven Images: New England Stonecarving and Its Symbols, 1650–1815.* Middletown, Conn.: Wesleyan University Press.

Lundin, Leonard. 1940. *Cockpit of the Revolution; The War for Independence in New Jersey.* Princeton: Princeton University Press.

Lurie, Maxine N., comp. and ed. 1994. *A New Jersey Anthology.* Newark: New Jersey Historical Society.

MAAR Associates, Inc. 1985. *Data Recovery at 28Ca50 Gloucester City, New Jersey.* Report submitted to the National Park Service, Mid-Atlantic Region, Philadelphia. Newark, Del.: MAAR Associates, Inc.

McCarthy, John P., and Jeanne A. Ward. 1999. "The Hexagonal Friends' Meetinghouse at Burlington, New Jersey: A Consideration of Form, Function, and Influences." Paper presented at the annual meeting of the Council for Northeast Historical Archaeology.

McGuire, Randall H. 1988. "Dialogues with the Dead: Ideology and the Cemetery." In *The Recovery of Meaning: Historical Archaeology in the Eastern United States*, ed. Mark P. Leone and Parker B. Potter Jr., 435–80. Washington, D.C.: Smithsonian Institution Press.

McKearin, Helen, and Kenneth M. Wilson. 1978. *American Bottles and Flask and Their Ancestry.* New York: Crown Publishers.

Marks, Geoffrey, and William K. Beatty. 1973. *The Story of Medicine in America.* New York: Charles Scribner and Sons.

Martin, John W. 1991. "Prehistoric Cultural Resources at the Old Barracks, Trenton, New Jersey." *Bulletin of the Archaeological Society of New Jersey* 46:19–30.

Merryman, J. H. [1880] 1981. *The United States Life-Saving Service–1880.* Reprint. Golden, Colo.: Outbooks.

Mitchell, James R. 1972. "The Potters of Cheesequake, New Jersey." In *Ceramics in America*, ed. Ian M. G. Quimby, 319–39. Charlottesville: University Press of Virginia.

Moonsammy, Rita Zorn, David Steven Cohen, and Mary T. Hufford. 1987. "Living with the

Landscape: Folklife in the Environmental Subregions of the Pinelands." In *Pinelands Folklife*, ed. Rita Zorn Moonsammy, David Steven Cohen, and Lorraine E. Williams, 65–230. New Brunswick: Rutgers University Press.

Morrell, Brian H. 1975. "The Evolution of the Rogers Locomotive Company, Paterson, N.J." *Northeast Historical Archaeology* 4(1/2):17–23.

———. 1994. "Rehabilitation of Historic Structures on the Delaware & Raritan Canal in Central New Jersey." In *Canals and American Cities: Assessing the Impact of Canals on the Course of American Urban Life*, ed. Ronald C. Carlisle, 87–102. Easton, Pa.: Canal History and Technology Press.

Mouer, L. Daniel. 1993. "Chesapeake Creoles: The Creation of Folk Culture in Colonial Virginia." In *The Archaeology of Seventeenth-Century Virginia*, ed. Theodore R. Reinhart and Dennis J. Pogue, 105–66. Richmond: Dietz Press.

Mounier, R. Alan. 1990. *An Archaeological Survey of an Abandoned Munitions Works: Block 688, Lot 1, Hamilton Township, Atlantic County, New Jersey*. Report prepared for Land Financial Services, Inc., Haddon Heights, N.J.

———. 1997. "Black and Dirty Work: Archaeology Amidst the Relict Charcoal Kilns of Southern New Jersey." *Bulletin of the Archaeological Society of New Jersey* 52:55–62.

———. Forthcoming. *Looking Beneath the Surface: The Story of Archaeology in New Jersey*. New Brunswick: Rutgers University Press.

Moynihan, Daniel. 1965. "The Negro Family: The Case for National Action." In *The Moynihan Report and the Politics of Controversy*, ed. Lee Rainwater and William A. Yancey, 39–124. Cambridge: MIT Press.

Mrozowski, Stephen A., Grace H. Ziesing, and Mary C. Beaudry. 1996. *Living on the Boott: Historical Archaeology at the Boott Mills Boardinghouses, Lowell, Massachusetts*. Amherst: University of Massachusetts Press.

Mudge, David C. 1986. "Charcoal and Iron: Some Interpretations of the Use of Charcoal by the Early Iron Industry in New Jersey." *Bulletin of the Archaeological Society of New Jersey* 40:33–37.

Mudge, David, and David Zmoda. 1982. *Raritan Landing Archaeological District (Addendum)*. National Register of Historic Places nomination form. On file, New Jersey Historic Preservation Office, Trenton.

Mulford, Isaac. 1853. "The History and Location of Fort Nassau on the Delaware." *Proceedings of the New Jersey Historical Society* 6:187–207.

Murtagh, William J. 1997. *Keeping Time: The History and Theory of Preservation in America*. New York: John Wiley and Sons.

Nelson, William. 1886. "Some Notes on Mattineconck or Burlington Island." *Pennsylvania Magazine of History and Biography* 10:214–16.

———. 1917. *New Jersey Archives*. Vol. 1. Paterson, N.J.: Call Printing and Publishing Company.

New Jersey State Museum (NJSM). 1972. *New Jersey Pottery to 1840*. Catalogue for an exhibit, March 18–May 12. Trenton.

Noël Hume, Ivor. 1976. *Historical Archaeology*. New York: Alfred A. Knopf.

Olsen, Stanley J. 1964. "Food Animals of the Continental Army at Valley Forge and Morristown." *American Antiquity* 29(4):506–9.

O'Reilly, Carey, Jeanne A. Ward, and John P. McCarthy. 1999. "Tea in God's Light: An Analysis of Artifacts from the Friends Meetinghouse Site, Burlington, New Jersey."

Paper presented at the annual meeting of the Council for Northeastern Historical Archaeology.

Parrington, Michael, Helen Schenck, and Jacqueline Thibaut. 1984. "The Material World of the Revolutionary War Soldier at Valley Forge." In *The Scope of Historical Archaeology: Essays in Honor of John L. Cotter*, ed. David G. Orr and Daniel G. Crozier, 125–61. Philadelphia: Laboratory of Anthropology, Temple University.

Pennsylvania Railroad System. 1927. *Operating Department Rules for Conducting Transportation, Effective, April 26, 1925*. Privately printed.

Pernick, Martin S. 1985. *A Calculus of Suffering: Pain, Professionalism, and Anesthesia in Nineteenth-Century America*. New York: Columbia University Press.

Pietak, Lynn Marie. 1995. "Trading with Stranger: Delaware and Munsee Strategies for Integrating European Trade Goods, 1600–1800." Ph.D. diss., University of Virginia.

———. 1999. "Bead Color Symbolism among Post-Contact Delaware and Munsee Groups." *Journal of Middle Atlantic Archaeology* 15:3–19.

Pollard, Sidney. 1999. "Factory Discipline in the Industrial Revolution." In *The Social Dimension of Western Civilization*, vol. 2, *Readings from the Sixteenth Century to the Present*. Boston and New York: Bedford, St. Martin's.

Pomfret, John E. 1964. *The New Jersey Proprietors and Their Lands*. New Jersey Historical Series, 9. Princeton: D. Van Nostrand.

Porter, Richard L., Carolyn L. Hartwick, T. Gregg Madrigal, Ian C. Burrow, and William Liebeknecht. 1995. *Archaeological Data Recovery N.J. Route 18 Extension Interim Improvements, N.J. Route 18 (River Road) Between Landing and Metlars Lanes, Piscataway Township, Middlesex County, New Jersey*. Prepared for the New Jersey Department of Transportation, Bureau of Environmental Analysis. New Brunswick: Rutgers University Center for Public Archaeology.

Prince, Carl E. 1958. *Middlebrook—The American Eagle's Nest*. Somerville, N.J.: Somerset Press.

Ransom, James M. 1966. *Vanishing Ironworks of the Ramapos: The Story of the Forges, Furnaces, and Mines of the New Jersey–New York Border Area*. New Brunswick: Rutgers University Press.

Rathje, William L. 1975. "Le Projet du Garbage 1975: Historic Trade-offs." Paper presented at the annual meeting of the American Anthropological Association.

Reckner, Paul E., and Stephen A. Brighton. 1999. "'Free from All Vicious Habits': Archaeological Perspectives on Class Conflict and the Rhetoric of Temperance." *Historical Archaeology* 33(1):63–86.

Robbins, Roland W. 1982. "Archaeological Site Reports at the Long Pond Ironworks (Report on a Preliminary Survey at the Site of the Buried Ruins of Blast Furnace, Located in the Hewitt Section of Ringwood Manor State Park, Ringwood, New Jersey) and (Report on the Initial Archaeological Exploration and Survey at Buried Blast Furnace Site, Hewitt Section Ringwood State Park, Ringwood, New Jersey)." *North Jersey Highlander* (Fall/Winter):25–59.

Roberts, Russell, and Rich Youmans. 1997. *Down the Jersey Shore*. New Brunswick: Rutgers University Press.

Rockman, Diana Dizerega, and Nan A. Rothschild. 1984. "City Tavern, Country Tavern: An Analysis of Four Colonial Sites." *Historical Archaeology* 18(2):112–21.

Rumbarger, John J. 1989. *Profits, Power, and Prohibition: Alcohol Reform and the Industrialization of America, 1800–1930*. Albany: University of New York Press.

Rutsch, Edward S. 1972. "The Cemetery Site, Jockey Hollow, U.S. National Historic Park, Morristown, N.J." *Bulletin of the Archaeological Society of New Jersey* 29:32–34.

———. 1974. "The Colonial Plantation Settlement Pattern in New Jersey: Iron and Agricultural Examples." In *Economic and Social History of Colonial New Jersey*, ed. William C. Wright, 10–23. Trenton: New Jersey Historical Commission.

———. 1975. "Salvage Archaeology in Paterson, N.J., 1973–1975." *Northeast Historical Archaeology* 4(1/2):1–16.

Rutsch, Edward S., and Brian H. Morrell. 1992. "An Industrial Archaeology Survey of the Long Pond Ironworks, West Milford Township, Passaic County, New Jersey." *Industrial Archaeology* 18(1/2):41–60.

Rutsch, Edward S., and Kim M. Peters. 1977. "Forty Years of Archaeological Research at Morristown National Historical Park, Morristown, New Jersey." *Historical Archaeology* 11:15–38.

St. George, Robert Blair. 1998. *Conversing by Signs: Poetics of Implication in Colonial New England Culture*. Chapel Hill: University of North Carolina Press.

Sanborn Map Company. 1911. *Map of Lakehurst, New Jersey*. New York: Sanborn Perris Map Company.

Santone, Lenore. 1998. "Resiliency as Resistance: Eastern Woodland Munsee Groups on the Early Colonial Frontier." *North American Archaeologist* 19(2):117–34.

———. 1999. "Selective Change and Cultural Continuity among the Munsee on the Colonial Frontier." *Journal of Middle Atlantic Archaeology* 15:21–34.

Sarapin, Janice Kohl. 1994. *Old Burial Grounds of New Jersey*. New Brunswick: Rutgers University Press.

Scharfenberger, Gerard P. and Richard F. Veit. 1999. "Archaeological Investigations at an 18th-Century Dutch-American Farm: The Johannes Luyster House, 28-Mo-261." Paper presented at the 30th Annual Conference on Historical and Underwater Archaeology.

Schrabisch, Max. 1915. *Indian Habitations in Sussex County, New Jersey*. Bulletin 13. Trenton: Geological Survey of New Jersey.

———. 1917. "General Knox's Artillery Park, Pluckemin." *Somerset County Historical Quarterly* 6(3):161–68.

Schrire, Carmel. 1995. *Digging Through Darkness: Chronicles of an Archaeologist*. Charlottesville: University Press of Virginia.

Schuyler, Robert L. 1999. "The Centrality of Post Medieval Studies to General Historical Archaeology." In *Old Worlds and New*, ed. Geoff Egan and R. L. Michael, 10–16. Oxford: Oxbow Books.

Scranton, Philip. 1997. *Endless Novelty: Specialty Production and American Industrialization, 1865–1925*. Princeton: Princeton University Press.

Seidel, John L. 1987. "The Archaeology of the American Revolution: A Reappraisal and Case Study at the Continental Artillery Cantonment of 1778–1779, Pluckemin, New Jersey." Ph.D. diss., University of Pennsylvania.

———. 1990. "'China Glaze' Wares on Sites from the American Revolution: Pearlware before Wedgewood?" *Historical Archaeology* 24(1):82–95.

———. 1995. "'Class Warfare': The American Militia System." In *Invisible America:*

Unearthing Our Hidden History, ed. Mark P. Leone and Neil Asher Silberman, 116–17. New York: Henry Holt.

Sekel, Clifford 1972. "The Continental Artillery in Winter Encampment at Pluckemin, New Jersey, December 1778–June 1779." M.A. thesis, Department of History, Wagner College, Staten Island, New York.

Shyrock, Richard Harrison. 1960. *Medicine and Society in America, 1660–1860.* New York: New York University Press.

Silber, Barbara, and Wade P. Catts. 2001. "'He Has a Very Fine Estate': The Beverwyck Site, an 18th-Century Plantation in Northern New Jersey; Morris County, New Jersey." Paper presented at the 2001 meeting of the Society for American Archaeology.

Sim, Robert J., and Arthur W. Clement. 1944. "The Cheesequake Potteries." *Antiques,* March, 122–25.

Sim, Robert J., and Harry B. Weiss. 1955. *Charcoal Burning in New Jersey from Early Times to the Present.* Trenton: New Jersey Agricultural Society.

Sivilich, Daniel M. 1996. "Analyzing Musket Balls to Interpret a Revolutionary War Site." *Historical Archaeology* 30(2):101–9.

Sivilich, Daniel M., and Ralph Phillips. 1998. *Phase I Cultural Resource Investigation: Neuberger Farm, Middletown-Lincroft Road, Monmouth County, Middletown, New Jersey.* Report prepared for the Monmouth County Park System, Lincroft.

Skinner, Alanson, and Max Schrabisch. 1913. *A Preliminary Report of the Archaeological Survey of the State of New Jersey.* Bulletin 9. Trenton: MacCrellish and Quigley.

Smith, Samuel. [1765] 1972. *The History of the Colony of Nova Caesaria, or New Jersey.* Reprint. New York: Arno Press.

Smith, Samuel Stelle. 1963. *Sandy Hook and the Land of the Navesink.* Monmouth Beach, N.J.: Philip Freneau Press.

———. 1975. *The Battle of Monmouth.* Trenton: New Jersey Historical Commission.

———. 1983. *Lewis Morris: Anglo-American Statesman.* Atlantic Highlands, N.J.: Humanities Press.

South, Stanley. 1977. *Method and Theory in Historical Archaeology.* New York: Academic Press.

Speert, Harold. 1958. *Essays in Eponymy, Obstetric and Gynecologic Milestones.* New York: Macmillan.

Springate, Megan. 2000. *Archaeology at the Allen House: An Introduction.* Freehold, N.J.: Monmouth County Historical Association.

Springate, Megan E., and Bernadette M. Rogoff. 1999. "Remains of the Blue Ball: A Late 18th–Early 19th Century Tavern Midden in Shrewsbury, New Jersey." Paper presented at the Middle Atlantic Archaeological Conference.

Springate, Megan E., and Carole Sinclair-Smith. 2000. "Minors in the Tavern: Summer Camp Excavations at the Allen House, Shrewsbury, N.J." Paper presented at the Middle Atlantic Archaeological Conference.

Springsted, Brenda. 1985. "A Delftware Center in Seventeenth-Century New Jersey." *American Ceramic Circle* 4:9–46.

———. 1999. "Murder Mysteries and Modern Archaeology: Early Experiments in Manufacturing Delftware at Burlington, New Jersey." *Journal of Middle Atlantic Archaeology* 15:95–123.

Springsted, Brenda L., Kurt Kalb, Janet Kopleck, and William Chittick. 1980. *Initial Results*

of Cultural Resource Survey of Route 18, Section 11B (Contract 4) Piscataway Township,
Middlesex County, New Jersey. Trenton: New Jersey Department of Transportation, Bureau of Environmental Analysis.

Stansfield, Charles A., Jr. 1998. *A Geography of New Jersey: The City in the Garden.* New
Brunswick: Rutgers University Press.

Stanzeski, Andrew J. 1974. "The Three Beeches: Excavations in the House of an Archaeologist." *Bulletin of the Archaeological Society of New Jersey* 41:30–33.

Starbuck, David R. 1986. "The New England Glassworks: New Hampshire's Boldest Experiment in Early Glassmaking." *New Hampshire Archaeologist* 27(1).

Stilgoe, John R. 1982. *Common Landscape of America, 1580 to 1845.* New Haven and London: Yale University Press.

Stone, Garry Wheeler, Daniel M. Sivilich, and Mark Edward Lender. 1998. "A Deadly Min-
uet: The Advance of the New England 'Picked Men' against the Royal Highlanders at the
Battle of Monmouth, 28 June 1778." *Brigade Dispatch of the American Revolution*
26(2):2–18.

Stryker, William S. 1882. *The Massacre at Old Tappan.* Trenton, N.J.: Naar, Day and Naar.

Tashjian, Dickran, and Ann Tashjian. 1974. *Memorials for Children of Change: The Art of
Early New England Stonecarving.* Middletown, Conn.: Wesleyan University Press.

Thomas, Ronald A. 1994. "An 18th-Century New Jersey Connection: Percivall Towle and
Thomas Scattergood." *Bulletin of the Archaeological Society of New Jersey* 94:111.

Thomas, Ronald A., and Martha J. Schiek. 1988. "A Late Seventeenth-Century House in
Gloucester City, New Jersey." *Bulletin of the Archaeological Society of New Jersey*
43:3–11.

Thompson, Jonathan. 1826. Letter to Stephen Pleasonton, 21 July 1826. Navesink Light
Station/Twin Lights Papers. Twin Lights Historic Site.

Tomaso, Matthew, Stanley Walling, and Richard Veit. 2001. "Class, Event Stratigraphy and
the Quotidian: Two Privies from Feltville/Glenside Park, Union County, New Jersey."
Paper presented at the annual meeting of the Society for American Archaeology.

Trollope, Frances. [1832] 1927. *Domestic Manners of the Americans.* Reprint. New York:
Dodd, Mead, and Company.

Turnbaugh, Sarah Peabody, ed. 1985. *Domestic Pottery of the Northeastern United States,
1625–1850.* New York: Academic Press.

United States Light-House Establishment. 1871. *Compilation of Public Documents and Ex-
tracts from Reports and Papers Relating to Light-Houses, Light-Vessels, and Illuminating
Apparatus, and to Beacons, Buoys, and Fog Signals 1791–1871.* Washington, D.C.: U.S.
Government Printing Office.

Veit, Richard F. 1963. *The Old Canals of New Jersey.* Little Falls, N.J.: New Jersey Geo-
graphical Press.

Veit, Richard F., Jr. 1992. "'Born a Slave, Died Free': The End of Slavery in New Jersey."
Bulletin of the Archaeological Society of New Jersey 47:23–29.

———. 1995. "'A Piece of Granite That's Been Made in Two Weeks': Terra-Cotta Gravemarkers from New Jersey and New York, 1875–1930." *Markers XII: The Journal of the
Association for Gravestone Studies,* 1–30.

———. 1996a. "Grave Insights into Middlesex County's Colonial Culture." *New Jersey History* 114(3–4):75–94.

———. 1996b. "'A Ray of Sunshine in the Sickroom': Archaeological Insights into Late

19th- and Early 20th-Century Medicine and Anesthesia." *Northeast Historical Archae-ology* 25:33–50.

———. 1999. *Dendrochronological Study of Merchants and Drovers Tavern, Rahway, NJ.* Report prepared for the Rahway Historical Society, Rahway.

———. 2000. "John Solomon Teetzel and the Anglo-German Gravestone Carving Tradition of 18th-Century Northwestern New Jersey." *Markers XVII: The Journal of the Association for Gravestone Studies*, 124–64.

Veit, Richard F., and Charles A. Bello. 1998. "4.4 Miles on the Morris Canal: Recent In-vestigations in Montville, New Jersey." Paper presented at the Middle Atlantic Archae-ological Conference.

———. 1999. " 'A Unique and Valuable Historical and Indian Collection': Charles Conrad Abbott Explores a Seventeenth-Century Dutch Trading Post in the Delaware Valley." *Journal of Middle Atlantic Archaeology* 15:95–123.

Veit, Richard F., and Paul W. Schopp. 1999. "Who's Been Drinking on the Railroad? Ar-chaeological Excavations at the Central Railroad of New Jersey's Lakehurst Shops." *Northeast Historical Archaeology* 28:21–40.

Vermeule, Cornelius C. 1936. "Raritan Landing That Was." *Proceedings of the New Jersey Historical Society* 54(2):85–115, 197–205.

Volk, Ernest. 1911. *The Archaeology of the Delaware Valley.* Papers of the Peabody Museum of American Archaeology and Ethnology, vol. 5. Cambridge: Harvard University.

Wacker, Peter O. 1971. "New Jersey's Cultural Landscape Before 1800." In *Papers Presented at the Second Annual New Jersey History Symposium*, 35–61. Newark: New Jersey His-torical Society.

———. 1975. *Land and People, a Cultural Geography of Preindustrial New Jersey: Origins and Settlement Patterns.* New Brunswick: Rutgers University Press.

Wacker, Peter O., and Paul G. Clemens. 1995. *Land Use in Early New Jersey: A Historical Geography.* Newark: New Jersey Historical Society.

Wall, John P., and Harold E. Pickersgill. 1921. *History of Middlesex County in Three Vol-umes.* New York: Lewis Historical Publishing Company.

Ward, Jeanne A., and Carey O'Reilly. 2000. "Archaeology of a Seventeenth-Century Gath-ering Place: The Burlington Friends Meetinghouse, Burlington, New Jersey." Paper presented at the annual meeting of the Society for Historical Archaeology.

Wasserman, Emily. 1972. *Gravestone Designs, Rubbings, and Photographs from Early New York and New Jersey.* New York: Dover.

Weig, Melvin J., and Vera B. Craig. 1955. *Morristown National Historical Park, New Jersey: A Military Capital of the American Revolution.* Historical Handbook Series, no. 7. Washington, D.C.: National Park Service.

Weiss, Harry B., and Grace M. Weiss. 1964. *The Early Promotional Literature of New Jer-sey.* Trenton: New Jersey Agricultural Society.

———. 1966. *Early Brickmaking in New Jersey.* Trenton: New Jersey Agricultural Society.

Welch, Richard F. 1987. "The New York and New Jersey Gravestone Carving Tradition." *Markers IV: The Journal of the Association for Gravestone Studies*, 1–54.

Wertenbaker, Thomas Jefferson. 1938. *The Founding of American Civilization: The Middle Colonies.* New York: Charles Scribner's Sons.

Weslager, C. A. 1961. *Dutch Explorers, Traders and Settlers in the Delaware Valley, 1609–1664.* Philadelphia: University of Pennsylvania Press.

Wilson, Budd. 1971. "The Batsto Window Light Factory Excavations." *Bulletin of the Archaeological Society of New Jersey* 27:11–18.

———. 1972. "The Batsto Window Light Factory Artifacts." *Bulletin of the Archaeological Society of New Jersey* 29:28–31.

———. 1975. "The Nature and Scope of Archaeological Observation." *Northeast Historical Archaeology* 4(1/2):39–43.

Yamin, Rebecca. 1988. "The Raritan Landing Traders: Local Trade in Pre-Revolutionary New Jersey." Ph.D. diss., New York University.

———. 1989a. "Squeezing Ceramics for More Than Their Worth: Boundary Maintenance at an 18th-Century Port in New Jersey." *Northeast Historical Archaeology* 18:49–69.

———. 1989b. "The Public and the Private Mr. Stockton: Morven's Commodore." *New Jersey Folklore Society Review* 10(2–3):3–7, 10–11.

———. 1992–1993. "Local Trade in Pre-Revolutionary New Jersey." *Northeast Historical Archaeology* 21–22:123–36.

Yamin, Rebecca, and Sarah T. Bridges. 1996. "Farmers and Gentlemen Farmers: The Nineteenth-Century Suburban Landscape." In *Landscape Archaeology: Reading and Interpreting the American Historical Landscape*, ed. Rebecca Yamin and Karen Bescherer Metheny, 175–92. Knoxville: University of Tennessee Press.

Yentsch, Anne E., Naomi F. Miller, Barbara Paca, and Dolores Piperno. 1987. "Archaeologically Defining the Earlier Garden Landscapes at Morven: Preliminary Results." *Northeast Historical Archaeology* 16:1–29.

Zmoda, David. 1985. *An Archaeological Survey for the Route 18 Extension, Piscataway Township, Middlesex County, New Jersey (07NJ820001)*. On file, New Jersey Department of Transportation, Bureau of Environmental Analysis, Trenton.

———. 1990. "Ceramic Reproductions in 18th-Century Salem County." *Bulletin of the Archaeological Society of New Jersey* 45:26–28.

Index

Nicolls, Col. Richard, 31
North American Phalanx, 168, 176

Ocean County, 128, 159, 187
Ocean Grove, 93
Ogden, John, 142
Old Barracks (Trenton), *64*, 79–83
Old Barracks Association, 81
Old Bridge, 144
Olden, Julia Boggs, 26
Old Tappan, 88
Olean-Bayonne Pipeline, *142*, 162–64
Olsen, Stanley, 76
Operation Archaelogy, 179
Osborne, Henry, 100
Osborne, Jonathan Hand, 100
outhouses, 3
ovens, 39, 70

Paca, William, 56
Palladio, Andrea, 54
parade grounds, 82, 83
parish houses: Christ Church (Shrewsbury),
   107–9; St. Michael's Episcopal Church
   (Trenton), 109–14
Parker Farm (Little Silver), *15*
Parsippany, 39
paternalism, 168
Paterson, 141, 168
Penn, John, 58
Penn, Thomas, 58
Penn, William, 31, 120
Pennsylvania Brigade, 76
Pennsylvania Line, 74
Perazio, Philip, 129
Perth Amboy, 41; British barracks at, 79;
   development of, 62; first settlements, 21;
   gravemarkers in, 95; health and nutrition
   in, 168
petroleum, 162–64
Philadelphia, 32
Philadelphia and Lancaster Turnpike, 117
Phillips, Ralph, 84, 85, *85*, 86, 87
photographs: aerial, 9, 71; historic, 9
phytoliths, 57
Pierson, Isaac, 73
Pietak, Lynn Marie, 58
Pine Barrens, 156–58
Pinelands, 4, 62, 91, 148, 156; Burr-Haines
   site, 39, 58–62

Pintard, Lewis, 57
Pintard, Samuel, 57
pipes: petroleum, 162–64; tobacco, 17, *17*,
   27, 28, 29, *30*, 37, 47, 53, 61, 157
Plainfield, 180
Pleasant Mills Cemetery (Batsto Village), *93*
Pleasonton, Stephen, 136
Pluckemin, 6, 63, *64*, 64–72
Pluckemin Archaeological Project, 70
Pompton, 152
Pond, Alonzo, 75
porches, 82
potteries, 28, 62, 69, 140, 141, 142–48. *See
   also* ceramics
Prentice Refining Company, 164
Price, Ebenezer, 98, 99
Price Pottery (Sayreville), 144
Princeton, 74; battle of, 63, 72
privies, 4, 174, 179, 180, 181, 182, *183*
Prohibition, 133
property deeds, 9
Puritans, 30, 93, 95, 97
Putnam, Frederick Ward, 26

Quakers, 30–34, 44, 59, 62, 104

radar, ground-penetrating, 9, 56, 71
Rahway Cemetery, *170*
railroads, 115; alcohol use and, 128–34
Ramapo Mountains, 154
Ransom, James, 153
Raritan and Delaware Bay Railroad, 115, *116*,
   128–34. *See also* New Jersey Southern
   Railway
Raritan Bay Union, 168
Raritan Borough (Somerset County), 10
Raritan Landing, 39, *40*, 41–44, 79
Raritan River, 41, 122
Rathje, William, 4–5
Reading, John, 4, 34–38
Red Bank (Monmouth County), 63
religious movements, 95, 97, 167
remote sensing, 9, 71
Richard Grubb and Associates, 106
Richards, Jesse, 159
Ringwood, 152
Ringwood Manor State Park, 151
River Vale, 88
Robbins, Roland Wells, 153, *153*, 154–55,
   165

About the Author

Richard Veit is an assistant professor of history and anthropology and a member of the graduate faculty in history in the Department of History and Anthropology at Monmouth University. He has taught at Monmouth since 1996. He also directs Monmouth University's Center for New Jersey History. In 1977, as a nine-year-old, at the suggestion of his father, a history and geography teacher, he volunteered on an archaeological excavation in Westfield, New Jersey. That experience left a lasting impression. After completing his undergraduate education at Drew University, he began working in cultural resource management. In 1991 he received his M.A. in anthropology from the College of William and Mary. He completed his Ph.D. in anthropology at the University of Pennsylvania in 1997. He has published widely in professional journals and encyclopedias. Recently he served as guest editor for a special volume of the *Journal of Middle Atlantic Archaeology* titled *Contact and Historic Period Archaeology in the Delaware Valley*. He is an active member of a variety of professional organizations and serves as an officer of the Archaeological Society of New Jersey.